THE STRUGGLE FOR SOUTH SUDAN

The Autobiography
of Gordon Muortat Mayen

*"A million patriotic years
separate us from the Arabs forever!"*
- Gordon Muortat Mayen

Edited by Aly Verjee

The publisher wishes to acknowledge and thank Dr. Douglas H. Johnson for his invaluable help and support for Africa World Books and its mission of preserving and promoting African cultural and literary traditions and history. Dr. Johnson and fellow historians have been instrumental in ensuring that African people remain connected to their past and their identity. Africa World Books is proud to carry on this mission.

All rights reserved. It is illegal to reproduce, duplicate or transmit any part of this book in either electronic means or printed format. Recording of this publication is strictly prohibited. No part of this publication may be reproduced, stored in a retrieval system, or transmitted, in any form, or by any means, electronic, mechanical, photocopying, recording or otherwise, without the prior permission of the publishers.

Copyright © 2025 The Muortat Family
Maps © MAPgrafix, 2024

Paperback: ISBN: 9781763683907
Hardcover: 9781763683938
eBook: 9781763873407

"Sudanese rebel asks Britain for asylum" by David Floyd, The Daily Telegraph, 1 July 1972 © Telegraph Media Group Limited, 2023, reproduced with permission of the Telegraph Media Group.

British Embassy, Foreign and Commonwealth Office, and Home Office documents in FCO 39/1154, "Exiles of Sudan", reproduced with permission of The National Archives of the UK (TNA), Kew.

Portrait of Gordon Muortat Mayen, February 1973 © Universal Pictorial Press and Agency / Avalon 2024, reproduced with permission of Avalon.

Every effort has been made to contact copyright holders of material reproduced in this book. We would be pleased to rectify any omissions in subsequent editions should they be drawn to our attention.

This book is sold subject to the conditions that it shall not, by way of trade or otherwise, be lent, re-sold, hired out or otherwise circulated without the publisher's prior consent in any form of binding or cover other than in which it is published and without a similar condition including the condition being imposed on the subsequent purchaser.

Cover design, typesetting and layout: Africa World Books
Unit 3, 57 Frobisher St, Osborne Park, WA 6017
P.O. Box 1106 Osborne Park, WA 6916

Table of Contents

List of Maps and Images   iv
List of Acronyms and Abbreviations   v
Editor's Note and Acknowledgments   vii

1. Early Life   1
2. Work in the Civil Service Before Independence   10
3. A Contested Transition to Independence   33
4. Intensification of the First Civil War   61
5. Joining the Liberation Struggle   88
6. The Nile Republic (1969-1970)   117
7. The Addis Ababa Agreement   156
8. Another Exile   182
9. The Formation of the Anyanya Patriotic Front (1974-1975)   211
10. Development of the Anyanya Patriotic Front (1976-1977)   233
11. Last Months in Ethiopia (1977-1978)   254
12. Second Waiting to be Recalled   294

Postscript and Thanks   *323*

List of Maps and Images

Cover image: Gordon Muortat Mayen, 1972
Back cover image: Gordon Muortat Mayen, Stephen Cic Lam, and Emmanuel Abur Matuong at the headquarters of the Nile Provisional Government, Bungu, Equatoria, 1969
Map of Southern Sudan, 1972
Gordon Muortat's cohort at the Sudan Police College, Omdurman, circa 1950
Hilary Akwang, Gordon Muortat Mayen, William Deng Nhial, and James Ajith, Wau, 1954
Gordon Muortat Mayen and Sarah Piath, Atbara, 1956
Gordon Muortat Mayen at Wau Airport, 1955
Police on parade in Wau, circa 1955
Map of the Southern Sudan-Zaïre border area, 1972
Letter from LG Faulkner, FCO, to Mr Kay, FCO, 19 May 1972
Letter from AR Grimes, British Embassy Khartoum, to JC Kay, FCO, 29 May 1972
"Sudanese rebel asks Britain for asylum", David Floyd, *The Daily Telegraph*, 1 July 1972
Letter from S Wright, Home Office, to DFB Edye, FCO, 11 July 1972
Gordon Muortat Mayen and Sarah Piath, London, 1972
Portrait of Gordon Muortat Mayen, February 1973

List of Acronyms and Abbreviations

S£: Sudanese pounds
AACC: All Africa Conference of Churches
ADC: Assistant District Commissioner
ALF: Azania Liberation Front
ANAF: Anyanya National Armed Forces
ANF: African National Front
APF: Anyanya Patriotic Front
APG: Anyidi Provisional Government
BCAR: British Council for Aid to Refugees
BIAS: British Immigration Advisory Services
CIA: Central Intelligence Agency
CMS: Church Missionary Society
DC: District Commissioner
DHSS: Department of Health and Social Security (UK)
DUP: Democratic Unionist Party
FCO: Foreign and Commonwealth Office (UK)
GUN: General Union of Nuba
MPs: Members of Parliament
NPG: Nile Provisional Government
NUF: National United Front
NUP: National Unionist Party
OAU: Organization of African Unity
PDP: People's Democratic Party

PMAC: Provisional Military Administrative Council (the Derg) (Ethiopia)
SACDNU: Sudan African Closed Districts National Union
SALF: Sudan African Liberation Front
SANU: Sudan African National Union
SDF: Sudan Defence Force
SF: Southern Front
SNF: Sudanese National Front
SPLM/A: Sudan People's Liberation Movement / Army
SPRF: Sudanese Popular Revolutionary Front
SSLM: South Sudan Liberation Movement
SSPG: Southern Sudan Provisional Government
SSU: Sudan Socialist Union (Nimeiri)
SUNF: Sudanese United National Front
SUP: Sudan Unity Party
UNHCR: United Nations High Commissioner for Refugees
WCC: World Council of Churches

Editor's Note and Acknowledgments

Gordon Muortat Mayen had an extraordinary life, participating in and bearing witness to some of the most important events in South Sudan's struggle for freedom. From Loka to Libya to London, his methodical, detailed documentation of what he lived through is almost as impressive. Muortat maintained a steadfast commitment to South Sudanese self-determination, while allowing his approach to evolve over time. My task as editor of Muortat's autobiography was to find a way to accessibly present this personal history while ensuring that Muortat's voice remained undampened. My principles were to edit for brevity and clarity, but not to substitute for the protagonist.

Muortat died in Rumbek in April 2008. There are obvious difficulties in editing the material of an author that cannot be consulted. As a personal history, revisions for fact-checking were kept to a minimum, and the views Muortat expresses are his own. Where there were inconsistencies (often concerning dates and places), I consulted the Muortat Family and other sources to determine what was most likely to be accurate. This work could not have been completed without the assistance of Gordon Muortat's family, who first had the vision for a book to be realized. Where there were factual questions, I drew again on the Muortat Family, as well as on secondary sources, and on my own knowledge of Sudan and

South Sudan, to try to find answers. With the tireless Jillian Luff of MAP*grafix*, much effort was spent poring over maps and location databases trying to accurately plot locations mentioned in the book, particularly in chapter 6.

For their support and encouragement, I would like to especially thank Peter Deng and the team at Africa World Books, as well as Angela Ainsworth, Avie Azis, Mark Bradbury, Kathryn Bubien at the *Associated Press*, Yeng Chang, Jacob Fodio Todd, Douglas H. Johnson, Chris Kwaja, Charlotte Martin, Ruth Marsh at *The Telegraph*, Scopas Poggo, Giorgio Rapanelli, Ana C. Rodrigues, John Ryle, Sabrina Salis, Michel Thill, Edward Thomas, the staff of the National Archives, Kew, London, and my family.

1.

Early Life

My parents did not know my date or year of birth. This was not unusual. They told me that I was born in the time of *Achiek e lek*. In that year, it was reported that an *achiek*, a spirit, had appeared in a sacred lake. People used to go there from the surrounding Dinka Agar country to pray and find healing. I later learned that the extraordinary events of *Achiek e lek* occurred in 1922. So, I deduced that I must have been born in 1922.

My father, Mayen Maborjok, and my mother, Akueng Mangu, were from the Athoi *wut* (section) of the Dinka Agar. My father's *gol* (clan) was Patiop, the "children of the earth." The Patiop *yath* (totem) is the fox. My mother came from the Pathoth clan. Their totem is fire.

We lived in the village of Aguarich, where we kept sheep and goats. When I reached the age of eight, I was taught how to tend the herd within the homestead, and once deemed good enough, was permitted to take the animals out for grazing. This responsibility came with risk. The animals could stray into someone's farm and damage crops. Such trespasses rarely went unpunished, both by the farm owner and probably again by a parent or a relative, if the youngster failed to show remorse. I was beaten on many occasions.

When I was about 10, I was taken to the cattle camp and put on a milk only diet, believed to be the best for children my age. I was tasked with clearing animal droppings to keep the camp clean. I also milked the cows, a task customarily designated to girls, women, and uninitiated boys like me. Each morning after the cows had been let out to graze, I spread the droppings to dry in the sun. In the evening, I gathered and burnt them. The smoke had the benefit of repelling mosquitoes. On the rare occasions when no suitable male adult or youth was present to bring the cattle back, I was asked to step in. The grazing fields were a good 10 miles away, which laid the cows open to attack by lions.

Two years later, I returned to Aguarich to resume tending to the sheep and goats. One day while I was watching the animals with my friends, we met two boys visiting from Rumbek, a town several miles away. They began to tell us about something they called school. I had never heard about school before. They said school was in the village of Akot, which was further away than Rumbek. Boys aged 10 and above were allowed into the school and taught how to read and write. If, after four years, one did well, one could become a chiefs' court clerk. Our visitors invited us to come with them to school. I knew of the mystery of writing but had never paid much attention to it. I had heard that court clerks could turn into *ajong*: man-eating lions. So, I grew a little uneasy standing next to the strangers. Humans who turned into lions were thought to possess some noticeable physical traits: they had no kneecaps, wore glum faces, avoided eye contact, and carried a rod blackened at both ends. This description seemed to fit one of the boys. Gripped with fear, I considered returning home. But on further reflection, I braved their invitation to accompany them to Akot.

When we reached Bakjiu, an old cattle camp three miles from the Naam River, it began to get dark. We decided to spend the night at Pulkuc village. We left the road and followed a path which led to a house at the edge of the village. I asked the owner if we could spend the night. We were given permission and went in. A woman there with her children told us that her husband had gone to the cattle camp. In the morning, we continued our journey to Akot arriving at 4.30pm. We could see the school building and hear the schoolboys.

In the first two years of school, the boys were given intensive tuition, with special emphasis on the Bible. Catechisms had to be learnt by heart. In 1937, I was baptized as Gordon, whom we were told was a devout Christian, a professional soldier, and an administrator. During these years, we were taught the early history of the Anglo-Egyptians and of the slave trade by the Northern Sudanese Arabs. The headteacher was a British missionary called Reverend Arnold.

I was permitted to return home for my initiation ceremony. At that time in Dinka Agar society, all boys between 14 and 16 had to be initiated into manhood. In August, about 80 boys from five surrounding villages gathered in one house. An adult relative or a guardian helped each boy to compose his own song, which he sang after the initiation. During the ceremony, which could last up to 15 days, the songs were rehearsed so that they could be sung together as a group. Boys were also taught how to fight. We used blunt wooden spears and blades of grass so as to not cause injury. Such training continued for over a month after our initiation.

On the day of our initiation, we got ready and were taken to an open place. We sat in a circle. Each boy sat with his legs crossed and dug a hole in front of him. The hole was used to collect the blood from the wounds. Four or more marks were cut across the forehead using a very sharp knife. Every Dinka sub-tribe has a distinct method of marking for identification. One of the main reasons for marking youngsters is to create what is called *rïc*, which means a generation or an age-set.

As we were waiting for our marking to begin, elders warned us against crying or showing any fear. Even blinking was taken as a sign of weakness. Any boy who cried or showed signs of fear would shame his family and damage the reputation of the clan. A close relative would stand behind each boy with a stick to hit him hard if he cried or made any fearful gesture.

Suddenly, the marker appeared. He approached from behind. He started with a boy on the right. As he was cutting the boy's forehead, the other boys began to praise or shout out the colors and names of their favorite bulls. Shouts of encouragement and people singing could be heard behind us.

I was seated in the middle. The marker held my head and began to cut from left to right. I heard the knife cut through the tissue and felt the blood pouring down my face, over my shoulders and the rest of my body. The pain was severe, but I was prepared to endure it. Although the blood nearly got into my eyes, I did not blink, for I was being closely watched. Five marks were made on my head; I bent my head forward so that the blood could reach the hole. Despite the pain, I felt very happy because I had successfully passed my initiation. One thing I was sure of was that nobody, except the elders, would call me a boy again. Sesame oil was rubbed on the wound with a sorghum leaf; later sisal leaves were tied on to cover the wounds. One of the cuts did not stop bleeding for three hours, so a medical treatment was applied: the root of a spider's web was used to cover the incision, and after a few minutes the bleeding stopped.

We returned to the house where we spent the night. Food was brought and we ate well as the pain slowly subsided. After two days, we were oiled with *lulu* and walked around the villages, parading ourselves in front of the girls and singing our songs. When all the songs had been sung, each girl was allowed to point at the boy she thought handsome and say loudly, "that is my husband!" The number of girls who picked a boy indicated how appealing he was to the girls. These activities were carried out over a three-month period after which we dispersed.

I returned to school towards the end of 1938. We moved to class four which was the final form. I was top of my class. The boys at Akot who achieved the best and second-best marks in the final examinations were allowed to go to Nugent Intermediate School in Loka in Yei District, Equatoria Province, for further education. When the results came out, Rev. Arnold informed me that I had topped my class and would go to Loka at the beginning of 1940.

Loka was one of the three intermediate schools (Bussere, near Wau, and Okavu in Eastern Equatoria were the other two) owned and administered by the Catholic Church and the Church Missionary Society (CMS). These schools offered the highest level of education available in the South until 1947.

In March 1940, I arrived in Akot to join the Loka boys so that we could travel together. Rev. Arnold then told me that my trip to Loka was cancelled. My health would be at risk because I was too slim. Since Loka was very cold, I would not be able to survive there. This was shocking news. But the decision had been made by the school authorities. I asked Arnold whether he shared that opinion. He said that he did and that my number two, a boy named Akec, from Yirol, would take my place. Arnold told me that I would go to forms five and six which had just been created at the Akot central school to train teachers. I told him that I was not interested in becoming a teacher and just wanted to continue my education. I was frustrated. He told me to see him again after two days.

Rev. Arnold was a considerate man. He understood that I felt betrayed. However, when I met him later, he said he would allow me to go to the Nugent School if I was able to obtain top marks at the end of the sixth year of the teachers' course. The whole affair felt unjust. Would the promise be kept? Would I be able to attain top marks? After persuasion by Arnold, I accepted the offer.

In 1941, the class moved to its sixth and final year. I was one of the students selected to attend the CMS synod in Juba in September. Rev. Arnold went with us. The students travelled in the back of a lorry. Just before we reached Lui Mission Station in Equatoria, there was a heavy downpour. My clothes were soaked, and I began to shiver.

Juba was the largest town in South Sudan, and this was my first ever visit. I felt completely lifeless. I thought I had malaria. I was taken to a doctor and diagnosed with pneumonia. Rev. Arnold was worried and decided to take me to Yei hospital, 100 miles west of Juba, where he thought the treatment would be better. We went in his saloon car, and I was admitted as soon as we arrived. After the doctor examined me and confirmed the diagnosis, Arnold prayed with me, gave me some pocket money, and returned to Juba while I underwent treatment.

By the end of October, I had fully recovered. A young missionary at Yei took care of me. He put me up in his house and showed me great kindness. He said that Rev. Arnold had arranged with the headmaster of Nugent School for me to attend lessons for two months, after which I would return to Akot to sit my final examination. I was sent to Loka where I was temporarily put in class one. I made a great deal of progress. I met friends from Rumbek and Yirol, some in their final year. I also became acquainted with boys from Equatoria, some of whom later became close friends, like Elia Lupe Waiwai.

In December, I returned to Akot and sat the final examinations. I maintained my top place. Rev. Arnold congratulated me and told me that I should prepare to enter Nugent School.

The next problem was how to get to Loka, as the school authorities did not arrange transportation. Boys from Rumbek and Yirol had to find their way to Shambe, from where we were provided with steamer tickets to travel to Juba. The journey from Juba to Loka was a nightmare. In most cases, boys had to walk over 60 miles. I had to walk 115 miles from Rumbek to Shambe, and then go from Shambe to Juba by steamer. In Juba, I would have to try and get a lift on a lorry to Loka.

Contrary to the fears expressed by the Akot school authorities in 1939, my four years at Loka were the healthiest I had experienced. Apart from the cold, the food and clothing were better. I found the environment and meeting people from different tribes fascinating. The Second World War was at its height. It was exciting to watch thousands of African troops in convoys passing along the main road. They were on their way to and from Ethiopia, fighting on behalf of the British colonial government against the Germans and Italians.

Communications and public transport were poor. Once a year, from December to March, boys from Rumbek and other areas far from Loka would go home for the holidays. In July 1944, I dreamed that my half-brother Dhaal Mayen had died. He was almost the same age as me. I was terribly upset, but as it was a dream, I had no reason to believe it. However, when I went home in December, I found that he had died in July when I had the dream. As Christians, we were used to dismissing the fulfillment of a dream as superstition. This experience changed my perspective.

In 1945, we went on strike to protest the inadequate provision of food and clothing and the lack of transport during the school holidays. There used to be fierce fights at Loka between boys from different tribes in South Sudan. This also happened in the secondary schools in Rumbek and Juba. There is a legacy of tribal conflicts among Southerners, which has survived all genuine efforts for peace and has continued throughout all stages of political and nationalist development in Sudan. Such conflicts have always threatened South Sudan's liberation struggle.

The church missionaries shouldered responsibility for education in South Sudan, while the colonial government did little to develop education. A few years before the end of the Second World War, the Church allowed a few boys who had completed their intermediate education to go to East Africa for further education and teacher training. At the end of my final year in 1945, I was one of a group of boys selected to go to Uganda to attend senior secondary school and teacher training. I declined this offer and decided instead to work in the civil service and train to become an administrative assistant.

In December, I returned to Akot and sat the final examinations. I maintained my top place. Rev. Arnold congratulated me and told me that I should prepare to enter Nugent School.

The next problem was how to get to Loka, as the school authorities did not arrange transportation. Boys from Rumbek and Yirol had to find their way to Shambe, from where we were provided with steamer tickets to travel to Juba. The journey from Juba to Loka was a nightmare. In most cases, boys had to walk over 60 miles. I had to walk 115 miles from Rumbek to Shambe, and then go from Shambe to Juba by steamer. In Juba, I would have to try and get a lift on a lorry to Loka.

Contrary to the fears expressed by the Akot school authorities in 1939, my four years at Loka were the healthiest I had experienced. Apart from the cold, the food and clothing were better. I found the environment and meeting people from different tribes fascinating. The Second World War was at its height. It was exciting to watch thousands of African troops in convoys passing along the main road. They were on their way to and from Ethiopia, fighting on behalf of the British colonial government against the Germans and Italians.

Communications and public transport were poor. Once a year, from December to March, boys from Rumbek and other areas far from Loka would go home for the holidays. In July 1944, I dreamed that my half-brother Dhaal Mayen had died. He was almost the same age as me. I was terribly upset, but as it was a dream, I had no reason to believe it. However, when I went home in December, I found that he had died in July when I had the dream. As Christians, we were used to dismissing the fulfillment of a dream as superstition. This experience changed my perspective.

In 1945, we went on strike to protest the inadequate provision of food and clothing and the lack of transport during the school holidays. There used to be fierce fights at Loka between boys from different tribes in South Sudan. This also happened in the secondary schools in Rumbek and Juba. There is a legacy of tribal conflicts among Southerners, which has survived all genuine efforts for peace and has continued throughout all stages of political and nationalist development in Sudan. Such conflicts have always threatened South Sudan's liberation struggle.

The church missionaries shouldered responsibility for education in South Sudan, while the colonial government did little to develop education. A few years before the end of the Second World War, the Church allowed a few boys who had completed their intermediate education to go to East Africa for further education and teacher training. At the end of my final year in 1945, I was one of a group of boys selected to go to Uganda to attend senior secondary school and teacher training. I declined this offer and decided instead to work in the civil service and train to become an administrative assistant.

Southern Sudan, internal boundaries shown circa 1972

2.

Work in the Civil Service Before Independence

Posting with the Police at Rumbek

In 1946, I was called to Juba to interview for the post of assistant administrative officer. I discovered that to qualify, I first had to work as a police officer for at least 10 years. If I did this successfully, I would be appointed to the post. I accepted these terms and joined the police service on 26 February. I went back to Rumbek to be issued with a uniform and a rifle and begin my training.

This was the first time I had lived in a town as large as Rumbek. Although I was born less than 12 miles away, I had visited Rumbek only once before, to see my uncle and his fiancée. People rarely visited government towns; the Dinka regarded them as bases of alien powers that had invaded their land and entrenched themselves by force.

After three months of police training, I was sent to Wau to undertake five months of military training with the Equatoria Corps. After this, I returned to Rumbek. It was now October.

Rather than working in the office as I expected, I was deployed to roadwork. Except for the Rumbek to Juba road, roads in and out of Rumbek district were only operational during the dry season from December to May. The road assigned to me was from Rumbek to the Tonj district boundaries, at least 50 miles long.

Local chiefs gave us about 200 laborers to work on the road. Each laborer's daily wage was 1½ piasters. The Dinka did not want to work for money, especially when the wage was so little. They found working on the road humiliating and detested it. The only option for the Anglo-Egyptian government was to force them to work. Policemen used to be sent to the villages and cattle camps to round up young men and take them to the roads. My role was to keep a list of the laborers and their chiefs. I had to conduct a rollcall every two hours. We used to stand in the intense heat of the sun for 12 hours a day, six days a week. Laborers constantly tried to escape. When this happened, their chiefs would be informed, and they would be forced back to work. If they did not comply, their cattle would be seized. One day, 75 percent of our workforce escaped overnight, and the roadwork stopped for five days.

In December, I was assigned to work as an assistant to an intelligent, experienced police officer and prison clerk. He could not rise to a more senior rank in the police or become an administrative assistant (the type of position I was aspiring to) because Southerners, whether educated or not, were not allowed to become senior police, prison, or military officers. The highest rank attainable by Southern Sudanese at that time was sergeant-major. There was one exception, a man called Michael Daffala from Maridi, who had studied at the police academy at Makerere University in Uganda. He was appointed as a police officer in 1946 in Juba but dismissed a year later.

The District Commissioner (DC), the highest-ranking post in the district, could only be a British national. The DC at that time was EH Nightingale. Nightingale was unpopular because he was a strict disciplinarian. All crimes were reported verbally to the sergeant-major, who was illiterate. He in turn reported these to the DC each day. Every Monday, new prisoners were paraded before the DC who wrote their names in a register and dealt with their cases. This was before we began investigating and prosecuting crimes in the magistrate's and chief's courts.

Nightingale told the sergeant-major that I was being recruited as a policeman as part of my training to become an administrative assistant. I had a special status which attracted others' attention. Moreover, my office work put some distance between me and most rank-and-file officers. Working under Sgt. Nekemia Mathiang Dhel was a positive experience as he wanted me to succeed. Sgt. Mathiang became a target for the illiterate policemen hostile towards the educated ones. In South Sudan, the police came from many different tribes. If I had taken up my position elsewhere, there may have been difficulties. That was why the selection board chose to send me to Rumbek. The whole colonial administration was based on the tribal structure.

There was a significant difference in pay between the Southern civil servants and their Northern Arab counterparts. This inequality absorbed the attention of Southerners in the years before and after the Second World War. We used to discuss this at Loka and our class had gone on strike over the issue. Southerners were paid much less compared to their Northern counterparts with the same qualifications and skills. For example, a Southerner who had graduated from intermediate school would receive a salary of S£1.50 per month after completing professional training school, while a Northern Sudanese with the same qualifications would start with a salary of S£15.00.

Discontent over pay was widespread and helped unify Southerners. In the middle of 1946, all Southern officials, policemen, prison wardens, soldiers and workers went on strike. This took the authorities by surprise. They reacted swiftly because they thought that this might be the beginning of a political awakening in the South. Two commissions were appointed to investigate the strikes, one regarding civil servants and police, and the second for the other workers. By the beginning of 1947, pay and conditions in the South were largely equalized with those of the North. A period of calm and normalcy followed, which convinced the authorities that political activity and discontent had died down.

I completed my second course of training as a police investigator in September 1947. I returned to Rumbek where I was assigned as a police investigator. When the DC received reports of my work, he was pleased and decided to promote me from police constable to full corporal. He then informed Sergeant-Major Philemon Majok Kuong. Kuong was not happy. He and the senior officers opposed my promotion on the grounds that it would discourage senior police constables, some of whom had served for more than 10 years. At that point, I had been in the police for only two years. The DC gave into the pressure and decided to only promote me to police lance corporal.

In 1947, several important events took place. On 12 June, the famous Juba Conference was held. At that time, there was no press or radio of any sort. As a result, even literate Southerners were politically unaware. No one knew what was going on at the conference at the time. I only later understood what took place after I met some of those who participated, and read extensively about it. At the Juba Conference, the issue of unity between North and South was presented and debated for the first time. The participants were drawn from the Sudan government, the Advisory Council, and pro-independence parties such as Umma. Some other political parties refused to attend the conference. Most of the Northern Sudanese who attended the conference were pro-independence. Those supporting the unity of the Nile Valley and unity with Egypt boycotted the conference.

The Juba Conference was hastily convened. There was no plan to consult Southerners, but the British in Khartoum were pressured by administrators who sympathized with the South. In the end, the decision to hold a conference in Juba was not about finding out the views of the South but to simply inform Southerners that South and North were to merge, whether they agreed or not.

Towards the end of the year, the Governor-General of Sudan visited Rumbek. I was asked to interpret from English to Dinka during his meeting with the Dinka chiefs. The Deputy Governor of Bahr al-Ghazal and the heads of departments in the province also attended. At the end of the meeting, the DC congratulated me and told me that my performance had been impressive.

Also in that year, a severe drought brought about a great famine. Many people in the Rumbek region perished. During the famine, the government began to import grain from Northern Sudan. It was then sold to the inhabitants through the Northern merchants.

Marriage

Another important event that year was my father declaring in October my engagement to Sarah Piath Ahoc. He did this with the agreement of my paternal uncles. The fact that I had been to school, learned to read and write, and lived and worked in town did not alter the importance of the Dinka traditions of marriage. However, my education did affect how I wanted to go about it. I decided that I wanted to choose the girl I would marry. I would then involve my parents and relatives at the contracting stage. However, before I had gone too far, I changed my mind. This was because I had observed that many marriages in which the young man made an independent choice were either full of serious problems or ended in disaster.

I called a meeting of my father and uncles. I informed them of my decision, and they praised me for having come to that conclusion. They were ready to help me choose my wife based on the Dinka tradition. I was asked to give the names of any girls whom I fancied. When my brothers had chosen their wives, they had given three or more names, so I did the same. The family background, character, and other essential qualifications of each of the girls were considered. In the end, Sarah Piath was unanimously chosen.

The next day, my cousin and I went to see what Sarah looked like. She lived in Acuolic village. When we arrived, we pretended that we were passing through from Pacong, a local administrative center, on our way to Rumbek. Her father, Ahoc Chol, knew me and my parents well. We were welcomed and asked to sit for a few minutes. We agreed, and Sarah brought us water to drink, which was the usual practice. This provided me with an opportunity to have a full view of her. I went away satisfied that a very good choice had been made. I realized that I had met her before, in her village in 1944. She was about 13 years old at the time. On that occasion, I did not hint anything to her or to the family, as doing so would be contrary to traditional practices. When I later told Sarah about the first time we met, she too was able to recall it.

I went straight home, met my father and some of my paternal uncles, and informed them that I was satisfied with the choice. Ten days later, my father led a delegation of elders from our clan to Ahoc Chol's house and presented a formal request of engagement. The request was accepted. The marriage contract was finalized between October 1947 and November 1948. It was a busy time. I used to go to Acuolic regularly to meet Sarah, and her parents, sisters, and close relatives. Sarah and I developed a deep love and an eagerness to marry each other during this time.

By August 1948, preparations for my marriage were nearly complete. At the end of October, a meeting between the families took place to negotiate the dowry and marriage. A dowry of 30 cattle was agreed; 25 to be delivered immediately and five later. In November, the bride would be delivered to my father and relatives. A huge ceremony with dancing and singing was organized for the afternoon. The women and men had two separate processions which then joined into one marriage dance. In the men's ceremony, I was placed in the center of the procession, which slowly moved to the house of the bride. The women's procession followed. Both processions were singing. The men's songs were composed by Akumduar Maluac, one of my paternal uncles, and the women's songs by Ajok Madheek, mother of my nephew, Moses Mading Anyijing. The marriage dance came at the end. This was also when the elders on both sides sat down together to conclude the marriage negotiations. In accordance with tradition, I was not allowed to participate in the discussions.

Sarah was at home, as decreed by tradition. She was sobbing in distress because dramatic changes were about to take place. She would be taken away from her parents and relatives to live with strangers in a new place. At midnight, Sarah was delivered to my father's house in Aguarich. Marriage was one of the important hurdles a Dinka man must clear. Now that I was married, I had to settle down and concentrate on my job as a policeman.

Police College in Khartoum

As I mentioned, I was recruited into the police force and promised that this would lead to an administrative position, if I did well, and after 10 years. 10 years in the police would take me to 1956. I had to work hard to secure my prospects for promotion to full police corporal and then sergeant investigator. I expected to complete a new advanced course of training under the police commandant in Juba, and began to prepare myself for the civil service examinations used to qualify officials for promotion. I felt well prepared for the exams, which I sat in August 1949.

Earlier in the year, I had sent a long petition to the governor of Bahr al-Ghazal. In my petition, I explained my conditions of recruitment into the police. I pleaded that my prospects for an administrative career be reconsidered. The petition was sent through the Lakes DC, RG McComas, who was impressed with my work. After two months, he called me to his office to say that the governor had received my petition and wanted to know whether I would like to sit a general knowledge entrance examination for the Sudan Police College. I accepted the offer without hesitation.

In early November 1949, I was called to the provincial headquarters at Wau, where Southern candidates sat the police college exam. After the exam, we were told to return to our districts and await the results to be conveyed to us as soon as they were received from Khartoum. In January 1950, the DC called me to his office. He told me with a big smile that I had passed. I was to prepare to leave for Khartoum at the end of February.

I was pleased, but my immediate problem was where to leave Sarah. I did not want her to go back to her or my parents' house in the village, which would mean losing contact with her for two years. Sarah had just given birth and she and the child would need constant care. I decided to leave her in the house under the care of my relative, Daniel Riak Dor, the headmaster of the government's boys' elementary school in Rumbek. Sarah accepted these arrangements.

On 1 March 1950, I left for Khartoum for the first time. I loved the wonderful views along the White Nile. I arrived in Khartoum by train from Kosti and enrolled in the police college the next day. Our cohort was the largest ever, comprised of 22 cadets: 19 from Northern Sudan, one from Aden, and two from South Sudan. As soon as I arrived, I met the other Southerner, Elia Lupe Waiwai from Yei, whom I had first met at Loka Intermediate School in 1941.

The college commandant was British, and his deputy was a Northern Sudanese, Senior Superintendent Khalifa Mohagoub. Mohagoub did not like that Southerners were enrolled at the police college. He was quite open about this and gave us a hard time. He especially did not like me. One day Mohagoub said, "Why did the British do this, sending chaps like you to institutions like this? They are definitely intending to make our rule over the South very difficult after independence. What we prefer is to leave things as they are until we take over, and then we shall decide which Southerners to send here for training." As students of the college, we declined to comment on his views.

Among the college staff, there was also one chief inspector, two inspectors, and several non-commissioned officers, headed by a sergeant. Their task was to drill the cadets in the use of firearms, physical exercise, and discipline. We worked and studied every day of the week, except Friday.

A very painful event occurred that year: our first-born baby girl died of malaria in Rumbek. I decided to bring Sarah to Khartoum. When I approached the college authorities, I was granted three weeks' leave to go to Rumbek and arrange for Sarah to join me. I flew by Sudan Airways, the first time I had travelled in an airplane. After three weeks, I returned to Khartoum; Sarah joined me later in the year. When Sarah arrived, I rented a house for her in Omdurman which I visited on weekends and holidays.

One of the ways that the Anglo-Egyptian colonial rule maintained law and order in the South was through the mounted police force in Malakal, the capital of the Upper Nile Province. The Upper Nile was a swampy and muddy region. It lacked infrastructure and there were no all-weather roads. Mounted police were used to keep the peace between tribes, collect taxes, and assist chiefs in administering their areas effectively. An animal husbandry course formed an essential part of police training, and all graduates were qualified in riding and maintaining the horses. Any police officer could be assigned to the mounted police.

Our cohort was sent to Malakal in early 1951. We remained there for three months. Most of the heads of department were still British nationals. We were warmly welcomed to the office of the Governor of Upper Nile, J. Long. He began to lecture us about the Upper Nile Province: its history, administration, and the problems facing the administration. Of all the cadets, four had jet-black skin. Despite this obvious fact, it had not occurred to Long that any of us were Southerners. He must have thought it too early to expect Southerners to be admitted to the police college.

After the lecture, there was time for questions. One Northern Sudanese asked Long why South Sudan was so neglected and undeveloped by the Anglo-Egyptian government. Long answered that because the Southern Sudanese were hostile to colonial administration, it had taken a long time to establish law and order, particularly in the Upper Nile and Bahr al-Ghazal Provinces. He went on to say that Southern Sudanese had killed men regarded as the cream of the colonial administration, hostility the British could not ignore. This was why the South was backward and dependent on the North and that all useful products or resources from the South flow North. He then showed us pictures of the British administrators and military officers killed during the uprisings in the South. Among them was the Governor of Mongalla, killed by the Aliab Dinka in 1919. There was also Capt. Fergusson, killed by the Agar Dinka in 1902; another who was assassinated by the Nuer in 1927, and one who was killed by the Zande.

At four o'clock, we had a tea party in Long's garden where he met every cadet separately. He was surprised to discover that I was from the South. He asked how I had entered the police college and I explained. He said that he was sorry he had not received the circular requesting applications for entrance into the college, and that he would not have supported an application from anyone whose mother tongue was not Arabic. I found out later that Long had had a similar exchange with Elia Lupe Waiwai.

In Malakal, we sat the college exam in horse riding. During the course, other cadets were highly impressed by South Sudan. They loved the greenness and the general environment. We told them they had not seen the real South that was south of Malakal, along the White Nile.

The final year of college was the hardest, as both the academic and practical aspects of the course intensified. But we were comfortable, and our morale was high. The food was good and so was the cadet allowance of S£522 per month. This was quite enough, particularly for the bachelors. The main subjects of our curriculum were criminal and statute law. Criminal law consisted of the penal code, code of procedure, and law of evidence. Statute law topics were police regulation and administration and detection and prevention of crimes.

Towards the end of the year, we sat more exams. We were given the rank of police sergeant and sent to work. Every other day, we were on the beat in either Omdurman, Khartoum, or Khartoum North. Cadets could be posted to any of the stations under the charge of a police officer. The officer would assign the cadet to patrol a two square mile beat for eight hours on foot. It was the duty of the cadet to prevent crime, apprehend would-be criminals, and prosecute them in court if necessary. Cadets needed to be conscious about what they did on the beat as it could have a profound effect on their future.

In October 1951, we completed our compulsory field training and were called back to the college. We then received reports on our performance from the respective station officer. My report was good; the only problem was my limited knowledge of Arabic, particularly because I was working in areas where most people could only speak and write Arabic.

At the end of the course, we sat the final and passing-out examinations. This covered everything we had learnt from car driving to veterinary and forensic skills. I passed. The passing out parade was held at the college at the end of November 1951, attended by many dignitaries and senior officials from the government and armed forces. Afterwards, we wore our uniforms with pride. We began with two stars. The sergeants-major, sergeants, and corporals who had instructed us since the course began came to congratulate and salute us. This was a powerful and important moment for us because some of these men had been harsh and abusive during our time in college.

During the course, South-North politics did not affect us very much. The differences and divisions were only just beginning to take shape and our political consciousness was still very limited. All of us were aware that relations between the Arabs and the indigenous Africans were strained. We discovered that most Northern Sudanese Arabs, whether educated or illiterate, regarded indigenous Africans as *abid:* slaves.

In our cohort of 22, skin color varied enormously. The very dark skinned, whether from the South or North, were regarded as *abid*.

Nearly all Southerners who had migrated to the North were angry about this and would react violently. The Arabs and Islamized black Northerners were less upset by it. Elia had decided that we would show how we felt if we were called *abid*. Fortunately, this never happened, and we both made friends with our Northern Sudanese Arab colleagues.

One day, Elia and I were invited by one of our Northern colleagues to visit his home for lunch. Our meeting point was in Omdurman, behind Brumble cinema. We arrived at the appointed time. Half an hour later, at 2pm, he arrived with a friend. The sun was very hot. He saw us and we saw them. As they walked towards us, we greeted them. Our colleague looked at us but did not answer and kept walking. When they were about to pass us, we called again, and again our colleague did not answer. We were astounded but decided to wait, hoping that he might be accompanying the friend to a place nearby and might return to us. We waited a further 40

*Gordon Muortat Mayen's cohort at the
Sudan Police College, Omdurman, circa 1950*

minutes, but he failed to come back, and we returned to the college. On Sunday, we asked him what had happened. He swore that he had come to the place but could not find us. We explained how he had walked past us with a friend, but he kept denying it. We decided to leave it there but any Southerner to whom we told the story saw it differently.

Our understanding of South-North politics was gradually developing through relations with older and more experienced Southerners. One of these was Michael Wata, from Yei. He was one of the South's greatest heroes and martyrs, killed by the army after the Torit uprising of 1955. Michael had been my history teacher at Loka Intermediate School. He was well versed in South-North politics and more knowledgeable than any other Southerner I had met. He and his colleague Zhiaba Toto abandoned their teaching jobs in 1945 and came to Northern Sudan in search of better-paid jobs in Khartoum.

There was discrimination towards us at the time of Ramadan. Whenever Ramadan arrived, Elia and I, as Christians, were the only individuals who would continue to drink and eat normally. This caused dismay to those who thought everybody in Sudan was a Muslim and did not like the fact that we did not fast. If arguments such as these cropped up in the presence of educated Northern Sudanese Muslims, they would defend us.

While I was on the beat in Khartoum, I received some wonderful news. Sarah had given birth to a daughter in Omdurman Hospital at 9pm on 21 September 1951. We named her Acol, which means replacement. Some people mistakenly thought we meant a replacement for our baby daughter who died in 1950. The name was meant to refer to my maternal grandmother, Acol Dut.

Posting in Rumbek (1952-1954)

After graduation, I was posted to Rumbek to be the first police inspector in charge of Lakes District (Rumbek and Yirol) Police Force. Everything was going well, and I was happy. Late in December 1951, I left with my family from Khartoum to Rumbek. We travelled by rail from Khartoum to Kosti. From there, we embarked on the steamer to the port of Shambe. When I was a police corporal, I used to travel in third class, but now my family and I were able to travel in second class. Sudan Railways was responsible for the good catering and meals on the steamer. Sarah loved the scenery along the river. After two days, we disembarked at Shambe, and the DC sent a car to take us to Rumbek. On the way, I stopped in Yirol to acquaint myself with some of the senior police, non-commissioned officers, and civilian officials with whom I would be working.

When we arrived in Rumbek, we met the Assistant DC, GRI Dees. He took us to our temporary accommodation, a small, newly built house. Dees was friendly. He told me that the budget provided for two good houses. One was for the sub-*Mamur* Administrator, Jervase Yak, and the other one was for me. The house was enough for Sarah, Acol, and I, but problems began when my numerous relatives and friends began to visit and expected to stay with us.

I was keen to start work immediately. Dees introduced me to the Lakes DC, Raven. Raven spoke at length about the administrative, judicial, and police structure of Lakes District and what my work would entail. It was my first real opportunity to practice what I had learnt at the police college. I was lucky to have the opportunity to do this among my own people.

My work was to maintain law and order and prevent crime. The nature of police work among the Dinka and the Nuer was different to elsewhere in Sudan. Crimes eligible for capital punishment were uncommon. Most crimes which involved death were categorized as culpable homicide not amounting to murder. Most of these cases were a result of a "fair" fight between individuals or groups, usually over disputes and feuds over the ownership of cattle or the abduction or impregnation of young women. A few cases ended in murder convictions and capital punishment. This could happen when two young men fought to the death. When one fell, instead of leaving him or allowing him to get up, the other hit or speared him fatally while vulnerable on the ground. That would then be treated as murder, punishable by death.

The most common crimes were fights during the dry season between December and May, mostly over cattle grazing rights or about bringing into the area infected cattle with diseases such as rinderpest. The police were sent to patrol the grazing areas soon after the end of the rainy season. There were cases of theft, but these were mostly confined to Rumbek or Yirol towns.

My most important innovation as a police officer was ensuring that every criminal case reported was investigated. This meant that the accused must be arrested, presented before a magistrate, and sent for trial by a magistrate. If it was culpable homicide or murder then the case would go before the chiefs' courts. Those sent before chiefs' courts were dealt with under customary law. In most cases of culpable homicide or grievous injury, the relatives of the deceased or injured persons received blood compensation in cattle. This reduced the term of imprisonment.

According to Dinka law, rape used to be punishable by the accused paying a heifer to the victim's parents. Later, rape became punishable by a long term of imprisonment; up to 16 years plus a heifer payable to the parents of the girl. We had not come across a case of marital rape, and this offence was not viewed as a crime. Only on a few occasions did I disagree with the chiefs over cases tried under customary law.

In 1953, I launched a successful campaign against hashish growers, traders, and smokers. The Dinka of Bahr al-Ghazal had known of hashish since 1930. Neighboring people such as the Zande, Moru, Jur Beli, and Bongo grew and smoked hashish like the Dinka smoked tobacco. In the 1940s and 1950s, some Dinka began to grow and smoke hashish too. Some became addicted and mentally damaged. Since possession and smoking of hashish was a crime, I drew up a program of action throughout Rumbek District during the rainy season of August and September 1953.

Before we acted, we collected information. We found out who the growers, traders, and smokers were and where they lived. Early one morning, we moved in with the intention of taking the culprits by surprise. We seized and uprooted large fields of flowering hashish and arrested the growers. However, we failed to capture the traders and smokers who were able to dispose of what they possessed when they heard us approaching. We were still satisfied as we had made it difficult to obtain new seeds to grow next year's crop. The seized hashish was dried in the sun and presented as evidence during the growers' trial. Many of the growers received heavy sentences. Later that year, I was invited to a police conference on hashish to talk about the seizure operation.

Most criminal cases throughout the Dinka and Nuer districts were straightforward. That is, although they may have been serious crimes, they were relatively simple to solve. In nearly all cases of culpable homicide and murder, the accused were ready and willing to confess. There were exceptions, though, particularly in Rumbek and Wau.

Throughout my civil service, I never missed taking my holidays. In 1953, part of my holiday was spent in my village with my relatives and the rest with my colleague and friend, Elia Lupe Waiwai, who worked as a police inspector in Yambio. We had studied together at Loka and at the Sudan Police College in 1950. It was the first time that I had visited Yambio.

Political and national cohesion took a long time to take root. One reason for this was that the colonial rulers had confined Southern Sudanese people, even educated ones, to their tribal areas. Elia confirmed that he was not always regarded as a South Sudanese. Despite this, the Zande people were very friendly and respected him. I was fascinated by what I saw at Yambio. The weather was pleasant and the rainforest much thicker and greener than we had at Rumbek. There was plenty of fruit, especially mangoes, bananas, and papaya, which I loved. Elia drove me around the villages, and I met other Southern government officials. At the end of the visit, I returned to Rumbek feeling happy and refreshed.

In 1954, I had another holiday with Jacob Cagai of Yirol, who was working in Rumbek as a local government officer. We went to Uganda. During our visit, we were lucky enough to meet Archdeacon Shaw, the founder of the Eastern Dinka Church Missionary Society. He gave us a lift in his car from Juba to Gulu in northern Uganda. He was old then, probably in his late seventies, and in the company of his servant Philip from Bor. We arrived in Gulu in the evening and drove straight to the rest house managed by the public works department. Under normal circumstances, indigenous Africans were not allowed to stay there. Archdeacon Shaw asked the British manager to allow us to spend the night at the rest house. The manager was reluctant at first but eventually agreed. We were given rooms. We changed our clothes and went down to the hall for dinner. Everybody was white, except for the cooks and the waiters. The waiter was unfriendly during dinner. He did not speak to us but merely sneered. Shaw suggested we continue our journey by train to Kampala, while he went to Nairobi. We said our farewells and thanked him for his help.

The only person we knew in Kampala was the former governor of Bahr al-Ghazal province, Thomas RH Owen, who had just retired and taken up a temporary job in Uganda. He was happy to meet us. We informed him that we hoped to see Queen Elizabeth II on her official visit to Uganda in the following days. Owen helped and drove us to Entebbe airport, where there was a huge guard of honor of African rifle troops. It was magnificent. All the dignitaries and chiefs were assembled to meet the Queen. When the Queen arrived, she disembarked her plane and inspected the guard of honor. We were able to have a close look at her: she was young, slim, and spoke in a clear, beautiful voice. I remember her wearing white gloves. When the parade was over, we returned to the hotel feeling satisfied.

At the end of May 1954, we went back to Sudan, with Owen. Owen booked us in second class cabins on the steamer to Nimule. He did this with some difficulty, as second class was exclusively for Asians. As black Africans we faced hostility, but no attempts were made to remove us. During the journey, our cabins became very hot. We opened the doors for fresh air, and the rooms became humid. The first-class cabins were much more comfortable, so we asked to be moved. The manager refused and a row broke out. We accused the manager of racism. He was furious and would have handed us over to the police. Owen, however, spoke to the manager who changed his mind and permitted us to move to first class on the condition that we paid the difference, which we did. Situations like this happened across Uganda. The way black Africans like us were mistreated caused us to have mixed feelings about coming back to Uganda for a holiday or for anything else.

Tonj and Wau: Sudanization, Relationships Between Southerners in the Civil Service

The governor of Bahr al-Ghazal was pleased with my work in Lakes and decided to transfer me to Tonj. I arrived in June 1954 and was put up in one of the teachers' houses at the intermediate school. The headmaster was Fahani Suleiman, a Northern Sudanese Christian. Although I did not stay long in Tonj, I had a good time there because the police force, chiefs, and people generally were cooperative. By this time, my family consisted of Sarah and two children, Rebecca Acol and Paul Madong.

In July, I was promoted to chief inspector. My promotion coincided with Sudanization being implemented in Bahr al-Ghazal. Nearly all the posts which British officials held in the civil and army services were taken over by Northern Sudanese. This was also the case in Equatoria and Upper Nile. Exceptions to this included the Assistant DCs of Wau and Yirol, Lewis Bey and Clement Mboro respectively. Some benefited from Sudanization; full *Mamurs* were promoted to Assistant DCs. This was the highest civil service post attained by Southern Sudanese. Also in that year, the two literate sergeants, Gabriel Kau Ater and John Akot, successfully passed their six-month officers' course. They had also been promoted to the rank of police inspector. I had recommended them for this course.

After my promotion, I was the senior-most police officer present in the district. The Bahr al-Ghazal Commandant of Police, Col. Abdul el Nur, frequently called me to Wau police provincial headquarters to carry out duties as acting deputy commandant. He was finding it difficult to get a police superintendent (who normally held the role of deputy) transferred to Wau. The Northern Sudanese were afraid of service in the South: they regarded it as a hardship posting. This included el Nur, who told me how scared he was to work in South Sudan. He would frequently take short holidays in the North.

In November, I was transferred from Tonj to Wau. I was assigned the duties of a superintendent and acting deputy commandant of the police in Bahr al-Ghazal. The Wau police force was also in need of reform and modernization. New structures needed to be devised to properly establish Wau as the police headquarters of the province. Every district police force was autonomous under its district commissioner; these forces needed centralization. We made a budget for the whole provincial police and ordered cars for police use, which were expected to be delivered in early 1955. We also set up a police training center and started courses for men from every district, although funds were insufficient to fully run this center.

At this time, there was more political awareness and activity in Juba than there was in Wau. In Juba, Southerners went on demonstrations against Sudanization and demanded better wages. Juba and Equatoria had been the initial force behind the general strike of 1946, after which salaries were equalized between North and South. The first Liberal Party conference also took place in Juba in October 1954. A key item on its agenda was condemnation of Sudanization.

In Wau and Bahr al-Ghazal more widely, there was little political activity in support of the Southern Sudanese cause. Some Bahr al-Ghazal members of parliament (MPs) in Khartoum, led by Santino Deng Teng, supported unity. The rest were either moderate or uncommitted. There were also many clerks, bookkeepers, and medical assistants who were only interested in carrying out their professional duties. This was especially the case after salaries of Southern officials were equalized with those of Northern counterparts. This did not mean that the Southern intelligentsia in Bahr al-Ghazal favored Northern Arab rule in Sudan. Many of them feared what would happen if Sudanization took place fully, thinking that there would be a re-colonization of the South by Northern Sudan. But they did not have sufficient political awareness to create initiatives like those taking place in Juba. The colonial government had banned civil servants from taking part in politics and the administrative laws prohibited it too. During those years of democratic rule, politics was the monopoly of a few politicians who had either been indirectly or directly elected to the parliament in Khartoum.

Most South Sudanese were not antagonistic towards each other, either on tribal or cultural grounds, until after the liberation struggle was launched in the early fifties. Most Southern government officials before 1947 were the products of missionary schools. Many of them had met during school days and were friends regardless of their tribal origins. I had many friends from other tribes at school. One was Erika Lakidi, an Acholi. After the Torit uprising of 1955, he migrated to Uganda where he became a cabinet minister. He was murdered by the Idi Amin regime in 1974. Other friends included Ezboni Mondiri and Philip Mboyo, both Moru, Kimindago, a Zande, and Elia Lupe Waiwai, a Kakwa. There was also Othwonh Bogo, a Shilluk, who died in a plane crash between Malakal and Khartoum in 1986, Hilary Paul Logali, a Bari, William Kile, an Acholi, Akwan and Hilary Akwong, both from the Luo of Bahr al-Ghazal, and Clement Mboro, an Ndogo.

There were outbreaks of tribal fighting at various schools, but these were usually settled by the school authorities. If these students met again as government officials, they and their families seemed to coexist peacefully with one another. When I was in Wau, many Southern officials ate lunch together and visited each other socially, outside of their jobs. There were no other means of socializing until after the so-called independence in 1956 when social clubs were

From left to right: Hilary Akwong, Gordon Muortat Mayen, William Deng Nhial, and James Ajith, Wau, 1954

introduced by the Northern Arab authorities. Examples of these included the tennis clubs which some Southern officials joined as members.

My father, Mayen Maborjok, died in hospital in March 1955. This happened just as I was beginning to settle down in Wau. My mother Akueng Mangu had died prematurely in 1941. My father still being alive had been a great source of happiness for me. I had started to pay him a monthly allowance of S£20, which he could use to buy cows or anything which would make his life better. I was informed that he was ill, so I went to Rumbek and brought him to Wau hospital for treatment. The doctor diagnosed his illness as liver failure. Sadly, his condition deteriorated, and he died on 15 March. He was about 65 years old.

3.

A Contested Transition to Independence

The Torit Uprising of August 1955

Northern Sudanese continued to migrate to the South, partly because of Sudanization and partly to set up businesses. The political atmosphere in the South, especially in Equatoria, was volatile. Tragic events took place, such as the killing and wounding of Southern workers by the authorities and Arab merchants following a strike at the Nzara cotton factory in 1955. No one knew what was going to happen. There was no evidence yet of an embryonic national liberation movement which could attack the new Northern Sudanese colonial government in the South. The only dissent was the denouncing of Sudanization at the 1954 Liberal Party conference in Juba.

Another administrative position of some significance in the Wau District was the *Mamur*. It was occupied by Paul Acire, a Southerner. This post was not affected by Sudanization because it was junior. My position as the police chief inspector at the provincial headquarters was also not affected by Sudanization. In Wau, the governor, Dawud Abdul Latif, and his deputy, Tigani Saad, were Northern Sudanese.

In early July 1955, my police commandant, Col. el Nur, went to Khartoum on holiday, leaving me as acting commandant. On the evening of 18 August, there was news of a military uprising at Torit, reported on all the international radio stations. Omdurman Radio did not broadcast the news, but it was in any case in Arabic. As many educated Southerners knew little Arabic, they depended on the foreign stations. Anyway, it was impossible to get the exact details of what was happening. There were all sorts of rumors. On 19 August, tension also rose in Wau. Nobody could act in support of or against the uprising because we had little knowledge of what was going on.

Fear and panic began to overwhelm the Northern Sudanese Arabs. They were afraid that what was happening in Torit would happen in Wau and Bahr al-Ghazal. They had been informed by their colleagues in Equatoria and Khartoum of what was taking place and learned that there were casualties among Northerners in Equatoria. This was a very delicate time. In my capacity as acting commandant of police, I called the governor regularly to reassure him. I told him that he and his officials need not feel afraid because the police were maintaining law and order. He looked worried and doubtful, even though he had always trusted me. The Prime Minister, Ismail al-Azhari, went on radio to order the rebels in Torit to lay down their arms. They did not obey his orders.

The British Governor-General of Sudan at that time was Sir Alexander Knox Helm, who had stayed on after Sudanization. On 20 August, he contacted the rebels. He too ordered them to lay down their arms. Helm said, "You have disappointed me very much because when I visited you recently, you impressed me as a well behaved and disciplined force. Now as the supreme commander of the Sudan Defence Force (SDF), I hereby order you to lay down your arms and accept your punishment as men." In reply, the spokesman and commander of the rebels Lt. Renaldo Loleyo said, "We have no desire to cause more bloodshed, but we are not willing to surrender our arms to the Northern troops because our lives will be in danger. We will surrender our arms to British and Egyptian troops". There was a short period of silence after which Helm replied, "No British or Egyptian troops will be sent. You must surrender your arms to the Sudanese troops. If you are afraid for your lives, I will send Mr Lewis, the former governor of Equatoria Province, to be present to ensure the safety of those surrendering their arms."

The rebels respected and trusted the Governor-General. They thought of him as neutral and sincere and agreed to surrender their arms. Other Southerners did not trust that the news broadcasts were impartial. We could not trust the information circulating about what was taking place in the negotiations between the Governor-General and the leadership of the Torit Mutiny. In Bahr al-Ghazal, we were able to hear news intermittently from Omdurman and Cairo. These bulletins mostly concerned the massive arrival of Northern Sudanese troops at Juba airport, which had not been taken by the Torit rebels.

Lt. Nyang Dhieu was an officer in the Equatoria Corps and a native of Bahr al-Ghazal involved in the Torit Mutiny. On 21 August, he arrived in Wau from Torit, via Yambio. Northern Sudanese civilian and military personnel fleeing the situation in Equatoria soon followed him. These Northern Sudanese accused Dhieu of having shot and killed a Northern Sudanese civilian between Yambio and Wau. This news circulated quickly and Dhieu's presence began to cause panic, especially among the high-ranking Northern Sudanese officials. I met Dhieu, who denied killing Northern civilians. He said that he agreed with those who sparked the uprising, but his advice to organize it properly was not heeded. I did not think that Dhieu was involved in the killing of civilians. Dhieu said that if he took over the force in Wau, he would order the closure of the airports throughout the province to prevent the government from landing troops and causing havoc. Despite Dhieu's good intentions, his presence in Wau still frightened the Northern Sudanese.

On the night of 23 August, all the Northern Sudanese in Wau fled in a small steamer headed for the North. Many Northern Sudanese officials left, including the governor, his deputy, who was also the officer commanding No. 3 Company of the Equatoria Corps in Wau, and army officers. This changed the situation completely. Dhieu took over as acting commander of No. 3 Company. Lewis Bey took over as acting governor. I assumed the position of commandant of the police.

The following day we convened a meeting of the chiefs and group leaders in Wau under the chairmanship of the acting governor. The meeting resolved to set up an ad hoc Provincial Council to maintain law and order and continue the smooth running of the civil administration. The rebels of the Torit Mutiny had complied with the Governor-General's order to lay down their arms. The meeting emphasized that no civilian should be killed, and no property looted. We resolved to telegram Prime Minister al-Azhari, warning him against sending Northern troops to Bahr al-Ghazal. If he failed to heed our appeal, clashes would ensue. We asked that confirmation be given to reassure the population. Within 24 hours, the Prime Minister confirmed that no troops would be landed in Bahr al-Ghazal.

After the meeting, Dhieu ordered the Equatoria Corps to occupy Wau airport and other strategic positions throughout the province. I deployed the police to maintain law and order in Wau town and in all the districts.

Gordon Muortat Mayen at Wau Airport, 1955

As the Provincial Council began to gain ground and the tension eased, Prime Minister al-Azhari sent his Minister of Wildlife and Animal Resources, Santino Deng Teng, to Wau. Deng Teng was a native of Aweil District. Soon after his arrival, he reassured the ad hoc Provincial Council that al-Azhari had agreed to their request and would not send troops to Bahr al-Ghazal.

There was a period of calm. Some policemen broke into the armory and removed weapons but did not use them. I responded by calling for a parade and ordering the return of arms to the armory. I warned them of the disastrous consequences for our people if law and order broke down. I reminded them of the binding commitment they had made to protect lives and property and maintain security. Some policemen had heard that police in Equatoria had looted property during the uprising in August. They felt that I was denying them this benefit by calling for restraint. When they realized that the leaders of the Torit uprising had accepted the

Police on parade in Wau, circa 1955

Governor-General's orders to surrender their arms, they agreed to return their arms.

Two days later, police reinforcements arrived from other districts and the situation returned to normal. One of my police sergeants, Alexis Bakomba, of Raga District, came to my house. He informed me that some Northern Sudanese armed with rifles had occupied a house in Hila Jebel and were threatening to shoot ordinary people. I left my house accompanied by my bodyguards. On the way, I decided to go and see a prominent Arab merchant, Sheikh Yussif el Malek. When we arrived in Hila Jebel, Sgt. Bakomba looked nervous and confused. I asked him where the house was, but he just looked around and shivered. Sheikh Yussif became suspicious. He believed that he would be ambushed by Bakomba's accomplices. In the bushes, we could not see anyone. Addressing me, Yussif burst out in Arabic, "You Gordon, I am ready to die. God is great. I have had many children. I am not afraid of death."

I immediately ordered everyone back to the car and told the driver to take us to the house of Lewis Bey. Bey questioned Bakomba, who insisted that there were some armed Northerners there, but that they may have run away when they saw the police car arriving. Bey asked Bakomba why he was shivering. He did not reply. I ordered Bakomba's arrest pending further investigation and thanked Sheikh Yussif and his friends.

The police investigation uncovered a story not backed up by much evidence. Apparently, there was a plot to lure me into an ambush planned by Bakomba and other policemen from Western Bahr al-Ghazal. The conspirators believed that I might go to the scene alone or with only one or two police bodyguards. When they saw me coming with a formidable force, they fled. The story of the armed Northern Sudanese was not true. However, Bakomba was released without charge.

There were rumors that began with the arrival of Lt. Dhieu that Southern policemen and soldiers had looted the property of Northern Sudanese traders. In addition, it was believed that Dhieu, Acting Governor Bey, and I were all denying people opportunities to loot the Arabs. This was thought to be one of the motivations for the ambush. Instead, we were insisting on the maintenance of peace in Bahr al-Ghazal. Meanwhile, Santino Deng Teng, the cabinet minister, claimed to be the one keeping peace in Bahr al-Ghazal. He regarded the three of us and other officials throughout the province as his subordinates.

The truth as far as we were concerned was that it was futile for Bahr al-Ghazal to rebel because it was unlikely to be successful. The Torit uprising occurred spontaneously. There had been no coordination between the leadership of the Torit uprising and the other provinces. There was also no clarity about objectives. Moreover, according to the latest reports from Upper Nile Province, No. 4 Company had obeyed the orders to disarm.

Bahr al-Ghazal remained under its own administration. It was free from Northern Sudanese Arab rule until November, when Northern troops occupied Bahr al-Ghazal from Equatoria through Yambio. Dhieu and I were replaced. I did not know where they took Dhieu, who was tried for his alleged killing of the civilian on his way to Wau in August. I did not hear then whether he was convicted.

Transfer to Atbara

In January 1956, I requested a transfer to Atbara. I did not want to work under forces of occupation. I loved my profession. But when the government is colonial and oppressive, it is not nice to be an agent of that oppression in your own community. I can remember how the Northern Sudanese police officers used to feel when they were ordered by the Anglo-Egyptian colonial government to persecute and oppress their own people during the campaign for the independence of Sudan in the 1940s and 1950s. The government knew that I would not be happy to continue to serve in the South and agreed to my transfer. One of the police superintendents, Ahmed Kanar, took over from me as the acting commandant of police in Bahr al-Ghazal. Col. el Nur was still on leave when I left Wau. He never returned to Wau or to South Sudan again.

I went to Atbara in early January and was assigned a non-officer job. This was not what I expected. The job was to disperse demonstrations by force, quell protests organized by the trade unions or other groups, and organize and command guards of honor. It was a job done by the rank and file. I developed some skill and a suitable physique. I did not like the job, but I could not see another option at the time. I think the authorities did not want me to have access to government secrets. In particular, they did not want me to know anything about how the South would be governed following the 1955 uprising.

I did not have sufficient knowledge of written Arabic, and this may have contributed to my being assigned this job. However, my spoken Arabic was not bad. I would never have graduated from police college if I could not understand Arabic at all. I was keen to learn Arabic as fast as possible, so I employed a Northern Sudanese man to teach me on a part-time basis. Although I made many Northern Sudanese friends, I was not exactly popular. I could be described as a lonely Southern Sudanese working among the Northern Arabs. I was treated with a certain degree of tolerance. Southerners were generally treated as alien and lacking certain qualifications, cultural and otherwise, which made them worthy only of being tolerated. This tolerance did not apply when the situation became aggressive and hostile.

A strange incident occurred towards the end of 1956. Sarah and I went for a walk one evening. She was dressed in Western-style clothing. I did not want her to wear the *tob* since we were Christians. When we reached the town center, children and some adults came out from their houses. They walked on either side of us and made rude remarks, "Look, the world is upside down, even the slaves have become high ranking officials and their womenfolk dress like *kawajat*." We walked on as if it was not happening. I asked one of my colleagues why people were behaving like that towards us, especially towards Sarah. He said that they had probably never seen black people dressed in European clothes walking in public and that they were ignorant.

My family was growing. We had three children when we arrived in Atbara: Rebecca Acol, Paul Madong, born in Rumbek in 1952, and Martha Nyanjur, born in Tonj in 1954. Another daughter, Yar, was born in Atbara in early 1956. In 1956, we went to Rumbek on holiday. Yar was six months old. A Dinka boy servant, Malwal, came with us and helped look after the children. Soon after we returned

GORDON MUORTAT MAYEN

*Gordon Muortat Mayen and
Sarah Piath, Atbara, 1956*

to Atbara from holiday, Yar contracted a serious illness and died. Sarah and I were shattered. We did not have any adult relatives to comfort us. Sarah and the children kept becoming unwell and we felt that the weather in the North did not suit our family. We both agreed that the only way out was to apply for a transfer back to South Sudan.

Two more junior Southern officers were transferred to Atbara. They were Inspector Gabriel Kau Ater, who had been transferred from Bahr al-Ghazal to Darfur before coming to Atbara, and Inspector Ibrahim Doulela, a young officer from Eastern Equatoria who had just graduated from the police college. Kau was from Rumbek and brought his family, so our social life improved. We ate together and discussed current affairs in the South. Kau used to relate to us the terrible experience he had had in Darfur. He had been insulted by senior police officers. They would say to him, "You mutinying slaves in the South, we will crush you." On several occasions, Kau's commandant had called to threaten him with dismissal. He compared Kau to the "brothers in Torit" who had done bad things to "our people." Kau asked for a transfer and after many months was placed in Atbara. I had the impression that he had lost interest in police work but could not afford to resign because he had a large family.

At the beginning of 1957, I applied for a transfer to the South. My application was rejected by the commissioner of police. Since the Torit Mutiny, government policy was not to transfer Southern police officers serving in the North back to the South. I was stunned, but resignation was not an option. So, I decided instead to apply for a transfer to the public administration at the rank of Assistant DC (ADC). I wrote to the commissioner of police and was informed that the matter would be discussed with the civil secretary's office.

Assistant District Commissioner of Jur River District: my early involvement in the struggle

The commissioner of police informed me that my transfer to the administration had been agreed. I was promoted to the rank of ADC and would be posted at Tonj, the headquarters of the Jur River District. I arrived in Tonj at the end of June 1957, happy to be back in Bahr al-Ghazal. I would spend six years in this post, serving until 1963. When I arrived, the DC was a Northern Sudanese Arab called Abushama. The second ADC's post was in Gogrial. This was filled by another Southerner, Tito Adibo from Upper Nile.

Sarah and I had a fourth child, a son, Mawan, born at Tonj soon after our arrival from Atbara in 1957. My cousin, Deng Kuwei Maborjok, gave him the name Mawan, meaning a relative of the fox, the totem of our clan. I also gave him the name Matom, which meant that he was born during the age of the atomic bomb.

I worked with the Dinka chiefs of the Jur River District. They were among the best in the province, honest, dignified, and respectful. The most senior chiefs included Giir Thiik, Aguer Adel, Arik Mawein, Cier Rehan, Benjamin Lang Juk, Parek Macar, and Wek Agoth, among others. They regarded me as their son, and I had high regard for them.

The most sensitive and important aspect of the district administration was to provide justice. There were thousands of Dinka civil and criminal cases about cattle. They comprised over 90 percent of the total yearly court cases, and they had to be processed under customary law, which fell under the supervision of the DC and the ADCs. If not well supervised and properly managed, these cases could result in corruption.

In Aweil, Tonj, and Gogrial, I introduced new rules which forbade court officials from preventing members of the public from entering the DC's or ADC's office when they were presenting their complaints. This enabled me to have direct contact with the complainants. I spoke to them in Dinka without any interpreters. Within a short period of time, I managed to clear up most of the cattle cases with the cooperation of the Dinka chiefs. In criminal cases, I used the same procedures whenever part of the case had to be dealt with according to customary law. Ordinary litigants were satisfied with the results.

By 1963, the atmosphere in the South was politically charged. A case of murder was brought before me. It involved a young Dinka woman from Thiet. She was married to a local Northern Sudanese trader. They had three children: one daughter and two sons. Her husband informed her that he wanted to take the children to visit his mother in the North. The woman wanted to go with them, but he would not allow it, saying it was unnecessary and that she should continue looking after the house in their absence. The woman became suspicious that the man might not return, and she might lose her children. She had heard of this happening to other Dinka girls.

The argument between husband and wife continued for several weeks. The woman then took a knife and cut the throat of her young son, aged about four, and her baby boy. She also tried to kill her eight-year-old daughter, but the girl managed to run away. The woman then walked with the bloody knife to Thiet police station, where she was arrested. In May 1963, she was brought before me in my role as magistrate. I asked her why she had killed her own children. She said she believed that killing them was better than losing them. She was convinced that her husband intended to escape to the North with her children and that if this happened, she would not see them again for the rest of her life. I took down the necessary evidence and charged her with murder. I sympathized with her, but there was no way I could help. Regardless of the degree of provocation, in the eyes of the law, this was murder.

During this time, there was an intensification of political activity among the South Sudanese, particularly in Equatoria. Still, Bahr al-Ghazal and Upper Nile were not completely dormant. The Torit Mutiny of 1955 and the election campaign of 1957 were carried out with vigor. Both these events raised the level of political consciousness in the South.

Sudanese civil servants were banned from political involvement. I was a government official, but I could not afford to refrain from political activities. It was especially important after the election of 1958. Continued political involvement was imperative because there was a strong expectation that the problems of the South could be solved if the South were granted federal status. Northern MPs promised the South in the 1955 parliament that their federal demand would be ratified by the constituent assembly of 1958.

Every politically minded and educated Southerner followed what was going on in parliament. There were no newspapers, but they listened to the radio. I also listened to the local and overseas radio and read various publications and magazines. Southern officials in Tonj, Thiet, Gogrial, Aweil, and Wau constantly debated South-North politics. At Tonj, we had students from the primary teachers training center and some from the government intermediate school. Most were politically conscious, such as Jok Run from Rumbek, who joined the Anyanya in the early sixties. At Tonj, there was a club where officials met to play tennis and discuss current affairs. Rumbek secondary school students were renowned, spearheading the campaigns for Southern political hopes and for Southern officials living in the South. They were a great influence and became the backbone of the armed liberation struggle which emerged years later.

Exile of Southern MPs and the Growth of an Underground Movement

In 1958, debates in parliament over federal status for the South polarized the country. The demand for federal status was reintroduced at the first session of parliament by the Southern MPs. The Northern MPs, however, opposed the demand during the debate; perhaps they were having second thoughts about their promise to the South in 1955. This culminated in a walkout by Southern MPs. In November 1958, the Sudanese army staged a coup d'état in Khartoum. All the South Sudanese were shocked and frustrated. They were committed to the demands for federation as the only possible peaceful and constitutional solution to the issues of the South. They were also angered by the arrogance and contemptuous attitude of the Northern Sudanese Arabs who monopolized the political and economic power of the whole country.

Some Southern MPs fled into exile to launch an armed struggle in response to the forceful repression by the army and Northern political leaders. Those who fled included Father Saturnino Lohure. They were later joined by some outstanding government officials, such as William Deng Nhial, Aggrey Jaden, and Akuot Atem, among others. As a result of this flight, the political situation in the South started to deteriorate.

A spontaneous underground movement emerged, quickly becoming established in Equatoria and Bahr al-Ghazal. The objective of the movement was to promote political awareness among Southern Sudanese at the grassroots. Objectives also included raising funds for the movement and encouraging young people, especially students, to join the guerrilla army to resist Arab neo-colonialism and repression. The leadership of this army was assembling abroad.

The Bahr al-Ghazal underground group soon took shape. I became the chairman and Salva Mawein Ariik, in Wau, was the secretary-general. The principles and rules by which the movement operated were laid down and coordinated throughout the South. One of the most important principles was absolute secrecy. Every member had to swear allegiance and loyalty to the South and to the liberation struggle. The movement was based on single cells, separate from one another. Every member had to contribute 10 percent of his or her income to the movement. This was remitted through foreign supporters in neighboring countries or through runners from the South who would take the money from one place to another. There was a coordinating committee based in Khartoum, which included Hilary Paul Logali and Darius Bashir, among others.

Part of the funds raised was retained in Bahr al-Ghazal to be spent on expenses for volunteers who journeyed on foot to join the movement outside the country. Most volunteers were students or young men from the countryside. These included Bernadino Mou Mou, who led the Anyanya attack against the government forces in Wau during the autumn of 1963, and Ferdinand Goi of Western Bahr al-Ghazal, who later became the overall commander of the Western Bahr al-Ghazal Anyanya. He fought hard against the Sudanese army.

The military regime became aware of these political activities and the situation became tense. We, too, became increasingly vigilant. The secret meetings of the Tonj committee continued. I also attended the meeting of the coordination committee in Khartoum whenever feasible. Whenever a meeting was to be held, word was passed around to the members informing them of the date, place, and time. For security reasons, we used to meet in a forest around 8pm. Every member had to arrive at the venue 15 minutes before the appointed time and lie down in the grass nearby. When the time was reached, everyone had to stand up. All would then move forward, and the meeting would begin. Meetings would last up to

15 minutes. When the meeting was over, attendees had to leave quietly one after the other.

In July 1962, somebody informed the police in Tonj that Sgt. Baak Aguot was a member of our committee. He was arrested. The committee went into session and resolved that we should help Baak escape to join the movement abroad. We were afraid that if Baak were tortured, he might confess everything. We contacted Baak secretly and told him to apply for bail, as there was no evidence against him. Since Baak was a senior non-commissioned officer and had several sympathizers from his area in the police, he was allowed to leave the cell and sit near the prison.

A group of recruits was leaving at night for the Congo. This was carefully conveyed to Baak so that he knew where to meet the group. Baak was to move at 8pm. He managed to get away as arranged and get to the meeting place. We held our breath. At 8.45pm, a bugle sounded, and the alarm was raised, indicating that there had been an escape of a prisoner awaiting trial.

I was the ADC and the magistrate concerned with prisoners of this type. Both Wau and I were duly informed of the incident, but I was not kept informed of the police activity that took place afterwards. At 1pm the next day, Constable Manin knocked on my door and whispered to me that Baak had run away. He said that he believed Baak had joined the group which was to leave the night before for Congo. Manin asked me if I thought that they had followed the route proposed in our last meeting. I replied that the route had been changed to the No. 14 all-weather road south of Tonj River, towards Juba. Manin thanked me and left. The following day, I heard that a car full of police had taken the No. 14 Road early in the morning. In the evening, news spread that a police car had overturned on the No. 14 Road and that several policemen were injured, though none seriously. There was a lot of police activity in

Tonj that week. A chief inspector from the special branch in Wau was brought to Tonj to conduct the investigation into Baak's escape. We were happy because Baak's escape had prevented the police from finding evidence of the existence of our committee.

A week later, Pastor Kedhikia Barac and I were sitting on the veranda of my house. We heard clapping coming from the shadow of a lemon tree in the garden. Much to my surprise, it was Baak, naked. Baak said that he had run along the track until he had reached a place two days west of Bussere. He was not able to catch up with the group because they were running too fast. He returned because he could not find them. I told him that if he reported to the authorities, his life would be in danger. He needed to get to Congo on his own. I gave him S£50, a lot of money at that time, as well as an updated map to help him reach Congo. He took these things and ran off. Shortly after, a police patrol passed by. That was the last time I ever saw Baak.

Why I Joined the Anyanya Liberation Movement
As a Southerner, I believed that unity between South and North had been imposed on us by the British and Egyptian colonialists. There was a lack of common feeling between us and much racial prejudice by the Arabs towards indigenous Africans. The inhuman, humiliating, and tragic history of the slave trade saw millions of Southerners carried away or killed. Today, the Northern Sudan Arab traders had a contemptuous attitude towards the Southern Sudanese.

In the few years after the so-called independence, I realized that there was no difference between the attitudes of these traders and those of the Northern Sudanese officials. These officials had come to the South to replace the British colonial officials. They arrived with the intention and determination to colonize and suppress the South by force, which they did. It would be possible for them to continue these actions as agents and executioners of successive governments in Khartoum.

Many Southerners realized during the run-up to the elections in 1957 that they were compelled to engage with the Northern Sudanese Arabs even if they did not want to. They had no option but to accept the federal status promised by the Arab MPs of the 1955 parliament. The Arab MPs, however, dishonored the promise of federalism at the 1958 Constituent Assembly. Under the military regime of Gen. Ibrahim Abboud, they proceeded to violently subdue the South. In 1958, I gave my unqualified support to the decision of the Southern leaders in parliament to resist re-colonization by Northern Sudan by all possible means. The Northern Arabs were using the state apparatus, including the army, to keep the South under their rule. The South, therefore, would have to use all means possible, including armed struggle, to resist, and achieve complete independence.

A military coup took place in November 1958 and the Southern MPs had fled into exile. I wanted to join them, but I had a large family. William Deng Nhial, Nikenora Manyok, and I discussed this problem in Tonj but were not able to find a solution. Yet our situation was becoming precarious. A small group of us decided to leave the country together. Shortly after, at the end of 1961, this became impractical. One of the people in the group was Zakaria Duot, a trader in Rumbek, originally from Bor, and among the staunchest and most patriotic Southern nationalists I met. Zakaria decided to leave on his own. He was sending his cattle to Maridi for sale, and I asked whether he could also take my five bulls. He said that he could, and I arranged to deliver my bulls to him. It was not long after that I heard that he had successfully left the country. After Zakaria left, he sent word that he had sold my bulls, but was not able to send the money, as he had given the proceeds to the movement. I did not mind that. I was sad to learn that sometime around 1963 in Uganda, Zakaria died from an asthma attack.

1962 was one of our most turbulent years. The underground movement was still secret. The government did not have concrete evidence about the movement and those involved. If individuals were arrested merely on suspicion, it would be explosive. Many people had fled the country. News circulated that the leaders abroad had set up a new liberation movement in Kinshasa. This was called the Sudan African Closed District National Union (SACDNU).

I had not abandoned the idea of leaving the country to join this movement. But I decided to devise a ploy to convince people that I had no intention of leaving the country. I sent Sarah to Rumbek to start constructing a semi-permanent house for us. I remained with some of our children at Tonj because it was closer to the mission school in Wau which they attended. On the weekends, I visited Rumbek to see how the building was progressing. I also had a mud house about 15 miles southwest of Rumbek on the way to the road to Juba. This house was situated next to my agricultural project in Makambalie, started in 1956 while I was in Atbara. I had planted mangoes, lemons, guavas, and other fruit. I transported the seeds of these trees from Wau or Tonj to Rumbek three times a year. My objective was to produce fruit on a commercial scale. I had dug two wells as the water table was less than six meters deep. A half-acre to produce green vegetables was being managed by my cousin Kaan Agok. My nephew, Moses Mading, would help while on holiday from school. Vegetables used to be sold at Rumbek market during the dry season.

My aim was to prove to the authorities that I was more concerned about my material wellbeing than I was with North-South politics. The reality, however, was that I was planning to leave the country together with my family. My plan was that towards October 1962, I would ask for a holiday to go to East Africa, and then join the movement. By then, all the children would also be on holiday.

In June, while I was visiting Sarah in Rumbek, I met my friend Nikenora Choor Malek, who had just arrived from Juba. Choor Malek was a trusted member of the underground movement. He told me that the military government knew about my activities in the underground movement and that I was being closely watched. He advised me not to go on holiday with my family, saying that it would be dangerous for us. He told me that he had been travelling with Col. Tahr Abd Rahman, the military governor of Equatoria, on his way to Wau and that throughout the journey from Juba to Rumbek, Col. Tahr expressed bitterness and anger. I was not surprised. We had already discovered that one of our members was a government spy. I changed my plans. Instead of taking a holiday, I decided to apply for a transfer to Nasir or Akobo. This would enable me to travel with my family to Ethiopia. I returned to Tonj and immediately applied for a transfer to Akobo. I also contacted Chief Deng Acuil to ask if he would look after my 90 cattle at Tonj. He agreed to do this for me.

The construction of the house was completed, and Sarah had returned to Tonj. We tried to decide what to do. The situation in Tonj had deteriorated. A rebel attack was imminent. There were rumors that the Anyanya had launched several attacks against the government forces in Equatoria. The rebels were thought to have established many camps in the rainforest south and south-west of Tonj town.

A group of rebels were rumored to have been seen during the night marching in the Tonj Primary School compound. As a result, many Tonj residents began to move out of town, on foot, to the surrounding villages. Some managed to hire cars to carry their belongings. We tried to explain that the reports were false, but people were so scared that they would not listen.

Transfer to Upper Nile

My transfer to Upper Nile was accepted, but not to Akobo District. I would have to go to Fangak. In August 1963, I left for Malakal where I met the governor, Abbas Fagiir. He was polite and seemed to know Southerners better than most other Northern Sudanese administrators. He had worked in Maridi for years. He told me I was to go to Fangak to help the DC deal with the floods. I went two days later. The whole district was flooded but the center of town was protected by a huge mud dike maintained by many Nuer laborers.

The only means of communication with the outside world was by telegraph and small steamers. Almost all the offices were closed. Controlling the flood was the top priority. At 9am every day, we sat outside to supervise the work against the flood. Occasionally, a whistle was blown to indicate that the water had broken through some part of the dike wall. Laborers had to run with mud to close the breach. This was unpopular work with the locals. During the night, many would run away and return to their homes.

One morning, the DC and I were watching the Nuer laborers carrying mud with their hands. The DC suddenly said, "These people are inferior. For them to emancipate themselves, their blood has to be mixed with that of a superior race." He added, "Their religion should be Islam and not Christianity, that is from countries thousands of miles away." I was enraged but tried to keep my composure. I said, "You should not say such things against other Sudanese nationals. If that is the attitude of all Northern Sudanese then the future of this country is quite bleak. Southerners are not inferior; they are among the most intelligent people in Africa. Yours is simply a racial prejudice like that of the South African whites.

You, yourself, are not pure Arab as you claim to be. More than half of your blood is that of the indigenous African whom you claim is inferior. These people whom you call inferior have their own way of life and culture, which they can claim to be superior to yours. They don't have either political and military power or formal education. If they had, you would not be sitting here ruling them." I continued, "these people have their own religion, which has not been written down and of which they are also very proud. Christianity is the right religion for the indigenous Africans because Jesus Christ was brought to Africa (Egypt) when he was a baby. He drank the water of the Nile, whereas Mohammed did not."

He then said, "I am sorry, I didn't know that what I said would offend you." The argument continued until eventually each of us threatened to write to the governor. Within a week, I wrote to the governor and requested a transfer from Fangak. The DC probably wrote to him too. I was called to Malakal where I met the governor and explained my encounter with the DC. The governor was conciliatory. He called the Fangak DC an opinionated and talkative man. The governor told me that I would not need to go back to Fangak and that he would consider sending me to Bentiu temporarily unless I had some objection. I told him that I had no objection. When I saw him again the next day, he said that the decision for me to go to Bentiu was finalized. I was to take over from Saad Zakir, who had just been transferred to Bentiu. A week later, I headed to Bentiu where I met Saad Zakir. He immediately went on leave, having removed the confidential files from the office. I reported this to the governor.

The two months I spent at Bentiu were pleasant. I was unable to move around the whole district because the flood had destroyed all the roads, but the town itself was dry. Another important official in Bentiu was Police Inspector Joel, a young man from Bor

District. It was a time of the year when things were quiet, like in Dinka districts. There were few cattle cases and tribal fights. The local church had been destroyed by the flood. I gave permission to the young pastor to hold prayers in my house since my family was away and I was alone. I knew a few words in Nuer and decided to take lessons. Two young, educated Nuer men volunteered to teach me regularly.

Bentiu was not greatly affected by the events of the liberation struggle. Yet most of the educated men were aware of what was happening. We held occasional meetings on political affairs in my house. I briefed them fully on what was going on in Bahr al-Ghazal, Equatoria, and among Southerners in Khartoum. They were happy to be taking part in these discussions and keen to learn.

The young men teaching me Nuer wondered why a branch of the South Sudan underground movement should not be established in Upper Nile. I told them that Enoch Mading de Garang, a church worker in Malakal, had paid a visit to Bahr al-Ghazal early 1962. During that visit, he had promised to establish a branch as soon as he was back in Malakal. I found out later that he had established an underground branch in Malakal, but it had not become fully operational.

Pochalla Attack
In the first week of September 1963, units of the Anyanya entered Upper Nile for the first time. They attacked the Pochalla police post along the Ethiopian border and inflicted some casualties. News spread quickly and fear struck the province. This was followed by a massive movement of people. Within a couple of days, I received a telegram from the governor when on the way to Wad Medani, where I had been transferred. The telegram ordered me to come to Malakal immediately. It informed me that Saad Zikir's leave had

been cancelled and he would be returning to Bentiu immediately to take over from me.

Bentiu was soon full of people, mostly citizens returning from other areas fearing impending hostilities. DC Saad Zikir arrived after three days. He took over from me and I left for Malakal by the same steamer. I met Governor Fagiir in Malakal on my way to Wad Medani. I reminded him that I had been denied access to the files while I was in the position of Bentiu DC. He said that he had been informed that I and other Southern officials were collaborating with the rebel movement abroad, and that we were not trusted. He added: "If I were the Sudan government, I would have dismissed all of you."

I asked him if there was evidence of our collaboration. If not, I said, "how do you justify this degree of distrust? If the distrust has become so great, how can the Southerners and the Northerners co-exist as citizens of one country?" He made no further comment except to say that he would forward my complaint to the Ministry of the Interior.

My Administrative Work in Blue Nile Province
I arrived in Wad Medani in October 1963. I was allocated a house and told it was only a matter of time until I was also given an office. In the North, administrators were known as local government officers, in posts such as executive officers and town clerks. The titles of DCs, ADCs, and *Mamur* had been abolished. They only existed in the South.

Every day, the executive officer sent a car for me. It brought me to his office, where a chair was provided at the side of his office table. I sat there from 9am until 2pm when the car would take me back home. It was boring and I regularly complained. I applied for special permission to go back to the South and bring my family over. By the end of November 1963, I was increasingly worried about their security. There was news of mass arrests, and the torture of educated Southerners accused of subversion. I was not surprised when the governor told me they were reluctant to allow me to go to the South in the current circumstances. I asked if he could tell me exactly what was going on, but he declined.

What kept me going were my occasional weekend visits to Khartoum, where I would meet colleagues such as Hilary Paul Logali and Darius Bashir. They would brief me on the situation in the South. They told me about the guerrilla attacks by the Anyanya units who lacked arms and ammunition. In Bahr al-Ghazal, Bernadino Mou, a native of Gogrial, had attacked Wau with his poorly armed men. His plan was betrayed. I was given a detailed report of the Anyanya attack on Pochalla and other successful attacks in Equatoria.

An attack on Wau by the Anyanya guerrilla forces took place in January 1964. The authorities then carried out mass arrests of Southerners suspected of being members of the movement in Bahr al-Ghazal. Nearly all the members of our movement were arrested and tortured. Under torture, two members named me as one of the leaders. But in court, they denied the allegations and explained that they had been forced to confess. No evidence proved that anyone was a member of the movement. Despite being under suspicion, I was able to go back to my family. In March 1964, I again applied for permission to go to Bahr al-Ghazal to bring my family to Wad Medani. This time my application was accepted. I left in April.

I found Sarah and my family safe. We hastily packed our things, as we only had two weeks. My work conditions in Wad Medani remained uncertain, so we decided to leave most belongings in the house in Rumbek. Among the valuable belongings left behind were a brand-new refrigerator, mahogany beds and wardrobes, five large wooden boxes of china, and kitchen equipment which we had accumulated over the years. We locked the house and appointed a permanent watchman with a monthly wage.

Many relatives and friends came to see us off. The war of liberation was looming. Nobody was sure as to what the future held, who would meet again, and who would not. The next day we went to Wau, from where we travelled in a first-class train carriage to Khartoum. On the train with us was my colleague in the underground movement, Salva Mawein Ariik, now a prisoner convicted by a court in Wau of being a member of the movement. The authorities believed that it was the underground movement that was responsible for the Anyanya attack on Wau. Mawein was later released after a successful appeal. He would die in the great massacre of July 1965 in Wau.

In Wad Medani, I reported to the governor, who promised that my assignment would soon be sorted out. I asked him why I had not been given a proper assignment. He said that it was because my transfer was so sudden and that he had not had enough notice. He also assumed that the reasons may have been connected to the outbreak of hostilities in the South. I talked to him about my interview with Governor Fagiir who had told me that I was one of the Southern government officials blacklisted because of my involvement in subversive activity in the South. I asked the governor if he was able to elaborate. He denied any knowledge of it, so I stopped asking.

Soon after, I was assigned to be the magistrate for the collection of business profit tax. Most Northern Sudanese merchants, as well as some foreigners, had failed to pay these taxes since independence in 1956. It was my responsibility to ensure the arrears were paid. I was given an office and some staff and the power to use police services. I began by instructing the staff to produce a list of the merchants with arrears. I called the defaulters to my office. Those who had admitted to not having paid were given up to two months to pay. I warned them that if they did not pay, I would be compelled to take further measures. Many of them left my office complaining bitterly. They accused me of behaving like the British imperialists that they had got rid of. They called me a *khawaja*. Some of their colleagues thought such comments unfair. They said that if they had been good citizens, they would have paid on time. Within a period of one week, thousands of Sudanese pounds were paid into the council treasury. After a month, more than two-thirds of the arrears were paid. The senior executive officer phoned and congratulated me on my success.

4.

Intensification of the First Civil War

The Fall of Abboud

One objective of the coup d'état in November 1958 was to impose Islamization and Arabization on the South. This turned out to be difficult to achieve. Many in Northern Sudan also expected the military regime to solve their political and economic problems. The public became disillusioned when there was no speedy solution to these problems.

In 1963, Provincial Councils were established throughout the country. The regime hoped to convince Southerners that they could share power and help run their own local administrations. Neither the North nor the South responded well to this idea. The dictatorship refused to recognize that there was a problem with the South. They continued to denounce the missionaries and the imperialists as the source of difficulties. They did not try to explore workable settlements to the conflict and were convinced that integration between the North and the South was achievable through force.

The government appointed a commission of inquiry in September 1964 to investigate the causes of unrest in the South and to make recommendations, without altering the constitution of the country. The appointment of the commission invited public discussion on the South Sudan question. For the first time, civil servants were asked to publicly share their views. Still, there were skeptics. The commission was denounced by the Sudan African National Union (SANU), among others.

The students' union of Khartoum University had long spearheaded opposition to the regime. They concluded that no solution to the Southern question was possible if the military regime remained in power. Following this conclusion, a ban was placed on further student meetings on campus. On 21 October, the students defied the order and staged another meeting. The police attempted to disperse the meeting, and a student named Ahmad al-Qurayshi was shot and killed. The following day, his funeral took place in Khartoum. A funeral procession of more than 30,000 people developed into a riot. The army was called in but was unable to bring the situation under control.

On 25 October, demonstrations spread to other major Northern cities. A group of teachers, lawyers, and students established what became known as the Professional Front. They were joined by other professional associations, trade unions, and the Gezira tenants. The executive council of the Professional Front was dominated by the Sudan Communist Party. A general strike was called, paralyzing the capital.

In Wad Medani, the massive demonstrations reached the civil hospital, less than half a mile from my house. The demonstration became a mob assaulting residents and looting shops. Fortunately, the demonstration did not proceed beyond the hospital.

As the situation deteriorated, the regime split between those who favored crushing the uprising through force and those who wanted power to be returned to civilians. The latter group was led by

Gen. Ibrahim Abboud and were convinced that even if they clung to power, they would be overthrown by junior officers in another coup. On 26 October, Abboud dissolved the Supreme Council and declared the resignation of the cabinet. The demonstrations and rioting throughout Northern Sudan then ceased.

Involvement with the Southern Front

Within 24 hours of the resignation of the military regime, Hilary Paul Logali, Darius Bashir, and other colleagues called me to Khartoum. When I arrived, I was briefed on the latest situation and its effects on the South. Negotiations were taking place between the army and the Professional Front. A transitional government was to be formed by the Northern National Front. They asked the Southerners present in Khartoum to join the National Front; in return, they might obtain some cabinet portfolios. The Southerners told the Northern National Front, however, that they had formed their own Southern Front (SF) to negotiate their terms of participation. I backed this strategy. I was a permanent civil servant and did not envisage joining the government, but I would support anyone nominated to join. I returned to Wad Medani.

The same week, the transitional government was announced. Sirr al-Khatim al-Khalifa, formerly a civil servant, was named Prime Minister. The South was to be represented by several Southerners. A senior portfolio, the Minister of the Interior, was for the first time held by a Southerner, Clement Mboro, formerly deputy governor of Kordofan. Other Southern ministers were Hilary Logali for public works and mineral resources, and Ezboni Mondiri for irrigation and transport. Abboud's position as the head of state was to be filled by a group of five, to be known as the Supreme Council of State. The provisional constitution in force prior to the Abboud regime returned.

As the Supreme Council of State was being formed, I was informed that SF colleagues had nominated me to represent the South in that body. I rejected this offer. I wanted to wait until there was a permanent solution to the South Sudan problem. I believed that if we rushed to take up positions, the ruling Northerners might assume we just wanted positions and money. They might think this our real motive for launching the political and armed struggle. After prolonged negotiations, the post in the Supreme Council was given to Luigi Adwok. Many SF members later blamed me for refusing to accept the position, especially after Adwok let the Front down. Adwok would vote in favor of elections in the South, contrary to the SF policy to boycott the elections.

The SF mostly comprised former members of the underground movement. It was supported by Southerners throughout the country. In Wad Medani, we formed our own branch, of which I was elected chairman. Traditionally, civil servants could not participate in politics, but the al-Khatim government declared that to find an acceptable settlement to the Southern question, all citizens must be allowed to air their views without fear. I had played an active role in the underground movement and so was co-opted into the main Southern Front in Khartoum. I attended meetings there nearly every weekend.

The SF objective was to bring about a compromise solution through negotiations. I was much opposed to this aim and to the role the SF had assigned itself. For the sake of solidarity, however, I did not step aside or speak out against this aim. I did continue to make my views on current affairs clear. The reason for my stance was that we were at the mercy of the Sudanese government. We were trying not to appear to pull the Southern political leaders in exile into a compromise agreement with the government. The government had declared to the world that the objective of SANU and the Anyanya was independence for South Sudan. The SANU leadership was also under pressure from foreign powers, including several black African neighboring countries, to enter negotiations with Khartoum.

Towards the Roundtable Conference
The transitional government made the first move towards starting negotiations. They sent SF members Darius Bashir, Abel Alier, and Alfred Lubari Ramba to Ethiopia, Kenya, and Uganda. The aim was to learn the reaction of the SANU leadership and Southern refugees to the changes taking place. At the same time, three other SF members reported back. Father Saturnino Lohure, then in Nairobi, and Aggrey Jaden and Joseph Oduho in Kampala, expressed reservations about the willingness and capacity of the transitional government to correct the mistakes of the past. Father Saturnino was particularly concerned about the exclusion of Southerners from Sudanization, and the dishonoring of the federal status pledged by the Northern political parties. He also expressed doubts about security of the political leaders in exile and the refugees. His view was that relations between the North and the South would not improve in the foreseeable future.

Aggrey Jaden, the newly elected President of SANU, promised the SF delegation that he would study the political changes that had taken place in Khartoum and consider what effects they would have on South Sudan. He shared Father Saturnino's concerns about the safe return of Southern refugees and politicians in exile.

The SF forged ahead and established itself as a political organization. It had already achieved recognition in Khartoum as the main organization representing the aspirations of the Southern people. It succeeded in securing embryonic representation of the South in the transitional government. The Front declared its stance as "self-determination for the South."

At the end of 1964, some SF activists, including myself, pushed the organization to hold a conference to clarify its policies and declare whether it would become a political party or continue as a political organization. The conference took place in Malakal in February 1965. Every branch throughout the South and the North attended, even though security in Malakal was precarious.

I led the delegation from Blue Nile province. I travelled with my friend Stephen Ciec Lam from Khartoum. Ciec Lam was a secretary to Clement Mboro and one of the best South Sudanese nationalists at that time. He confided to me that the issue of differences between the Dinka and the Nuer would be raised at the conference. He told me that he was not formally a delegate, but this issue was why he was going.

The evening I arrived, Ciec Lam, Natale Olwak, and two other Nuer men came to my room. Ciec Lam said, "Uncle Gordon, there is a problem between the Nuer and Dinka. We have decided to present it to you for resolution since we know you are one of our impartial South Sudanese leaders." Before he went further, I asked him to tell me whether it was the whole Dinka and the whole Nuer tribes he was talking about or just certain sections of them. He said that he was talking about all of both the tribes. I said that if this was so, I was not able to provide a solution; as I was a Dinka, I was bound to be prejudiced. I advised him to raise the matter at the conference so that other South Sudanese could give their opinions.

Olwak continued, "Uncle Gordon, don't throw away the opportunity and the confidence placed in you by the Nuer. Please reconsider." I told Olwak that I was not going to change my mind but that I would listen. Ciec Lam and another man began to explain that ever since the liberation movement started, the Dinka had prevented the Nuer from participating in the movement. They did this by humiliating, contradicting, and undermining Nuer. It was alleged that William Deng had mistreated Philip Pedak and Enoch Mading de Garang, the secretary of the SF.

The relaying of the story did not alter my stance. I told them to prepare to explain their side of the story the next day to the chairman and the delegates. Ciec Lam and the others said they were not prepared to raise the issue. I said that if they did not, I would.

Two days later, I raised the issue at the conference. The chairman supported my stance and asked the Nuer to present their complaint. The Nuer claimed that it was their right to have five delegates at the proposed Roundtable Conference. The chairman told them that the basis of representation at the Roundtable Conference was not by tribe, but by capability. This meant that if five brothers who were capable were found, then they could in principle represent the South. Selection on merit became one of the policies of the SF.

My conference speech was written by the Medani SF branch committee. The main point was the need for Southerners to unite behind the SF and its goal of the right of self-determination for the South. What divided us, such as belonging to different tribes, sections, clans, provinces, and districts had to be resisted. I ended my speech by appealing to delegates to not put too much hope in the upcoming Roundtable Conference. I felt the transitional government would try to deceive the South. They would say that the important positions given to the SF in the cabinet and in the Supreme Council of State should be enough for the SF to persuade the Anyanya to scale back its armed struggle.

Bona Malwal was one of the most prominent and active members of the SF and was also the deputy editor of the Front's newspaper, *The Vigilant*. Three days before the conference ended, he arrived and told everyone that I had been selected by the Front as a delegate to the Roundtable Conference. The motion was agreed. Hence, I proceeded to Khartoum to prepare for the Roundtable Conference even though I felt that I should have remained in Malakal until the end of the SF conference.

As soon as I had gone, Bona Malwal and others tabled a motion that I should also replace Ezboni Mondiri as a cabinet minister. Ezboni had been dismissed after striking a Northern Sudanese messenger for insubordination. I had been opposed to the idea of luring Southerners into high positions, particularly to ministerial posts, because it would dilute the vigor of such persons to work for a lasting settlement of the conflict.

In early February, I heard on Radio Omdurman that the SF conference had recommended I be appointed to the transitional government as Minister of Works and Mineral Resources, to replace Ezboni. I was shocked. I regarded this as an unfriendly act on the part of my colleagues. I quickly made up my mind to refuse. However, several friends and colleagues, including Gordon Abyei Makuac, president of the SF executive committee, intervened and pressured me to accept the portfolio. Reluctantly, I accepted, not because of the pressure but out of respect for the unanimous resolution of the Malakal conference. If I had stayed at the conference as I had wished, there might have been a different outcome.

One of the principal resolutions of the Malakal conference was to declare that the SF become a political party with a constitution. The objective of the SF would be to continue to demand the right of self-determination for the South. Although the SF headquarters would remain in Khartoum, its base of activity would be in South Sudan.

Massacre of Southerners in Khartoum
In November 1964, Clement Mboro started a tour of the South to persuade SANU leaders to attend the Roundtable Conference. He was expected to return to Khartoum on the morning of 6

December. A huge crowd of Southern Sudanese planned to receive him at Khartoum airport. His plane was delayed, and the crowd began to be impatient. Rumors began to fly that Mboro was the victim of a government conspiracy. The crowd dispersed and violence erupted. Property was damaged at the airport and in other parts of Khartoum. The reaction from the Arab residents was swift and brutal. All over the city, they attacked the rioting Southerners using firearms, swords, and other weapons. Hundreds, if not thousands, of Southern Sudanese were killed. It is not known exactly how many Southerners were killed or injured as the authorities refused to investigate.

The massacre took place in broad daylight and in view of the world. The next day, the transitional government stepped in. The Southern survivors in Omdurman and Khartoum were placed in Khartoum football stadium under police protection.

In Wad Medani, reports circulated that massacres would continue. A small committee of our SF branch monitored the situation. One evening, they reported that the police had disappeared from the streets. In their place, northern Sudanese civilians were in groups carrying swords and other traditional weapons. They had no guns. I went out to look and found that it was true.

I drove to the house of the deputy governor and briefed him. He assured me that he would contact the commandant of police and ask him to intervene. Two hours later, the street was cleared of the mobs. The deputy governor later confirmed that their objective was to repeat the acts of violence which had occurred in Khartoum. It was fortunate that we had been able to nip the violence in the bud.

Why had Southerners rioted in Khartoum on 6 December? One reason was that the Northern Sudanese had succeeded in overthrowing the Abboud military government by demonstrating and rioting, and some Southerners may have thought they too could achieve their aims through the same means.

William Deng Nhial, still the secretary-general of SANU, wrote a letter to the Prime Minister. He proposed negotiations with the aim of finding a solution to the question of the South. He suggested three things. Firstly, that amnesty be granted to those in exile. Secondly, that the closed district ordinance and the 1962 Missionary Societies Act be repealed. Thirdly, that SANU be recognized as a political party inside Sudan.

Deng was generally well regarded by Southern Sudanese for the sacrifice he made when he deserted his post as an administrator and joined the movement in exile and the role he played in founding the liberation struggle in 1962. His letter, however, received a mixed reaction. Some thought the letter represented the official SANU response to the changes in Sudan. Those who knew about the splits in the SANU thought Deng might be acting out his frustrations in the letter.

SANU was split between Father Saturnino, the patron, with Joseph Oduho, the president, on one side and William Deng, the secretary-general, on the other. Another split was between Aggrey Jaden and Joseph Oduho. A conference to elect a new SANU president had been convened in the absence of William Deng. The first aim of the conference was to abolish the post of the secretary-general, to get rid of Deng. Although the motion passed, Deng refused to acknowledge his dismissal. Then, the SANU conference unexpectedly elected Aggrey Jaden as president.

Many Southerners feared that if Deng was merely acting out his frustrations, the transitional government might take advantage of this to further divide the SANU leadership. In December 1964, the transitional government issued a statement: general amnesty was granted to all Southerners in exile as well as to other citizens involved in the rebellion.

Another joint government and SF delegation, of Abdin Ismail

and Ezboni Mondiri, was sent to Kampala in January 1965 to hold talks with the government of Milton Obote. An agreement had already been reached on the repatriation and resettlement of refugees. SANU had by now consented to the holding of a conference, provided it took place outside Sudan.

The transition government predictably reacted to Deng's letter by sending another delegation, comprising Dawud Abdel Latif, Mou Gier (aka Muondit), and Akec Mohamed to meet Deng in Kinshasa. Deng refused to allow the transitional government to exploit the differences between him and the other SANU leaders. He told the delegation that he would eventually return to Sudan, but his immediate concern was the convening of the conference. He returned to Kampala to join the members of the SANU Executive Committee. He decided to show unity with other colleagues to restore solidarity within the SANU leadership. He presented proposals for a future SANU strategy considering the prevailing political developments in two parts. First, SANU should return to Sudan and participate as a political party given the demise of the military regime. Second, SANU should reactivate the campaign for federal status of the South. These proposals were rejected by the other members and SANU continued to be deeply divided. The only point on which most of the SANU leaders did agree was that there should be a conference. It was undecided where this should be held.

Deng had few options because the SANU leaders had failed to agree. On 27 February 1965, accompanied by SANU members Ezekiel Macuei Kodi, Peter Muoranyaar Biet, Elia Duang Arop, Rizgalla Ibrahim, and Joseph Bol, Deng left the party.

It was eventually decided that the venue for the conference would be Juba. Joseph Oduho and Aggrey Jaden were persuaded of this by a delegation which included Hilary Paul Logali. The venue, however, was later switched to Khartoum as the security in Juba was judged to be not good enough.

The prospects of the conference were overshadowed by the December massacre of the Southerners in the streets of Khartoum. There was also the effect of the aggressive attitude of the Northern traders and civil servants in the South. They had invited the Northern Arab army present in the South to take strong measures against the Southern political activists. The morale of Southerners was also low because of reports of divisions among the leaders in exile. When William Deng arrived in Khartoum, his SANU faction returned to the country with the SF delegation. Other SANU colleagues decided not to return. Deng engaged in dialogue with the SF leadership to try and merge his SANU faction with the SF. The SF, however, were not helping efforts to promote unity among Southerners. Deng and the SF were not able to come to terms, but relationships remained friendly between the SF and the two factions of SANU.

Pressure began to build on the rest of SANU in exile which included Joseph Oduho, Father Saturnino, and Aggrey Jaden. They were all due to attend the Roundtable Conference in Sudan. On 3 March, Ugandan minister of interior Felix Onama made a statement in the Ugandan Parliament in support of the efforts being made to bring about a political solution for South Sudan. He criticized the attitudes of Southern leaders in exile and accused them of being under foreign influence.

The Roundtable Conference

The prime minister called a meeting and declared that the government was going ahead with arrangements for the conference. The SF, the Sudan Unity Party (SUP) of Santino Deng Teng and Philemon Majok, and William Deng's faction of SANU, decided that the conference would be held in Khartoum on 16 March, irrespective of whether the leaders in exile attended or not. They appealed to leaders outside the country to attend and contribute.

Faced with this pressure, the SANU leaders in exile began to organize a delegation. A compromise was reached: SANU would have a single delegation comprising four from the Deng faction and five from the Aggrey faction. With the goodwill between the SANU and SF, it was also agreed that the SF should have nine delegates at the conference, meaning that between us we had 18 delegates out of the 27 agreed for the South. The other nine were to represent other shades of political opinion in the South, such as the SUP. The Northern political parties had 18 delegates. It was also agreed that Egypt, Uganda, Ghana, Kenya, Nigeria, Tanzania, and Algeria would observe the conference. The conference had a secretariat and a chairman, Professor El Nazeer Dafalla, Chancellor of Khartoum University. The SF first opposed but later accepted his chairmanship.

On 15 March, a deadlock developed between the SANU and SF delegates. We needed to agree a common strategy for the conference and a single leader for each delegation. For the SF, there was no difficulty. I had been selected prior to the meeting. But when it came to SANU, the five who had come from exile had decided that Elia Lupe Waiwai should lead. But as William Deng Nhial wanted to lead the delegation, he rejected Elia. The SF mediated a long discussion, which lasted until the early hours of 16 March 1965. A compromise was reached: SANU would have a single delegation with two heads: Deng and Elia.

The South then entered the Roundtable Conference united by a common strategy and having rejected the Southern delegates sponsored by the Northern political parties and the transitional government. The leaders of the unity parties were Ismail al-Azhari of the National Unionist Party (NUP), Sadik el-Hamdi (Umma

Party), Ali Abd el Rahman of the People's Democratic Party (PDP), Abdel Khalig Mahgoub of the Sudan Communist Party and Hassan al-Turabi of the Islamic Charter Front.

The delegations of the three Southern political parties were composed as follows:
1. SANU: William Deng Nhial, Elia Lupe Waiwai, Lawrence Wol Wol, George Akumbek Kwac, Oliver Albino, George Lumoro, Hillary Uchalla Akuono, Nikanora M. Aguer, and Elia Duang Arop.
2. SF: Gordon Muortat Mayen, Abel Alier, Gordon Abyei Makuac, Othwonh Dak, Othwonh Buogo, Natale Olwak, Lubari Ramba, Bona Mawal Madut, and Romano Hassan.
3. SUP: Philemon Majok, Riiny Lual, James Bol Kamal, Edward Amum, Gordon Soro, Charles Ali Bilal, and Yusif Diku.

The conference opened with an address by Prime Minister al-Khatim, who, among other things, identified the root causes of the problem as physical, racial, and cultural differences exacerbated by British colonial policy, missionaries, and the military regime. He ended by appealing for a new approach and a peaceful solution. The Northern speeches that followed were along the same lines. Many asserted that the problem would be resolved by the North granting regional government to the South. In the same speeches, they rejected Southern calls for separation and a federal government. The stance of the Northern political parties, the Khartoum government, and the Northern armed forces towards the South was unanimous.

Southern opinion was more divided. Aggrey Jaden spoke on behalf of SANU to denounce Northern domination of the South and call for independence. William Deng, co-leader of the SANU delegation, explained political grievances which had led to the violent conflict between the South and the North and called for federal status for the South.

I delivered the Front's speech. I gave the historical background of relations: slavery between the North and the South, and the decision by Britain and Egypt at the Cairo Conference of 1953 to annex the South permanently to the North without the consent of its inhabitants. That the unity declared between the North and the South at the 1947 Juba Conference had no mandate from the Southern people. That the 1955 Torit uprising was a result of this decision. That the trend by successive Northern governments to impose the will of the North on the South by force was corroborated by the events of December 1964 when hundreds of Southerners were massacred in the streets of Khartoum, as well as other mass killings of Southerners in the South. I ended by requesting the conference grant the right of self-determination to the people of South Sudan.

Proposals were put forward after the speeches. SANU and the SF proposed that the people of South Sudan be allowed to decide their future through a plebiscite, with three possible choices: federation, unity with the North, or independence. This proposal should satisfy the wishes of everybody: unionists, those seeking independence from the North, and federalists. To reach an impartial result, we proposed an independent body be appointed to supervise the plebiscite. We suggested that the present African observers be assigned this task; the results of the plebiscite be binding on both the South and the North; that a copy of the agreement be deposited with the Organization of African Unity (OAU) and the Arab League; and that the delegates and observers visit the three Southern provinces.

We also proposed that the state of emergency imposed on the South be lifted and the army return to their barracks in the North. SANU and the SF would work to end present hostilities in the

South by appealing to the Southern fighters. We wanted the security powers presently in the hands of the army to be transferred to civilian administrators and the Southern administrators presently in the North to be transferred to the South. We requested that the agreement between the governments of Uganda and Sudan for the safe return and resettlement of Southern refugees be implemented.

Joining the Cabinet

The euphoria which followed the fall of the military regime was reduced considerably by the failure of the Roundtable Conference. Nevertheless, our main tasks were to ensure that the resolutions adopted by the Roundtable Conference were carried out before the transitional government came to an end, to organize the SF into a political party, and to make sure that the conference reconvened when recommended by the relevant committee.

One issue that hindered progress in South Sudan was tribalism, even though the SF had increasingly risen above such antagonism. As I have noted, for the first time, three cabinet ministries and a post in the Supreme Council of State were held by non-Dinka Southerners: Clement Mboro, Hilary Paul Logali, Ezboni Mondiri, and Luigi Adwok. Rumors circulated of a Dinka conspiracy designed to put the post holders at risk. I observed some relief and joy from Mboro, the first Southern Minister of Interior and a man of extraordinary honesty and integrity, when he heard that I had accepted to join them as a minister. In April 1965, I took up my Cabinet portfolio as Minister for Works and Mineral Resources. Mboro became one of my closest friends and colleagues through the years. We agreed to maintain solidarity within the Cabinet. Whenever one of us submitted a ministerial proposal or project, the rest would give unqualified support. Occasionally, some Northern ministers lobbied us first to get our collective support before making their own proposals.

The resolutions of the Roundtable Conference were to be implemented within three months. We also sought, while in the government, to politicize the masses in South Sudan to understand why violent armed struggle had been unavoidable, to educate them about South Sudanese nationalism, and to promote support for the SF. A program of action was drawn up and I was assigned to address rallies in Juba, Wau, and Malakal.

A good number of SF members, despite being strong Southern nationalists, had some confidence in the Northern Sudan Arab leadership and hence believed that a lasting solution was possible. This explained the strenuous efforts some of the members made in the early stages of the dialogue between SANU in exile and the transitional government to bring about the Roundtable Conference, even on the government's terms.

Not only that: even though the SF was an internal wing of SANU in exile, and entirely in support of a call for the independence of South Sudan, many did not believe in the possibility of the South achieving independence. Some members remained glued to their views despite their bitter experiences with Northern Arabs. While not quite a majority in the Executive Committee, an absolute majority in the grassroots was completely committed to the original SANU and Anyanya principle of independence for South Sudan.

Prime Minister al-Khatim was appointed by the North because of his so-called expertise on the South, where he worked for many years as an educationalist. At first, he appeared to be quite constructive and open, especially when he admitted wrongs perpetrated against the South by the North and the existence of social and cultural differences. He resolved to find an acceptable solution for the South. But when the transitional government was faced with implementing reforms and preventing the army from carrying out atrocities in the South, he was ineffective.

The End of the Transitional Government and Elections

Elections were due at the end of the term of the transitional government in 1965. Pressure began to mount against the transitional government as soon as the year began. Spearheading it were the main sectarian political parties: Umma, the NUP, and others such as the Muslim Brotherhood. Various methods, including demonstrations by paramilitary elements of the Ansar, were used.

Clement Mboro, the Minister of Interior, believed the promises made to us and that those reforms agreed at the Roundtable Conference would be implemented. He worked day and night to ensure that these resolutions, especially the enrolment of cadets in the military, police, and prison colleges, were put into action.

Prime Minister al-Khatim feared our solidarity in the Council of Ministers and as a result, Council meetings were reduced or even cancelled. Instead, the Northern Sudanese senior ministers used to meet separately under the chairmanship of al-Khatim to make decisions on security matters such as sending troops to the South. Mboro, despite being a senior minister, was excluded from such special meetings.

In late April 1965, there were reports of atrocities committed by the army in the South. We received one telegram stating, "if you are unable to ensure security of the people of the South from the army, it would be better for you to resign." Soon afterwards, we heard that a village near Tonj was burnt down by the army and that several people were killed. We were angry and disappointed. We felt we were being reduced to puppets.

We met al-Khatim many times and appealed for action, but he did nothing. We called for meetings of the Council of Ministers to discuss the situation, but al-Khatim became evasive. At this point, the three Southern ministers met and issued a press statement condemning the transitional government and atrocities against civilians in Tonj and other places in the South. Al-Khatim reacted angrily. He told us our statement was a breach of collective responsibility as members of the government. We replied that we were aware of this, but that complying with the rules would be turning our backs on our people. The three of us were ready to be dismissed, but the prime minister did not penalize us.

The political parties were more concerned with the election. The October Charter stated that elections would be held not later than March 1965. The power to hold elections was vested in the five-member Supreme Council of State of which one member was a Southerner, Luigi Adwok.

In a meeting of the SF Executive Committee in December 1964, it was resolved that the three Southern provinces would not participate in the general elections. The prevailing lack of security meant that conditions were not conducive for Southerners to vote freely. Moreover, thousands of Southerners were in exile. We wanted a peaceful resolution of the Southern question to be achieved first. Luigi Adwok was present in the meeting and was instructed not to vote for the elections by the SF Executive Committee. But contrary to his instructions, Adwok voted for elections. The Umma and NUP favored elections, but the PDP, the Sudan Communist Party, and the SF were opposed. Adwok's vote for elections created a majority in favor of the elections. Thus, Adwok made it possible for elections to take place, not only in the South but throughout Sudan. Adwok was a popular member of the SF, but his betrayal of the cause and insubordination angered many. He quarreled with many senior members, including me. He was eventually asked to resign from the executive committee rather than be dismissed.

The elections were won by the Umma Party. Despite this, many Northern Sudanese expressed doubts over the wisdom of electing a parliament in which the South was not represented. They feared that doing so would aggravate the split between the North and the South. However, the worst development resulting from the elections was that 21 Northerners, most of them traders resident in the South, represented the South in parliament. They simply nominated themselves in the Southern constituencies and were declared to have been elected unopposed. To our disgust, their election was upheld by the Supreme Court. The Southerners felt that the seating of these 21 Arabs as representatives of South Sudan was illegal, a breach of the promises made by the North, and proof that Northern Sudanese rulers did not recognize the desire of the Southerners for self-governance. As usual, protests by Southerners fell on deaf ears.

In June 1965, the Umma and the NUP agreed to form a coalition government, as Umma had not emerged from the elections with a majority. Muhammed Ahmad Mahgoub of the Umma Party, one of the most anti-South of Northern leaders, became Prime Minister. Former Prime Minister Ismail al-Azhari of the NUP became Chairman of the Supreme Council of State. This marked the end of the transitional government and our time as ministers.

Soon after we were out of the transitional government, the SF transformed into a proper political party. A new executive committee was formed, with Clement Mboro as president, I as vice-president, and Hilary Paul Logali as secretary-general. William Deng also converted his SANU into a political party, with himself as president. There was another SANU in exile whose president continued to be Joseph Oduho.

Massacres in the South

Soon after becoming Prime Minister, Mahgoub gave an ultimatum to the South Sudanese rebels to surrender within 15 days or face serious consequences. When the deadline expired, Mahgoub ordered the army in the South to deal firmly with the outlaws and their supporters. The army fully complied with those orders. In July 1965, news of more massacres of Southerners began circulating in Khartoum.

On 9 July, the news of a massacre of Southerners in Juba by the army was published in *The Vigilant*. All the Southerners in Khartoum and Omdurman were distressed by reports of enormous casualties.

The reports were discussed in the SF executive committee. Mboro and I volunteered to visit Juba and see things for ourselves. When we approached Ahmed al-Mahdi, now the Minister of Interior, he warned us that if any misfortune befell us, he would not be responsible. We told him that we did not care, and our lives were not better than the lives of our people being massacred in Juba.

On 13 July, we flew from Khartoum to Wau and Juba. At 10am, we arrived in Wau, where we were met by Isaiah Majok Akoc, the SF secretary for information. Majok gave us the shocking news that the army had shot and killed over 200 Southerners at a wedding party on 11 July. Many of the victims were friends and others were well known to us. The incident was a severe blow to Bahr al-Ghazal Province and the South as a whole, politically and intellectually.

At the airport, there were many top Northern government officials including the officers commanding the Wau garrison. While chatting with the garrison commander, Clement Mboro suddenly started weeping and shouted, "You Southerners who are here and in Wau town, I call upon you to go into the bush because the government whose responsibility it was to give you security has turned against you." As I was standing by Mboro at that time, I looked at the commander and saw that he too had become emotional; his knees started to shake. At the same time, he tried to calm Mboro.

It was time for our plane to take off for Juba. We advised Majok to come with us to Juba as there appeared to be no security for him in Wau. He agreed and flew with us. From Juba, he returned to Khartoum that day on the same plane. We instructed him to give a detailed report on the Wau massacre to *The Vigilant*, the Southern community in Khartoum, and to other domestic and foreign media.

During the seven days we spent in Juba, we were visited by the surviving South Sudanese intelligentsia, officials, notables, and chiefs. They were undeterred by the threat of government spies. The authorities were anxious about what we would do. We knew the government would do everything in its power to prevent our reports on the massacre reaching the outside world.

Southerners gave us information about the Juba massacre and how it had been executed. The army had gone on a rampage shooting ordinary civilians with automatic weapons mounted on cars. People ran in every direction in absolute terror. Some threw themselves into the Nile and drowned. Two days after we arrived, we were taken to the health workers' quarters. 45 of them had been shot and killed by soldiers during the massacre. The bodies remained unburied.

We asked if we could see the officers commanding the troops based in Juba, both of whom were Northern Sudanese Arabs. Their common response was that it was the Anyanya guerrillas who started the violence by ambushing the troops. No evidence was provided to substantiate this allegation. We took notes of the information given to us, concentrating on gathering the names of those Southerners who were reported killed by the Northern troops or who were missing. At the end of our stay in Juba, we had recorded 2,500 names.

The government was aware of our activities. They had planned to upset any attempts to take written materials to Khartoum, as we might give these to the press. We advised most of the Southerners with whom we had associated during our stay to leave Juba for their own safety, especially after we left for Khartoum. I asked my nephew, Moses Mading Anyijong, who was a student at Juba Commercial Secondary School, and who had survived the massacre, to come to Khartoum with us. Since Mboro and I knew we might be searched and arrested on arrival in Khartoum, we asked Moses to help us. We put all the documents, including the list of the victims of the massacre, in a briefcase we gave to Moses. We told Moses to take it somewhere safe from where we would collect it in due course. He did as he was told.

Many Southerners in the three towns and elsewhere in the North came to the airport to welcome us back. They wanted to know about the massacres of Juba and Wau and felt anxious about their own security.

While we were still on the plane, a senior security police officer, Abd El Malik el Tash, my colleague from the Sudan Police College, boarded. Mboro also knew him well from when he was Minister of Interior. Abd El Malik headed for us. He politely informed us that our bags would be taken by the police and that we would be taken to police headquarters for further investigations. He then escorted us off the plane. Most of the Southerners looked concerned. To clarify the situation, we asked Abd El Malik whether we were under arrest. He replied that we were being taken for questioning and would be released soon after. This was conveyed to the Southerners and the atmosphere improved. We were taken to police headquarters where our belongings were searched thoroughly. Then we were searched. They found nothing except a list of 12 names in my jacket pocket, which they took away without asking me whose names they were.

We were interrogated about why we went to the South, what we were doing in Juba, and so on. We explained that as the leaders of the SF, we could not afford to sit back, after having heard that the army had massacred thousands of our people in Juba and in other areas in the South. We also told them that we met many people including the commanders of the army and senior civil servants during our stay in Juba. These people gave us firsthand information. At the end, we were asked whether we had any documents; we said we did not. At 2am, we were told we could go.

The following day, *The Vigilant* published a report of our trip to the South. Just before our return from Juba, the authorities had opened a criminal case against *The Vigilant*, accusing it of false publication and seditious reporting in reference to the massacres of Wau and Juba.

In early August 1965, Mboro and I held a press conference in Khartoum South, attended by newspaper reporters from inside and outside Sudan. We presented our detailed report on the Juba and Wau massacres together with the list of 2,500 Southerners killed or missing smuggled into Khartoum. This took the Mahgoub government by surprise. It was the first time that reports of atrocities committed by government soldiers in the South had been presented to the press by Southerners.

Reports continued to arrive concerning more massacres committed by government forces in various parts of the South. This included a Shilluk village in Upper Nile raided by government troops on 5 August: 187 people were killed. The motivation, it was alleged, was to prevent villagers from joining the Anyanya. In the same year, Paul Nur, a prison officer, was shot and killed in his house in Rumbek by soldiers. More than 20 Southern teachers were killed. Their bodies were thrown into holes on the Rumbek-Mvolo Road. An unspecified number of Southern Sudanese officials were massacred in Yirol, Akobo, Yambio, Maridi, Bentiu, and elsewhere. 37 chiefs were killed because of Sadiq al-Mahdi's instigation at Bor before he became prime minister. Yet, when he visited Bor, he only wept on the grave of a young Northern officer reportedly killed by the Anyanya.

Losing Faith in a Political Settlement

SANU had been established as a political party in the country by William Deng Nhial. Since Deng's arrival, every effort had been made to bring SANU and the SF together. Many Southerners believed that this would strengthen their unity and the position of the Anyanya. But as usual, when Southerners disagreed, it did not happen.

The dividing factors were fundamental. The SF recognized Deng as one of the founders of the movement in exile. We worried that his return to Sudan would be exploited by the Northern government to divide the Southerners. Further, the SF was loyal to the leaders of the movement abroad and was reluctant to take sides in the disagreement by merging with Deng's SANU party. The SF advised all of SANU to unite and agree to either come back together or all remain in exile.

From Deng's perspective, SANU did not need to continue to operate in exile following the fall of the Abboud regime. SANU could return home and resume a political and peaceful struggle for federal states for the South. This was unacceptable to the SF whose objective was self-determination for the South. For SANU in exile to wage an armed struggle was impossible because no foreign power was willing to provide them with military aid.

The SANU leaders in exile believed that an armed struggle would lead to the liberation of the South. They disagreed with Deng's approach on the grounds it had been tried by the Southern politicians of the fifties such as Benjamin Lwoki, Bullen Alier, and Buth Diu. They had failed. SANU in exile accused Deng of being manipulated by the Sudanese government.

This SANU and SF rivalry inside the country reached its peak during and after the massacres in the South. Soldiers killed several of Deng's outstanding SANU members, including Ring Mabuoc. Elia

Duang Arop, a prominent member of SANU in Sudan, returned to exile in 1965 to rejoin the Anyanya movement. Deng refused to do so. By 1966, rivalry between SANU and the SF had reached its peak. Both had established clubs in the Khartoum New Extension. Each had rented houses and was paying maintenance allowances for members of their executive committees. Even though every Southerner was a member or supporter of the SF before Deng arrived, Deng gradually won over many Southerners, mostly from the Dinka districts of Tonj, Gogrial, and Aweil. He was slowly gaining ground in Rumbek, but not Yirol. He failed to recruit many in Upper Nile and Equatoria. As the level of political consciousness was still low among Southerners, support for the two parties was based on tribe and personality rather than on differing objectives.

While Deng was campaigning actively, the SF leadership assumed that Southerners would not rally behind a demand for federal status, since the Northern Sudanese had previously rejected it. However, towards the middle of 1965, the SF leadership began to realize that Deng's campaign was gaining ground. It then launched its own campaign in the North. Neither party could campaign effectively in the South because of the war although there was clandestine activity by SANU, tolerated to a certain extent by the government.

The SF achieved many successes in the north. In 1966, Joshua Dei Wal and I were sent to Eastern Sudan as part of a program to maintain support among Southerners. We held huge rallies in Gedaref, Kassala, and Port Sudan and got thousands to declare their membership of the Front. A few speakers blamed the SF for taking things for granted. They admitted that while the SF's cause – the right of self-determination for the South – was very popular among Southerners, William Deng was a shrewd campaigner.

In the same year, both Southern parties acquired links with Northern political parties, partly for financial backing and partly to win support for their political goals. SANU had a link with the Umma Party which dated back to the time William Deng returned from exile. SF forged a link with the PDP of Sheikh Ali Abd el Rahman.

I initiated a meeting of the SF Executive in August 1965 and proposed that in view of the government massacre of thousands of Southern intellectuals and civilians, the SF be dissolved, and the executive committee go into exile and join the Anyanya. It was clear that that this government or any other government which might follow would not be interested in a genuine peaceful solution, and as such we were wasting our time and effort.

After lengthy discussions, a majority did not accept to dissolve the SF nor to merge with the Anyanya. Instead, the Party resolved that it be left to individual members to decide. If members wished to volunteer to join the movement in exile, the Front would not oppose them.

When the meeting was over, Abel Alier, the SF vice secretary-general, called me aside and said, "Though I did not speak, I was entirely in support of your proposal… I will follow you if you join the movement any time from now. What I would do initially as my contribution would be to raise funds for the movement, through legal practice which I shall undertake in East Africa. Then eventually, I shall join the movement and will be ready to work in any capacity." Unfortunately, Abel Alier did not fulfill his promise. I never had an opportunity to ask him why.

Immediately after this meeting, I, Ciec Lam, and Arkangelo Barri Wanji decided to join the Anyanya. Unfortunately, we could not leave the country legally, because SF members were banned from travelling abroad.

5.

Joining the Liberation Struggle

Going into Exile

At the end of 1966, Clement Mboro was granted an exit visa and left for Europe. I still faced the problem that had haunted me since 1959; how I could safely move into exile with a large family? After discussing it with friends and relatives, I decided to leave alone. I arranged for the family to be smuggled out after me.

When Mboro returned in November 1966, I applied for a visa to visit Ethiopia, where it would be possible for my family to cross the border. My application was refused without explanation. The *Vigilant* newspaper took up the matter by publishing an article accusing the government of racial discrimination. Only a small number of Southerners were allowed to travel abroad, compared to many Northern Sudanese.

A few days later, I was summoned to the Ministry of the Interior. The Minister explained that my visa application was refused due to a recent incident at Addis Ababa airport. Anyanya rebels had been caught with large quantities of ammunition. I was told that I would be given an exit visa for any country other than Ethiopia.

I decided to apply for a visa to Kenya and in January 1967 I received an exit visa. My plan was to go from Kenya to Tanzania and ask for asylum. I would then go to Ethiopia, travel to the border of Sudan and wait there for my family, from where we would return to Tanzania. I would then join the Anyanya.

On 13 February 1967, I flew to Nairobi. I had 50 Sudanese pounds in my pocket. There were no longer South Sudanese political exiles living in Nairobi. This was because some South Sudanese had demonstrated at Nairobi airport against Muhammed Mahgoub. They shouted hostile slogans and Mahgoub became furious. He accused the East African leaders, including Milton Obote and Jomo Kenyatta, of supporting the South Sudanese outlaws. Obote and Kenyatta responded by ordering the Southern political leaders in Nairobi and Kampala to leave. Joseph Oduho had gone to South Sudan, fleeing arrest by the Kenyan government.

By 1 March, I was in Dar es Salaam. Majok Barnaba Riak, a native of Rumbek, whom I had known since he was at Rumbek Secondary School, had been granted political asylum in Tanzania. He welcomed me and put me up in his house. After a few days, I applied for asylum in Tanzania with Majok's help. Julius Nyerere was one of my political heroes. I felt there was more law and order in Tanzania compared to many other countries. I was optimistic that the result would be positive, but after three months my application was rejected. I was ordered to leave the country. I was terribly upset but not surprised. A Tanzanian minister had told me that while they sympathized with the people of South Sudan, their sympathy was curtailed by the fact that we allowed tribalism to divide us. My reply was that while I agreed, he should accept that tribalism was a common problem in Africa, although Tanzania might be an exception, to an extent.

Going to Uganda seemed out of the question. Father Saturnino had been assassinated by a soldier believed to be working for the Sudanese government. Obote had rounded up the Anyanya leaders in the country as a response to Mahgoub's threats to East African leaders. There had also been clashes between the Anyanya and Ugandan army units.

I returned to Kenya and applied for asylum. While I awaited a response, Paul Acire and I carried out some political activities. The Arab-Israeli war had just broken out, and the Sudanese government, as usual, was dancing to the tune of anti-western music, to the extent of expelling US diplomats and closing the US embassy in Khartoum. Paul and I thought it might be beneficial for our movement to visit the US embassy to discuss the possibility of American policy changing in favor of the oppressed Southerners. We were politely received but told that it was too early to expect a change of policy. We also went to the Soviet and Chinese embassies but did not get encouraging responses.

During this time, I received the Kenyan government's decision rejecting my application. I had to leave the country. In any case, I had little to eat and did not have a decent place to stay. Moreover, I did not know whether my family had crossed into Ethiopia. I was faced with the choice of going to Uganda to wait for news of my family or returning to Sudan.

I decided to proceed to Uganda. At the beginning of July 1967, I went to Uganda and met Othwonh Dak, a student at Makerere University. We had met previously at the Roundtable Conference. Dak told me that his friend Sarafino Wani, a SF supporter, could put me up in his house for four weeks. I intended to apply for asylum. Southerners could register as refugees. I learned that leaders such as Joseph Oduho, the President of the Azania Liberation Front (ALF), and Aggrey Jaden, President of the Sudan African Liberation Front (SALF), had returned to the Anyanya controlled areas inside South

Sudan due to the insecurity caused by the Ugandan government. Since the Anyanya military wing was not only decentralized but operating on a tribal and regional basis, each leader had to return to his own district or regional headquarters to be well received.

I was given a brief picture of the situation in exile just after the Roundtable Conference and prior to the fleeing of the political leaders into the Anyanya controlled areas inside South Sudan. After the Roundtable Conference, all the political leaders who attended, except William Deng, returned to exile. As William Deng had registered SANU as a party in Sudan, Joseph Oduho's SANU faction adopted the ALF name with Oduho as president and Aggrey Jaden as vice-president. The post of secretary for defence was held by Ezboni Mondiri. Political differences, fed by tribal feeling, soon developed between Oduho and Aggrey which culminated in Aggrey forming a breakaway political organization, the SALF. When the governments of Kenya, Uganda, and Tanzania ordered the arrest of Southern politicians, Oduho went to the Anyanya headquarters in his home region of Torit, Eastern Equatoria, and Aggrey went to the Anyanya headquarters in Moroto, Central Equatoria, in his home region. There was a faint hope that the movement might re-establish operational political bases in exile when the political climate normalized.

Another South Sudanese I met was Lawrence Wol Wol, then a student at Makerere University. Othwonh Dak assisted me in locating Wol Wol, whom I had also met at the Roundtable Conference. Wol Wol also briefed me on the events before and after the formation of ALF and SALF. It was not long before I also found Arkangelo Wanji in Uganda. We discussed how to join the movement. We agreed that since the offices of the Southern political organizations were closed due to harassment by the East African governments, we had no alternative but to enter South Sudan to join the liberation movement there.

In Kampala, we received reports that the Anyanya forces in Eastern Equatoria had arrested Oduho and sentenced him to death. We were worried that the execution of a Southern political leader by his own forces would have adverse effects on the movement. Sarafino Wani, Othwonh Dak, Wol Wol, and I resolved to send a letter from us to the senior Anyanya officer in command, appealing to not harm Oduho. We warned that if such a thing happened, we would not only have lost a great leader, but our liberation movement would be written off internationally as anarchist. If there was any charge, it should be investigated fully and tried by a neutral tribunal. The accusation, apparently, was that Oduho had committed adultery with a soldier's wife. We also resolved that Arkangelo Wanji should deliver the letter by hand. Wanji took it and returned after a fortnight with the good news that Oduho was fine. The allegations had been false.

The Khartoum government was dismayed by the way the case of Oduho ended. I was blamed for having championed his cause. According to reports from Khartoum, Clement Mboro was being harassed and accused of sending his vice-president to aggravate the war. Mboro denied this. I decided to write to Mboro, saying that I had resigned from the Southern Front. This letter was posted to Mboro with a request to show the letter to those concerned in the government. It eased the pressure on Mboro.

One Southerner who tried to persuade me not to join the movement was Ezekiel Macuei Kodi, an important member of William Deng's SANU. He was one of the five young men who returned with Deng from exile in 1965. He argued that joining the Anyanya to boost the armed struggle was a mistake because no country would arm the Anyanya. The only alternative was to intensify the political struggle to bring about a federal solution. This was SANU's argument. However, I believed that demands for federal status throughout the late fifties and sixties had yielded nothing. The Northern Sudanese Arab rulers would not give us freedom on a silver platter. We had to struggle using both political and military means.

Despite our political differences, Kodi and I maintained cordial relations. I consented to his marriage to my immediate sister-in-law, as I was empowered by my father-in-law to have the last say in the matter. As Kodi rendered much service to my family in later years, I did not regret this decision.

Joining the Anyanya

I resolved to join the Anyanya forces at their nearest camp. Wanji and I preferred Oduho's camp in Eastern Equatoria rather than Aggrey's, which to reach required passing through the Democratic Republic of Congo. However, while preparing to leave Kampala, I heard the Anyanya political and military representatives from all three Southern provinces were holding a convention three miles from the Congolese border, just inside South Sudan, on 20 August 1967. A runner had arrived with an invitation. He explained how to get there. One obstacle was that I had no money to buy a bus ticket. The boy assured me that if I could get a ticket, we could go together.

The next day I visited Wol Wol and explained the situation. He gave me 40 Uganda shillings and I bought a bus ticket. Unfortunately, the runner had changed his mind and would only return after two weeks.

I decided to go alone, despite the dangers. On 15 August, I left Kampala for Aba on the borders of Sudan and Congo. After our bus passed Arua, Congo, we were ambushed by Congolese soldiers. We had stopped at a roadblock when the soldiers emerged from both sides of the road aiming their automatic weapons at us. They took money, beer, and other valuables from the passengers before allowing us to proceed.

When we arrived in Aba at 7pm, it was completely dark. I was not sure how to locate the reportedly numerous South Sudanese. The driver advised me to go to the Catholic mission and showed me a road. I followed the road, and as I walked along I saw a red light. I followed it and came to the mission station. A man came who knew very little English. I told him that I was from South Sudan. He came back with a young South Sudanese. The South Sudanese took me to his place and offered me a bed and food. We had a long, happy conversation during which he explained the situation of the Southerners and informed me that political leaders such as Aggrey Jaden were in Aba and that he would take me to them tomorrow morning.

The next day, he took me to Aggrey. Aggrey and I had first met at Loka Intermediate School in 1942, when he was in his final year, and I was in my first. We met again in Khartoum in the early fifties, when he was at Gordon Memorial College, and I was at the Sudan Police College, as well as in 1965 at the Roundtable Convention. With Aggrey were Daniel Jumi, Marko Rume, and Elia Lupe Waiwai.

I explained that I had decided to join the Anyanya, as I had concluded that the massacres perpetrated in the South by the Sudanese government had proved that nothing could be achieved through political activity in Sudan. While I failed to arrive on time for the convention, Aggrey told me it had been successful and had been attended by members of the liberation movement from all three provinces.

The convention was convened at a time when the liberation movement was in disarray. Political organizations set up in exile such as the ALF and SALF had been broken up by the Kenyan and

Ugandan governments. The national headquarters set up at Ngili in Moruland by Ezboni Mondiri had been overthrown by mutineers. Ezboni himself was detained by his own soldiers.

The convention resolved to set up a Southern Sudan Provisional Government (SSPG) to become an umbrella organization with a political wing and a military wing. The political wing would be non-partisan and composed of an executive council of 15 ministers, five from each of the three provinces. The military would be known as the Anyanya National Armed Forces (ANAF). It was to be organized in brigades, with one in each of the provinces and two at the national headquarters. Aggrey Jaden had been elected president and Camillo Dhol Kuac, a former official in the ministry of agriculture and a MP in 1958, vice-president. The minister for defence was Akuot Atem Mayen. Aggrey said I would be appointed as a minister, despite arriving late. I was to be taken to the Anyanya transit camp at Angundri, the temporary headquarters of the SSPG.

After three days I left for Angundri, 12 miles inside South Sudan and a one-day walk from Aba. I was accompanied by several civilian members of the movement and some soldiers. On arrival at the border, we were received by a guard unit of 15 Anyanya soldiers. The commander was Sgt. Dut Manyiel Dut from Rumbek. It was 1pm when we entered South Sudan, walking along a footpath winding through the bush. At 6pm, we arrived at Angundri and were met by Camillo Dhol. Camillo explained that a decision would be made about my assignment when the president arrived. He had heard that I had left Sudan and wondered why I could not attend the convention. I explained the obstacles I had faced.

The following day, I met the military and political heads of the district camps running the arms and ammunition black markets on the border. Each district transit camp at Angundri had a separate committee. There was no central coordinating body. Each district camp received money from its district commander to buy arms and ammunitions in the Congolese black market. There were plenty available following the defeat of the Simba, the pro-Lumumba army in Congo. The decentralized Anyanya meant each district had its own force meant to be able to sustain armed attack on its local Sudanese military garrison.

After one week, Camillo and I returned to Aba for further consultation. Aggrey appointed me as the acting minister for defence until Akuot Atem, the minister appointed in absentia, arrived.

Aggrey said he would remain in Aba to await foreign contacts. He wanted Camillo, Daniel Jumi, and I to return to Angundri to establish a national headquarters. Camillo would be acting president. As acting minister of defence, I was tasked with establishing the ANAF.

Not all the appointed ministers and senior Anyanya officers were present at the camp; many of them left after the convention but were expected to return. A meeting was called of all the ministers, senior Anyanya officers, Anyanya district officers and their political officers present at Angundri. I was the first speaker. I said,

> *"I was made to believe that with your 6 years of political and armed struggle backed by our political struggle inside the country, a just and lasting solution of the north-south Sudan conflict within one Sudan was a possibility. But after I witnessed the massacre of the Southern Sudanese civilian population in Khartoum in 1964 and in Juba and Wau in 1965, I came to the conclusion that the Northern Sudanese Arab rulers and oppressors would not accept such a thing. Thus, in my view, the South has to choose between surrender and carrying on the armed struggle."*

The best move would have been for the SF to dissolve itself and join the struggle, but some SF members felt that internal political activity was still worthwhile.

Now, despite all the Anyanya's military achievements, there was still a lot to be done. Above all, we needed unity in the movement and for the Anyanya's military and political wings to be properly organized.

I could see that there were numerous arms and ammunitions black market camps and that they had nothing in common except an agreement to form a common front against the enemy whenever it attacked Angundri. This was good but we needed to immediately implement the Angundri resolution by contributing men and arms. This would allow the ANAF headquarters to be moved inward into South Sudan and further organized to spearhead the liberation of the South.

The immediate problem facing the SSPG was a lack of funding and arms to establish a modern and effective liberation struggle. Moreover, Yei District, where the SSPG was to be launched, had been devastated by war in the past five years. Very little money was in circulation. From mid-1966, Sudanese currency started to come from Bahr al-Ghazal and Upper Nile for use in the black market. Some of this money found its way into the hands of the local people through the purchase of food and other commodities in the open market. That was how the situation slowly began to improve.

Since the districts of Tonj, Gogrial, and Aweil had large transit camps with funds available for black market purchases, Camillo and I called a meeting of the commanders from these districts. We presented the problem the president had conveyed to us, namely the lack of funds. The commanders agreed to raise up to 600 Sudanese pounds. At that time, the Sudanese pound was almost equivalent in value to the British pound sterling. Within 3 days, 600 pounds was delivered. We immediately took the money to Aba and delivered it to President Aggrey. He was pleased and surprised, in view of the poverty of the movement.

The SSPG was set up because it was felt that the time was ripe for a provisional government in exile. This provisional government would probably have been set up in Kampala if political splits and the harassment of the political leaders by the governments of Uganda and Kenya had not occurred in 1965 and 1966. Aggrey and the leaders resolved that since it was most desirable for the politicians who had gone into the bush of South Sudan to struggle together inside the motherland, it was appropriate to set up there a provisional government comprising both political and military wings.

While Aggrey was still away, the provisional government and ANAF functioned with reasonable efficiency under Acting President Camillo Dhol. The Council of Ministers met regularly. Brig. Ali Guatala was the Acting Commander-in-Chief of the ANAF. At the end of 1967, Gen. Emilio Taffeng arrived from Eastern Equatoria and took over command from Guatala.

The Council of Ministers sent a circular to all Anyanya units informing them of the outcome of the Angundri Convention and the formation of the SSPG. All letters and other messages used to be taken on foot. It took two to four months to reach Bahr al-Ghazal and Upper Nile on foot. The letter instructed all units to step up guerrilla operations against the enemy. It was reiterated that they were required to send their financial contribution to the SSPG urgently.

Generally, there was cooperation between the SSPG, the ANAF, and the transit camps despite occasional tribal and sectional tensions. One day, I was asked by the Anyanya black market transit camp if I could meet them. At the meeting, their local commander told me that in the years they had been in Angundri, they had always been badly treated by leaders from other tribes. They wanted me to take charge of Rumbek and Yirol with the responsibility of sorting out the black market. I said I was sad to learn that there were some South Sudanese leaders who persecuted other Southerners because of their tribe or sub-tribe. I joined the movement to contribute to the liberation of South Sudan. I did not join to become a tribal leader. Part of this meant ensuring that no one was subjected to injustice because of belonging to a particular tribal group. This did not mean that I denied being an Agar Dinka or being from Lakes district.

They listened but continued to explain the difficulties they were facing in the black market. They asked if I was willing to talk to some of the leaders responsible for the discrimination. The leaders I spoke to said that they would help whenever the Dinka were in need. I relayed this back. I promised that I would always take up their case in future if they faced tribal or sub-tribal prejudice again.

Lagu Takes up ANAF Chief of Staff Position

President Aggrey Jaden appointed Col. Joseph Lagu as the ANAF chief of staff, but Lagu was reluctant to take up the appointment. As ANAF chief of staff, Lagu would inherit the guerrilla forces in Eastern Equatoria formerly under the control of Father Saturnino Lohure. Saturnino had been assassinated by a Ugandan soldier allegedly hired by the Khartoum government in 1966.

Aggrey had made some important, positive contact with a foreign power sympathetic to our cause through its embassy in Kinshasa: Israel. Lagu had also made contact with the Israelis via an embassy in East Africa, a contact he intended to keep independent of that made by Aggrey. However, the Israelis advised Lagu to coordinate with Aggrey. Lagu was surprised by this development but had no option but to comply.

In November 1967, Lagu made a surprise visit to the SSPG headquarters in Angundri. He was given a rousing welcome by the acting president, the commander-in-chief, and the senior ANAF officers. They hoped that he was coming to take up duties as ANAF chief of staff. Lagu met the Council of Ministers, which told him that the Israelis must have been convinced that because he was the ANAF chief of staff, there was no contradiction between his contact with them and that of the SSPG president.

That evening, Lagu met all the ANAF officers. He spent the night with them. A meeting was organized for the next morning to reconcile Lagu and Gen. Taffeng. In the meeting, both Taffeng and Lagu spoke at length. Taffeng referred to Lagu as his son. He said that for the sake of the country, he was willing to forgive Lagu. It ended with vigorous hugging and handshakes between the two officers.

The next day, Lagu and I, in my capacity as the acting foreign minister of the SSPG, left Angundri for Nairobi. We phoned the Israeli embassy to ask for an appointment to meet the ambassador, and the following morning we met the ambassador in his office. I explained the purpose of our mission and delivered a letter from the acting president of the SSPG. The letter appealed to the ambassador to accept the coordination of contacts of Col. Lagu and President Aggrey Jaden. I said that from this moment onward, Lagu would be known as the chief of staff of the ANAF. Lagu's contacts with them would not contradict those made in Kinshasa or elsewhere by the Aggrey. The ambassador assured me that he would inform his government accordingly and that I and Lagu were welcome in his office any time. I returned to the SSPG headquarters leaving Lagu in Nairobi. Lagu planned to return to his district headquarters in Eastern Equatoria.

Before I accompanied Lagu to East Africa, Lt. Col. Naanga

Marik, Commander of the Anyanya Lakes regional headquarters, arrived in Angundri with an accompanying force. Naanga reported to the Minister of Defence, Akuot Atem, that a few mutinying corporals had placed him under house arrest. After 3 days, a loyal force released Naanga and escorted him to the ANAF national headquarters.

After a lengthy debate, the Council of Ministers resolved that an ANAF military tribunal be set up at Rumbek, comprising neutral officers from all three Southern provinces, to thoroughly investigate the incident. The Council of Ministers fully empowered the tribunal to resolve the case. It was to try all persons accused of crimes and breaches of military discipline. It was decided that if Naanga was found innocent, he should be returned to office and any other accused brought to the ANAF national headquarters.

This resolution was passed on to the minister of defence, but the situation in Lakes remained confused. The resolution was not implemented, for reasons unknown. I did all I could to persuade Akuot to speed up implementation, but he did not listen. Camillo instead assigned Naanga to duties at the ANAF national headquarters.

The Return of Aggrey Jaden
In March 1968, President Aggrey returned from Kinshasa. Aggrey thanked Acting President Camillo and all the ministers for laying the foundation of the liberation movement. He felt the essential parts of the 1967 Angundri Convention had been implemented. However, Aggrey said that his program in Kinshasa was not moving with the pace he expected. He was not feeling optimistic, although he stressed that the contacts being made were encouraging. He spoke in detail about the obstacles that needed to be overcome. Aggrey was asked whether the Israelis had informed him of Lagu's contacts with their embassy in East Africa. Aggrey confirmed that

they had, and he had told them that Lagu was his chief of staff.

The Council of Ministers and Camillo then briefed Aggrey on the contact with Lagu. It was acknowledged that there was lingering mistrust between Aggrey and Lagu. Despite this, Aggrey said that he was pleased with how things had been dealt with in relation to Lagu.

The Relocation of the National Headquarters
Several important resolutions were passed by the Council of Ministers. One of these was to relocate the SSPG headquarters to inside South Sudan, but not too far from the borders for storage and supply reasons. Bungu, east of Yei, was chosen. Towards the end of March, the national headquarters was moved from Angundri to Bungu. Romano Hassan from Western Bahr al-Ghazal, meanwhile, declined to come to the bush and take up his office. President Aggrey appointed me to act in Hassan's place as full-time foreign minister while retaining my position in the Ministry of Agriculture.

The ANAF was growing. Food shortages began to be felt at the headquarters. I invited chiefs of Yei and the neighboring districts and the Anyanya political officers to attend a food-production conference.

The conference was a success. There was a spirit of nationalism and approval for what we were doing. Many praised the efforts we were making to unite the people of South Sudan. I explained to the chiefs that the Anyanya was being forced to stage a guerrilla war as our arms and resources were not equal to those of the Northern Sudanese Arab government. For us to do this and win our freedom, the Anyanya needed food. The chiefs could supply this. I wanted them to agree to cooperate and work together with the leadership of the movement. I proposed that every able-bodied adult must set aside a plot or two on which to cultivate food for the Anyanya. On this plot, just one kind of food should be planted, such as grain,

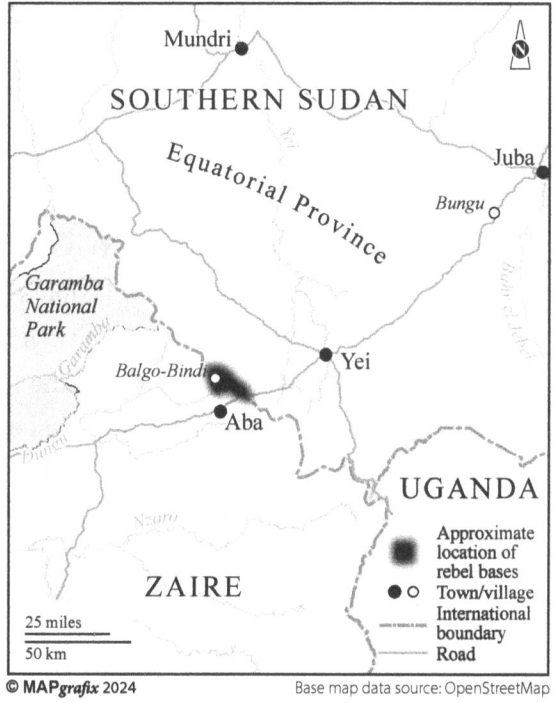

Key locations on the Southern Sudan-Zaïre border, 1972

beans, cassava, or groundnuts. The householder must construct a store for this foodstuff after the harvest. This food would be for the Anyanya whenever they needed it. All the chiefs and the political officers agreed to this proposal. It was also agreed that once this policy was put into action, the guerrilla forces must no longer collect food by force from civilians.

After this, a meeting was held with the chiefs, spiritual chiefs, and elders, alongside the president, the vice-president, 10 ministers, the commander-in-chief, his deputy and senior officers. The spiritual chiefs conducted wonderful ceremonies and rituals. They asked for samples of our weapons to be brought. They spat on the weapons as a blessing and said, "Our children, we are very pleased with what you are doing. We were longing to see the people of South

Sudan united. We want unity irrespective of tribal and cultural differences. God will bless these weapons of yours for their quantity and effectiveness against our common enemy."

The agreement reached with the chiefs of Western Equatoria worked. Over the next few years, there was plenty of food for the Anyanya. There was no problem of foreign NGOs and the use of food as a weapon of war which the Sudan People's Liberation Movement / Army (SPLM/A) would later face. I wrote a letter to all the Anyanya regional headquarters explaining the food agreement. I would like to have toured all the Anyanya controlled areas in the South myself to put the final touches to the food production program, but there were other demands on my time.

Funding the Rebellion

President Aggrey Jaden remained at the headquarters waiting for the result of his contacts in Kinshasa. I began to search for foreign assistance in East Africa. I kept the president informed of my findings. I was told by the Israelis that their government would welcome a visit from Lagu, but that they would not be able to provide travel documentation for him. They wanted to know whether the SSPG would be able to provide the documents needed for travel. When I informed the president, he did not hesitate to give his approval. He was not happy, however, with the way our foreign friends were going about it. Within two weeks, our SSPG representative in Zaïre, Francis Mayar Akon, confirmed that he would be able to obtain documents soon. He advised that Lagu should come to Kinshasa using a laissez-passer. Lagu flew to Kinshasa from Nairobi with a travel document secured by Mayar and was later able to visit Israel.

The SSPG was getting more arms and men from the regional Anyanya headquarters, particularly from Western Equatoria. The Western Equatoria forces had many modern weapons. They had purchased or received these from the Simba forces that had been fighting in Congo, following their defeat by the pro-Mobutu forces in 1965. These weapons enabled the Western and Eastern Equatoria Anyanya forces to escalate their campaigns. The enemy suffered large casualties and many of their vehicles were destroyed by landmines. However, by the time the SSPG was established, much of the Western Equatoria guerrilla activity had slowed down because there were no more Simbas coming through.

The two ANAF headquarters brigades were growing rapidly. In May 1968, we had a force of about 1,000 men. There were frequent successful attacks on the enemy. The three regional brigades were also taking shape in Bahr al-Ghazal and Upper Nile. That same month, the Council of Ministers decided to integrate the ANAF across the three Southern provinces. This would begin at headquarters. After integration, the mixed troops were to contain members of every tribe. The forces and arms which came from the national headquarters had to be integrated with those of the provinces. Surplus arms were to be returned to the headquarters. This was put into action successfully in the surrounding areas without too many difficulties, although there were problems with the Zande, Moru, and in Eastern Equatoria. Two large ANAF integrated forces assembled under Akuot Atem, the Minister of Defence, and Simon Mandis. Akuot volunteered to head the forces going to Upper Nile Province and Mandis, those going to Bahr al-Ghazal.

Arkangelo Wanji and I began teaching members of the ANAF. Wanji's classes were about guerrilla tactics and political science in general. I lectured on the historical background of the conflict between the Northern Sudan Arab government and the indigenous oppressed Africans of Sudan.

Uncertainty Due to a Lack of Foreign Support

Uncertainty due to a lack of foreign support was undermining morale. Promises and visits were made to the president, but these were followed by silence. There was a lot of false hope among the Anyanya and the people of South Sudan. This was damaging. There were a few countries that sympathized with the people of the South in their current plight. They had pledged military, material, and humanitarian assistance. Hopes among the people were also raised from signs of unity in the movement and the joining together of the SSPG and ANAF.

These developments had a demoralizing effect on the president and his ministers. The president was fearful that if the promises were not going to be fulfilled, his leadership might be threatened. This was what had happened to his predecessors. He was worried about a possible challenge to his leadership from Lagu and was aware that Lagu was in regular contact with several foreign powers. Foreign powers continued to maintain the Northern Arab rule over the indigenous Africans. It was felt that these foreign powers, therefore, would tend to oppose radical leadership in the South's liberation movement.

Fighting Breaks out in the Headquarters

A fight broke out at the national headquarters while I was away in East Africa. Lt. Col. Naanga, still the commander of the Anyanya battalion in Rumbek, had been sent to Angundri transit camp to round up and return Anyanya deserters to the headquarters. When he arrived at Angundri, he met Gabriel Kau Ater, the former police inspector, former MP in Sudan and former justice secretary under Joseph Oduho. Kau was on his way from Rumbek to SSPG headquarters to take up his new post as Minister of Justice. Naanga had a grudge against Kau, arrested him, and escorted him to Bungu.

When Defence Minister Akuot Atem learned this, he arrested Naanga, placed him under detention, and freed Kau.

When the supporters of Naanga at Rumbek heard, they came to the SSPG headquarters and attempted to release him from detention. There was a clash between these supporters and the ANAF troops at headquarters. Three soldiers died, two from the ANAF and the other from Rumbek. Naanga's supporters withdrew to Rumbek, leaving him in detention.

Some reacted angrily because they felt that the attack had endangered the president. These were mainly officers from the Western Equatorian ANAF, Anyanya, and others from Aggrey Jaden's tribe. They were skeptical of the Dinka ministers, so they took the president to a hideout deep in the jungle to provide proper security for him, as they saw it. Anyone who wanted to see him had to be physically searched first. I returned after nearly a month to find that to see the president, I too, had to be searched.

I visited Naanga in detention. I assured him that I would speak to Akuot Atem and President Aggrey. I met Akuot and warned him that under no circumstances should Naanga be executed. Justice must prevail. I did not say this because Naanga was from the same tribe as I, but because Naanga was not the principal accused. He did not abet the killing or the attack at the headquarters. Akuot replied that Naanga was one of the best officers we had. He was only being detained for his own safety, as protection from relatives of those who were killed in the fight. He would be released as soon as it was certain that his life was no longer in danger. I also met the president and expressed concern about the safety of Naanga. He assured me that Naanga would be treated with justice.

Negotiations Between the Government of Israel and the SSPG Leadership

Aggrey Jaden and I proceeded to Nairobi and formed a delegation comprising him, Joseph Lagu, Sarafino Wani, the SSPG representative in East Africa, and I, the SSPG Foreign Minister and Minister for Agriculture and Food Production.

We met the Israeli ambassador to discuss support for the SSPG on 18 June 1968. We requested the following assistance along with modern weaponry to liberate South Sudan from Sudanese colonization: food, clothing, medicines, means of communication, and vehicles. We also asked for funding along with diplomatic support and help to influence other states in Africa and abroad. We especially needed funding and could show the specific amount required and the annual SSPG expenditure.

After making our requests, the ambassador adjourned the meeting for several hours. He came back to inform us that his government had accepted all our proposals. Funding had been approved but would be staggered. The ambassador said that the only problem he could see was how assistance could be delivered as South Sudan was landlocked. As far as we knew, there was no neighboring country which would be willing to allow passage of material.

We told him that we would do our best to persuade the neighboring countries. We also asked him to ask his government whether they would try to convince neighboring countries to help. We identified some countries we felt were possibilities. The ambassador promised to try.

The discussions continued the following day. The long-term relationship between Israel and the liberation movement was discussed. We talked about what to do when South Sudan emerged as an independent state. No document was signed, but both sides solemnly promised to respect the agreement reached between the two delegations.

We were told that implementation of our agreement would take several months. We requested urgent funds to buy food for the ANAF and vehicles to transport them. Fortunately, our friends agreed to give us some of what we needed now. The president took receipt of this help. Joseph Lagu asked the president if he could be paid a lump sum to take to Eastern Equatoria to feed the ANAF soldiers there. The president agreed to this. He then decided that the whole delegation should return and brief the Council of Ministers and senior ANAF officers of the outcome of the negotiations. After this was done, the amount requested would be paid and Lagu would be allowed to return to Eastern Equatoria. However, Lagu refused to submit to the authority of the president. I advised the president to pay and let him go to avoid a potential disagreement. The president took my advice. Lagu promised to return to the SSPG national headquarters as soon as possible.

Implementation of ANAF Integration
While we were in East Africa negotiating, the SSPG Council of Ministers began integrating the ANAF. Vice-President Camillo Dhol was in Zaïre at that time, so Minister of Defence Akuot Atem was Acting President.

The Council of Ministers had dispatched an integrated ANAF force to Bahr al-Ghazal. Akuot was supposed to leave for Upper Nile with another integrated force. Before he went, he ordered a court-martial for Lt. Col. Naanga. The charge was that Naanga's troops from Rumbek had attacked the national headquarters. Naanga was sentenced to death along with three of his junior officers. Akuot sent instructions to have them shot by firing squad.

On 26 June 1968, the president, several SSPG officials and ANAF officers, and I, left for SSPG headquarters. We stopped in Moroto the next day. Lt. Col. Michael Lorwe told us that Naanga and three of his officers were executed the previous morning at

Moroto. We were shocked. The president was terribly upset and angry. I told the president that this was what I had feared would happen. We also learned that Arkangelo Wanji, the Deputy Minister for Defence, was in Moroto. The president sent for Wanji. Wanji gave us a full account of what had taken place during Akuot Atem's time as Acting President. This included the trial and execution of Naanga and his associates.

On 28 June, President Aggrey surprised me by saying he had decided to return to East Africa to meet the Israelis and urge them to speed up the implementation of the agreement. I did not think this a good decision. it was important that he led the delegation to headquarters to brief the Council of Ministers and the ANAF general staff of the success of our negotiations. This would boost morale. But the president did not heed my advice. He told me to proceed to the headquarters and brief on his behalf. He assured me that he would return in July.

Northern Troops attack Moroto

Moroto was one of the best planned and most secure Anyanya camps in the South. It had streets, officers' quarters, barracks for soldiers, married women's quarters, and places for children. At 1pm on 29 June, Arkangelo Wanji and I were speaking with some senior officers in the shade of a *rakuba*. Then, a man ran over to inform us that the Arabs were coming.

There was only one way to enter Moroto and that was from the south. The north, east, and west sides were thick with jungle. The reported attack was supposed to be from the north. Some officers were skeptical about such a possibility. Wanji called for Lt. Col. Lorwe and instructed him to send a force to intercept the enemy, which he did. The rest of the force, numbering more than 2,000, was instructed to be ready to defend the camp.

Wanji and I were impressed with the arrangements, but there was a lack of ammunition and effective guns. Six men were assigned to the ministers as bodyguards. None of us had guns. The officer commanding our bodyguards advised that it was better we move several hundred yards outside the main camp to avoid being captured. It was likely that the Anyanya forces would have to withdraw when their ammunition ran out. We moved 200 yards outside the camp. As soon as we did, the shooting began. We picked up the pace until we were out of range. After 15 minutes the shooting died down; we then saw a thick cloud of smoke. Anyanya forces had retreated and Moroto had been set alight by the enemy. Some soldiers told us that the Anyanya forces had withdrawn after inflicting heavy casualties against the enemy. No Anyanya guns were captured. The Northern troops withdrew under the cover of darkness, afraid of becoming a target of a nighttime guerrilla attack in the thick jungle.

We set up a temporary camp, three miles away. Anyanya soldiers began to slowly arrive. After three days, 75 percent of the original force had re-assembled. Lt. Col. Lorwe supervised the construction of this camp, which became known as New Moroto. The morning after, we went to view the scene of the battle. We saw part of a human skull, a dead body, many blood stains, and large quantities of spent ammunition. The body was of a young man with both hands tied behind his back. He was identified as an Anyanya deserter. He may have acted as a guide for the enemy as he was believed to know the location of Moroto. The blood was that of the dead and injured enemy forces retreating and the skull belonged to a major of the enemy forces, who was shot in the head and killed.

There was an old man living in the village. He advised us not to move and we complied. Despite our insistence that he be unharmed, he was killed by the Anyanya soldiers. We went back to

New Moroto. Wanji and I congratulated Lorwe and his officers and men for their gallantry at the battle of Moroto. They had inflicted serious casualties on the enemy forces. We wrote an account of events to be sent to President Aggrey in East Africa.

Four days later, Wanji, Marko Rume, and I, together with more than 100 ANAF officers and men from Moroto, left the new camp for the national headquarters at Bungu. It was a nine-day walk. News had already spread that negotiations with our foreign friends had been successful. What prevented morale from being even higher was the absence of President Aggrey Jaden.

Camillo Dhol, the Acting President, was in Bungu when we arrived. The next day, Wanji and I briefed the Council of Ministers, the ANAF Commander-in-Chief, Gen. Taffeng, his deputy, Brig. Guatala, and other senior officers on our negotiations, including what we thought the foreign military and material assistance would be. We explained why Aggrey had not returned with us and told them he would join us soon. News of the execution of Naanga was given, affecting nearly everyone's morale. Despite this, everybody seemed quite happy. They expected that year to be one of unity and solidarity among the Southerners. At that moment in the history of our struggle, levels of patriotism and unity were at their peak.

Aggrey Jaden Departs
In the middle of August 1968, Aggrey Jaden and Elia Lupe Waiwai, the Minister of Interior, arrived at headquarters. For a few days, no large meetings took place, but each minister visited Aggrey's residence, except for Akuot Atem and the two ministers presently in Bahr al-Ghazal. During these encounters, the president expressed anger about the execution of Naanga and his associates. Aggrey had made it clear that Akuot was to not to send the case to trial before his return from East Africa.

On 25 August, Aggrey informed us that his cousin in a village near Bungu was ill and that he and Elia Lupe Waiwai were going to see him. They would return the same evening. They took one bodyguard. The president spent the night away. We did not think this significant. Then he spent a second night away. The officer in charge of security tried to contact him but was unable to do so.

We found Elia at his house at Aba. He failed to provide information on the whereabouts of Aggrey. Anxiety swept the national headquarters. No one knew where he had gone and why. Four days later, a letter for Camillo arrived from Aggrey, stating that he had left because he did not want to be a rubber stamp for the Dinka.

Camillo called the Council of Ministers to discuss the situation, how to proceed, and how to persuade Aggrey to return. The atmosphere was gloomy. It was decided that a letter should be written to Aggrey by the Council of Ministers, to be delivered by me in person, as I was close to the president. The letter appealed to Aggrey to change his mind and return to his duties. Southerners were happy and gradually uniting under his leadership. Also, it was the first time in the history of the liberation movement that a foreign power had agreed to provide military assistance.

Camillo addressed over 700 officers and men of the ANAF at the headquarters. He broke the news that the president had left the leadership, but that he did not know the details of why Aggrey left. He appealed to everyone to remain calm and maintain loyalty to the ongoing struggle. He reminded everyone that in the last 13 years their comrades in arms and civilian compatriots had laid down their lives for the struggle. He very much hoped that this event did not signify the beginning of another rift among the leaders of the movement. He appealed in particular to the military wing of the movement to not allow itself to be subverted on tribal grounds.

Camillo explained the Council of Ministers had written to

Aggrey appealing to him to return and resume his leadership of the movement. The letter said that if there were persons in the Council with whom he disagreed, he should still come back. He would have the authority to remove those individuals and we would give him our total support. The letter warned Aggrey that his departure was likely to push the movement to the brink of collapse.

In Kampala, I met Aggrey and gave him the letter. He read it carefully. I told him that his ministers were upset and wanted to know why he had decided to leave. I stressed that abandoning the leadership would threaten the movement with collapse because tribal differences would be likely to flare up. I addressed his complaint that he was merely a "rubber stamp." I noted that I did not remember any occasion on which Dinka members had either ganged up to oppose his policies or imposed ideas different from his. I said, "I have observed complete love and respect for you from all of us. This is why we have asked you to come back and sack anyone with whom you feel you cannot work."

Aggrey said that he was pleased by the letter. He had no differences with any of the ministers except Akuot Atem, of whom he spoke at length about the lack of discipline and respect. He gave a few examples, such as the trial and execution of Naanga. He also spoke of his differences with Joseph Lagu, whom he saw as having an ambition to take over the leadership. Aggrey ended our discussion by thanking the Council of Ministers for their concern. He also thanked me for delivering the letter and appeal to him personally. He finished by saying that he was angry but not yet ready to abandon the movement. He assured me that he would return to the headquarters soon.

The next day, Aggrey and I had another discussion. One issue we discussed was the second convention, which the Council of Ministers had instructed me to bring to Aggrey's attention for his opinion. In August 1967, a resolution was passed that there should be another convention in early 1969, approximately one year after the meeting in Angundri. The convention would elect a fully representative SSPG. Aggrey Jaden had been convention chair when he was elected president a year ago. He said that he would stand for another term of office, which was expected. It was thought that his chances of success were high, especially because foreign military aid had been obtained during his tenure. I requested that he come to lead the preparations for the 1969 convention. He agreed to both lead the preparations and attend the convention.

I reminded Aggrey of the agreement for military and material assistance that was reached with the government of Israel in June, which I regarded as an outstanding achievement, a turning point in our struggle. He thought so too. Aggrey had returned to East Africa alone in June. I asked if he had reminded the Israelis of the urgency of the implementation of the agreement. He said that he had, and they had reassured him they were doing everything to expedite it.

This was the last session we had together. I bid him goodbye and returned to the headquarters. I reported the results of my mission to the Council of Ministers. All were happy about Aggrey's promise to return to the leadership.

Time passed but Aggrey did not return. Morale was declining. Acting President Camillo appealed for calm. Individual Anyanya soldiers from Western Equatoria were deserting. Some left their guns behind with a note saying, "I am leaving the liberation armed struggle to the Dinkas." We continued to write to Aggrey pleading for his return. The number of deserters continued to grow; most took their guns with them. The security of the headquarters was in jeopardy, and the armed struggle was slowing. The War Council met to discuss the absence of Aggrey. It was resolved that deserting soldiers must be stopped from taking away guns, by identifying possible deserters and disarming them.

The news from Bahr al-Ghazal and Upper Nile was that ANAF integration was not making much progress. Gabriel Kau and Simon Mandis were both stuck at Rumbek with their integrated forces. Akuot Atem had transformed the Bor battalion headquarters into a military base. He was launching regular raids against the enemy garrison in Bor town. This was contrary to the policy which stipulated that the Anyanya forces in all of Upper Nile must be fully integrated before any attacks were launched.

At headquarters, there was still tension after the death of Naanga. Some advocated revenge. They wanted a fight between the ANAF elements from Bor and Rumbek. The Council of Ministers attempted to suppress this, stating that anyone instigating tensions would be dealt with harshly. Even though Naanga was dear to our hearts and a great hero in the struggle, starting a fight with the forces from Bor would have been devastating to the movement. Fortunately, the situation calmed after a few weeks.

Contact between Aggrey Jaden and the ministers reduced further. People began to think that he was not going to come back. The question that remained was why? Everybody was aware that his commitment to South Sudan nationalism was second to none. In my view, Aggrey was not the type of leader who gave in to provocative behavior or aggressive demands. He was well educated and not naïve. Aggrey was also not "anti-Dinka."

6.

The Nile Republic (1969-1970)

An important resolution of the 1967 Angundri Convention was to hold a second convention to elect the president of the new provisional government. The second convention was set for 19 April 1969, to be held at Balgo-Bindi.

Letters were sent to the Anyanya provincial and district headquarters instructing them to send delegates to the convention. An invitation was sent to Joseph Lagu and senior ANAF officers in Eastern Equatoria. A letter was also sent to Aggrey Jaden in Kampala, asking him to attend. This letter highlighted that there was a good chance Aggrey would be elected unopposed as president. I was again asked to deliver the letter to Aggrey by hand. The ministers wanted to show Aggrey that they were unanimous in their desire for him to return.

In November 1968, I again met Aggrey in Kampala to convey just how much his abrupt departure had lowered morale in the movement. He assured me that he would attend the convention as a candidate for the presidency. Aggrey was not hostile to most of us, except Akuot Atem and Joseph Lagu. I returned to the national headquarters and informed the Council of Ministers that Aggrey had assured me he would attend. However, he did not turn up. We waited beyond the date set for the convention to start. Eventually, we had no choice but to begin without him.

We first had to deal with the positions of president and vice-president. The general view was that if Aggrey did not return, I should be elected president. Vice-President Camillo Dhol, ANAF officers, and those working in the civil administration also held this view. The process had to be democratic. I would have preferred Camillo become president if Aggrey did not return. There were other leaders who could have been nominated, including Joseph Oduho, Ezboni Mondiri, and Joseph Lagu, provided he resigned from his army position. However, these three did not respond to the invitations sent to them.

In the first session, many people expressed satisfaction with the work of the SSPG in its first two years. They were dismayed at the way Aggrey had abandoned the leadership. Most delegates from Equatoria felt that since Aggrey had not explained to the people why he left, the next president should come from Upper Nile or Bahr al-Ghazal. After lengthy discussion, Camillo nominated me for the presidency. I objected as Camillo was my senior and had been in the movement longer than me. When the matter was put to a vote, I was unanimously elected. Marko Rume was unanimously elected vice-president. While Camillo should have been vice-president, this could not happen as the Angundri Convention had decided that the president and vice-president should be from different provinces.

Another important item on the agenda was the name of South Sudan. Some argued that it was logical for the Southerners to fight and die in the name of the South, as a distinct entity. Eventually, all agreed it was necessary to select a new name. If the political conflict was won, this name would be that of the new independent state.

Many names were proposed. These included Juwama (Juba, Wau, and Malakal), Nilotia, Sue Republic, Imatong Republic, and Nile Republic, among others. Nilotia was almost accepted. It was dropped because some Equatorian delegates argued that the republic would be thought to belong to Nilotics, potentially excluding other ethnic groups. Juwama was rejected as too artificial. It was the plain name, Nile, which received unanimous support. The River Nile was a unifying element. Its tributaries flowed through every Southern village. If it became independent, South Sudan would thus be known as the Nile Republic.

The new government was accordingly named the Nile Provisional Government (NPG). It was resolved that when independence was attained, the name would be confirmed by the people, who retained the absolute power to change the name if they so wished. We also agreed that at least 75 percent of the revenue contributed to the movement would be spent on ANAF equipment, food, health, clothing, and welfare. Annual budgets would be drawn up. Food production would also be stepped up to enable the movement to become self-reliant.

We reaffirmed our commitment to the struggle, resolving that "we the Nilean delegates deliberating at the NPG Convention held at Balgo-Bindi in April-May 1969 do hereby resolve that the ongoing Nile State Liberation struggle, spearheaded by the NPG with the ANAF as its military wing, is uncompromisingly determined and committed to continue the armed struggle until complete independence for the Nile State is attained," in line with the aims that SACDNU and the original SANU adopted in Kinshasa in 1962, by the Azania Liberation Front, and by the SSPG at the Angundri Convention of 1967.

The Formation of the Nile Provisional Government

A difficult step was the formation of the NPG Council of Ministers. I consulted my colleagues and the ANAF commanders. I decided to leave intact the previous government's civil and military institutions such as the ANAF general staff, the War Council, the commission for ANAF national integration and so on. In forming the Council of Ministers, I was careful to avoid the traps of tribalism, nepotism, and other types of prejudice. I needed to ensure that ethnic interests were well balanced. This did not mean preserving tribal representation as implied at the 1967 Convention. I drew from my experience at the Southern Front, where we reduced tribal prejudices to a minimum. Positions in the executive were allocated based on qualification, capability, and commitment to nationalism.

The NPG Council of Ministers constituted me as President, Marko Rume as Vice-President, Clement Moses as Minister of Finance, Camillo Dhol as Minister of Interior, Arkangelo Wanji as Minister of Foreign Affairs, David Koak as Minister of Defence, Akuot Atem as Minister for Cabinet Affairs, Stephen Lam Ciec as Minister of Health, and Gabriel Kau Ater as Minister of Justice.

The attainment of arms was the top priority. A committee was set up and assigned this important task. Usually, the committee was chaired by the Minister of Defence but occasionally I chaired because it was so important. The first action we undertook was to resume contact with Israel, via its embassies in Nairobi and Kampala. This followed our previous contact in June 1968. An NPG delegation of myself, Wanji, and Elia Duang Arop, the Deputy Minister of Finance, went to meet the Israeli ambassador in Nairobi in May 1969. We briefed the ambassador on the departure of Aggrey Jaden; he already knew about it. We also told him about the developments leading up to the formation of the NPG and that the only difference between the two provisional governments was the new name. We made it clear how desperately we needed the implementation of the June 1968 agreement, so that the liberation movement could move forward. The ambassador thanked us for the visit and asked for documentation regarding the formation of the NPG and a written explanation as to why Aggrey had left. He said that these were necessary to present to his government so that a decision could be made regarding the implementation of the June 1968 agreement. He assured us there would be no change of policy as far as his government was concerned. Both sides agreed to keep in touch until the agreement was implemented.

On our way back to the NPG national headquarters, through Kampala, I initiated contact with the French embassy, which had shown some sympathy for our plight in the past. When we arrived, we were well received. We presented our request for military and material assistance in writing. The ambassador agreed to forward our request to his government, with a strong recommendation to grant assistance to the NPG. He told us that his government would give a definite, possibly positive, response to our request within a month. We then returned to the national headquarters to await the result of the two contacts.

Within a month, our representative in East Africa informed us that the French ambassador in Kampala had requested we visit. When we returned, the ambassador informed us that his government had agreed to grant us military and material assistance. The ambassador asked us to build an airstrip near our headquarters. We also had to send two young officers to France to be trained on how to drop loads, such as arms, from a plane. The French government would send a military officer to NPG headquarters to help train our Anyanya forces and help with the airdrops.

After three months, the airstrip was complete. Our young officers had left for France, and the military trainer had arrived and started work. We discovered later that the military trainer had been a mercenary in the Congo in the early sixties. Despite this, our attitude towards him did not change. Morale was on the rise and new recruits for the ANAF were arriving in their hundreds, mostly from Bahr al-Ghazal and Upper Nile. Our tribal politics meant that the Shilluk were reticent. There had been no Shilluk representative in the Council of Ministers since the time of the SSPG. Othwonh Dak had been offered defence but declined. Another senior Shilluk leader, George Kwanai, had also declined to join the SSPG and the NPG.

Three months had passed, and nothing was forthcoming from the Israeli ambassador in Nairobi. We did not give up hope. A committee was assigned to buy weapons from the black market in Zaïre. The main problem was that the Zaïrean soldiers were unscrupulous. In addition, white mercenaries would sometimes forcibly take back the arms from the Anyanya after the sale was completed. Occasionally, they would kill or beat up the Anyanya soldiers in the process.

Both the SSPG and the NPG had tried to raise funds through taxation, in the same way as the rural councils had done during the British and Arab colonial administrations. The difficulty was that the Anyanya did not have the experience to organize this. What the Anyanya was able to collect would be spent on their own arms purchases. The Anyanya were reluctant to pay such funds to the NPG, as they thought that the NPG should obtain financial and military aid from foreign sources rather than depend on locally raised funds. They did not listen to the national leaders who tried to explain why it could not be done in that way.

We received another offer from two former white mercenaries. They asserted that there was a source of support in southern Africa. This source promised to aid the NPG representative in Zambia, Enoch Mading de Garang. Mading de Garang advised the NPG to negotiate with the two mercenaries. I met the men in Kampala. They reassured us that the source was reliable and was backed by a government in southern Africa. They also told us that they were personally sympathetic to the cause of the South Sudanese. They said that they were keen to come to the bush to provide military training. If the promised aid materialized, they would train the ANAF in the use of those arms. We were interested in the mercenaries' offer but suspected them of being spies. We remained skeptical about the arrival of military assistance. Despite these concerns, we urged them to follow up. We said that we would like to submit the issue to the Council of Ministers for approval first. We also told them that we already had one foreign military training expert. Within two weeks, the proposal was approved by the Council of Ministers. After this, the two men were allowed to come to the NPG headquarters and started training immediately.

The NPG had now recruited three foreign military expert trainers, all former white mercenaries in Africa. They trained our forces as effectively as they could. They began in August 1969, with the last trainer arriving in September 1969. As the training progressed, the food, medical, and clothing situation became more critical. In June 1969, large numbers of forces were coming from the provinces to the headquarters expecting to be trained and to participate in the new liberation struggle. They had heard that it was being aided militarily and materially by foreign sources and sympathizers.

Obtaining funds so that the movement could grow was vital. Without foreign support, the only source of revenue for the NPG was S£300 sent from the ANAF provincial brigades, meant to be paid annually by every district into the central treasury. Few districts, however, were able to pay their contributions. Problems compounded when the Sudanese currency was changed by the Nimeiri regime. As a result, what we had lost its value. Some of our foreign supporters tried to exchange it for the new Sudanese currency but had little success.

Another fundraising scheme was charging foreign television teams to cover ANAF and NPG activities. This was on the condition that they paid 10 percent of their proceeds to the NPG. Unfortunately, the TV crews never honored these agreements. Another source of revenue was to shoot elephants, rhinoceros, and buffaloes and sell the tusks and meat. This scheme was successful until July 1970, when the NPG was disbanded.

The Council of Ministers took several decisions to cope with the situation. Urgent messages were sent to the provincial and district commanders and civil administrators in Bahr al-Ghazal and Upper Nile to ask them to send sufficient funds to feed the large numbers of ANAF undergoing training. We explained that it was not enough to send forces for training without the resources to feed them. We also asked them to encourage the local chiefs to increase their efforts to supply food. The chiefs remained supportive of the movement and their response was positive. A large amount of food, particularly cassava flour, started to come in.

The Structure of the NPG, ANAF, and the Civil Administration
The NPG president was the overall head of the movement, including the civil administration. The ANAF was militarily structured, but the NPG and the civil administration were democratic. Each ministry had its own committees. The minister of each portfolio was also the chairman of its committee, except for defence, for whom the chairman was the president.

As a guerrilla movement, the ANAF was not autonomous. It was not yet an established army of an independent state. The NPG created a War Council, chaired by the NPG president. The NPG ministers for defence, finance, foreign affairs, and interior were ex-officio members. The War Council had the power to initiate war policies. It discussed issues like the size and development of military units, military food supplies, equipment, and training.

The ANAF general staff were independent. They planned their own military operations and how they worked. Their plans, however, had to be based on the general guidelines laid down by the War Council. This also needed final approval from the War Council and the Council of Ministers. Members of the ANAF general staff were the Commander-in-Chief, Gen. Emilio Taffeng, the Deputy Commander-in-Chief, Brig. Ali Guatala, and the Chief of Staff, Col. Maggot Dongoro. Joseph Lagu should have been chief of staff, but he was absent. There were also two or three other senior officers.

The ANAF was founded on four brigades: Brigade 1 in Bahr al-Ghazal, Brigade 2 in Upper Nile, Brigade 3 in Equatoria, and Brigade 4 at the national headquarters. It was decided that the Equatorian and headquarters brigades would deploy together at the headquarters to defend it against enemy attack, until the headquarters brigade developed to the strength and size required to work alone. The Equatorian brigade patrolled the entirety of Western Equatoria, carrying out regular ambushes against the enemy.

The integration of the ANAF continued despite major obstacles. There was also tension between the tribes caused by the departure of Aggrey Jaden and the chronic lack of funding. Despite this, implementation of this policy of integration was achieved by the NPG. In Bahr al-Ghazal and Equatoria, the ANAF was integrated. In Upper Nile, the commander of the Bor Battalion brought his forces to the NPG national headquarters and integrated them with the ANAF. This happened despite Col. Gai Tut's attack at Bor on the integrated forces operating under Akuot Atem and Lt. Col. Aquilla Manyuon.

Hostility to the NPG

That foreign military experts were training the liberation forces of ANAF was a powerful morale booster. It also contributed to the belief that foreign military and material aid would eventually materialize. However, after several months, the goodwill and patriotic attitude of the villagers of Yei District began to decline. The food supply was also dwindling.

Leaflets started to appear calling on the NPG and its leaders to return to their areas in Bahr al-Ghazal and Upper Nile. The NPG was regarded as Dinka, but most of it was not: the leaflets were false. The NPG responded with a counter leaflet. This stated categorically that it would not leave Equatoria because it was an integral part of the Nile Republic. The NPG leaflet pointed out that since 1955, thousands of patriots from Equatoria, Bahr al-Ghazal, and Upper Nile Provinces had laid down their lives.

Eventually, the food supply virtually stopped. The ANAF had to be sent into the surrounding countryside to collect cassava. They were under strict orders not to molest the villagers. A small ANAF unit was formed specifically to fetch meat from the Garamba Park in Zaïre. The former Zaïrean Prime Minister, Moïse Tshombe, had issued an order that the Anyanya were permitted to kill 20 animals per year in the reserve for food. This did help the NPG to solve the meat shortage. Unfortunately, the privilege was abused by the Anyanya. Despite these difficulties, the training program of the ANAF continued. Everybody involved was determined to see it through.

Major Clashes Between the ANAF and Sudanese Government

The NPG policy was to increase training and obtain better equipment, rather than concentrate on military operations: we knew that our arms were poor in both quantity and quality. However, this did not mean abstaining from combat: the ANAF was always ready to retaliate. There were several attacks on our Bungu headquarters by the Sudanese army. The heaviest was in August 1969, while a French TV crew was visiting.

That August, the War Council was in session under a huge tree at the Bungu headquarters. It was attended by all the senior ministers, Gen. Taffeng, Brig. Guatala, and other senior officers including Col. Dongoro, Lt. Col. Paul Awel, and his deputy Lt. Col. Emmanuel Abur Nhial. A full battalion was deployed at the headquarters half a mile away.

At 1pm, an administrator ran towards the meeting. He said that the Arabs were coming. I closed the meeting and ordered Gen. Taffeng to take charge of the ANAF. All the officers went to their units. The ministers and I moved swiftly to our quarters, located on a small stream. Brig. Guatala shouted at us to go down the stream, which we did. We did not have a special security force or guns to defend ourselves. All our weapons were in the hands of our fighters. We later realized that this was a grave mistake.

Word came that the enemy forces were advancing towards the headquarters on three fronts. Our camp was within the rainforest next to the Congo-Nile divide. There was an expectation that the enemy would attack the ANAF headquarters south-east of the presidential quarters. At exactly 1.30pm, the enemy forces opened fire. One force attacked the presidential and ministerial quarters, the second attacked the main ANAF base, and the third followed the stream from the south with the intention of cutting off the presidential quarters. We discovered later that the attacking forces were guided by Anyanya members who had deserted.

The usual practice in Anyanya operations was to retaliate against all attacks. If the ammunition ran out or the enemy firepower proved superior, the ANAF would tactically withdraw. At

Bungu, the ANAF returned fire, and the enemy slowed. Within five minutes, the enemy opened fire on our position on the stream. We ran across the stream quietly and crawled in the tall grass. Our only bodyguard, a Luo man, returned fire. Bullets rained down on us, but no one was hit. We retreated approximately 400 yards, then stopped. The enemy did not pursue us.

The battle continued for more than one and a half hours. When it stopped, we saw smoke coming from the presidential quarters which had been captured by the enemy and set on fire. Smoke was also coming from the direction of the ANAF headquarters which had also been captured and set on fire. The ANAF had no radios and coordination in battle was impossible. Gen. Taffeng arrived with a small force. Taffeng was worried about my safety and that of the ministers. Ammunition was running low, so the ANAF tactically withdrew. Taffeng and his men advanced towards the presidential quarters, moving along the stream. They met the enemy and exchanged fire. One of Taffeng's officers, Capt. Kothea Kedit Muortat, was shot. He sustained a fracture to his thigh and was taken to the ANAF's new base.

I ordered Taffeng to organize the ANAF guerrilla units. Each unit was to continuously attack the enemy's position. This was to happen at different places and at different times throughout the night and the next day. The enemy appeared to have concentrated its forces on burning down the presidential quarters. I also instructed Taffeng to organize security for the French TV crew.

Just before 7.30pm when it was dark, the ANAF counterattacked. The enemy responded with a barrage of fire. The enemy could not advance quickly because they did not know the geography of the area or the location of our positions. The enemy continued to fire heavily against the ANAF who fired back for three minutes. The fighting continued throughout the night, but the enemy did not send reinforcements. We later learned that the enemy force attacking us believed the forest was full of Anyanya fighters.

We were able to keep the situation under control because Taffeng and I had coordinated prior to this event. I issued further orders to Taffeng to lay a series of ambushes along the known routes to Yei town. This route would be followed by the enemy if they decided to withdraw during the night or at dawn.

We were expecting the enemy forces to use mortars as they had done earlier, but this did not happen. After 2.30am, the enemy firing ceased. We assumed they were withdrawing to Yei. But we discovered that the enemy forces had slipped out of Bungu altogether, avoiding the ambushes organized earlier. After consulting me, Taffeng sent out a force to pursue the withdrawing enemy. At 4am, heavy shooting was heard from the direction of Yei. Our guerrilla units had engaged the enemy forces as they were withdrawing to Yei, causing them heavy casualties.

The next day, the ANAF carried out a mopping up operation. More than 10 enemy soldiers had been killed by the ANAF. The number of wounded was unknown. Some wounded were carried to Yei by the retreating forces. Only one ANAF officer was wounded.

After returning from the bush, the French TV team was invited in. I explained to them how the ANAF had foiled the attack by Khartoum's military dictator Nimeiri. We apologized and said that it had not been possible for them to film the battles. This was because we did not have enough arms and ammunition to guarantee their security during such operations. They said that they had been able to record the sound of the battle and that they also intended to film me, together with the government, in action. They gave us antibiotics which saved the life of the wounded Capt. Kothea, who was then carried to Aba in Zaïre for further treatment.

During the Anyanya movement, when a base was attacked or burnt down, a new base was immediately established. Bungu was therefore abandoned, and Balgo-Bindi became the new national headquarters.

Growing Divisions in the Movement

Several incidents reveal the tensions in the movement. For example, when an integrated ANAF unit from Bahr al-Ghazal arrived at Balgo-Bindi headquarters in October 1969, a quarrel broke out between the soldiers from Lakes District and Aweil District. A woman from Rumbek had left her husband and run away with a soldier from Aweil. Feelings ran high along sectional lines. The two factions were well-armed and took up positions facing each other. Gabriel Kau Ater and I stood between the two sides as they were about to open fire. We told the two sides that if they were going to shoot, they would have to kill us first. We were the elders and were not prepared to stand by and witness our young men butcher one another. We said we did not want the cause of South Sudan to be destroyed by the citizens of Lakes and Aweil. Fortunately, no fighting took place; only insults were exchanged. This continued from 10am until 6pm. After that, both sides stood down and dispersed. The leaders on both sides said that if it were not for us, they would have fought each other.

There was low morale at headquarters and among the ANAF soldiers. This was partly because of delays in obtaining arms and partly because of a propaganda campaign being stepped up against the NPG in Equatoria. Divisions were inherited from the SSPG, and tensions were growing between tribes in Western Equatoria and the Dinka. Aggrey Jaden was involved in this despite the good relationship we had with him previously. As a result, many ANAF soldiers from Equatoria left. I called military parades and delivered long speeches appealing for unity, as disintegration would weaken the struggle, but nobody was listening.

We successfully defended our headquarters for several weeks against enemy attacks. After this, Gen. Taffeng asked if he could take a few weeks off. He explained that he wanted to visit his ill daughter in his village. I gave him permission to go, although I remained suspicious of his intentions. He assured me that he would be right back. Taffeng's departure was followed by more Equatorian soldiers leaving the ANAF. The majority of the ANAF soldiers who remained at the headquarters were Dinka and Nuer. Hundreds more Anyanya troops arrived from Bahr al-Ghazal and Upper Nile Provinces because news of military aid to the movement had spread. The number of soldiers had increased, but the Equatorian villages which had supplied food were becoming unfriendly. Food was increasingly scarce, and hunger was a serious problem.

Many were opposed to South Sudan becoming independent. These included elements within the north, the international media, the OAU and many foreign governments. They interpreted the desire for independence as extremism. It was the view of the opposition that many Anyanya military leaders, including Joseph Lagu, were moderate enough to accept a united Sudan. The Southern political leaders labelled extremists included Joseph Oduho, Father Saturnino, Aggrey Jaden, and me.

After the election of the NPG, I met Lagu in Uganda. I was aware of his hostility towards the NPG. I asked why he refused to take up the post of ANAF chief of staff offered by President Aggrey in 1967. I offered Lagu the post again in the NPG in 1969. Lagu made it clear that he no longer wanted to serve under the leadership of any Southern Sudanese person. This was related to his military service under Father Saturnino and Joseph Oduho. He was also opposed to the political wing leading the movement. He declined to explain why. The only reason I could think of was that some foreign media suggested that the Anyanya military wing would find more support. I asked Lagu if he was fighting for an independent South Sudan or for a compromise settlement within one Sudan. He answered that he was fighting for independence, but that foreign friends who knew better than us were advising him differently. They said that we would not be able to sustain a long war. It became clear to me that Lagu was giving in to foreign pressure.

Delivery of Arms to Lagu

In September 1969, the Israelis began delivering arms to Lagu. This was the result of the deal negotiated by the SSPG delegation in June 1968.

The NPG Council of Ministers decided that the NPG should dissolve and allow the ANAF to merge with Lagu's forces. We felt there were no other possible sources of military assistance. Joining with Lagu's forces would prevent any further infighting between the Anyanya.

It was my job, as President, to convey this decision to the ANAF general staff and hear their views. I met the NPG senior ministers and explained events from the time the arms supply was negotiated in 1968, to when the arms were delivered to Lagu. I said that acquiring arms had been a top priority, and that it was my view that we needed to dissolve the NPG and allow the ANAF to merge with Lagu's forces. The ANAF members of the general staff rejected this NPG resolution. They argued that the ANAF must not surrender to Lagu. They felt that Lagu was being imposed on the people of South Sudan. They asked me to order them to overrun Lagu's headquarters. They said that they thought that they could take it within half an hour. They would take all the arms delivered by the foreigners and arrest Lagu. I rejected this request as I thought such an action would ignite a tribal conflict and destroy the liberation struggle.

In the end, a compromise was reached. We would try to learn

whether sympathetic countries would accept to deliver arms to the ANAF to fight separately, but alongside Lagu's forces, against the common enemy, until such time as the factions might be reconciled. I told the meeting that I would lead a NPG delegation to East Africa to meet the Israeli ambassador to discuss this proposition. I instructed the commander-in-chief to try and maintain morale in the ANAF. Morale had improved ever since reports of the delivery of arms to Lagu began to circulate.

In Kampala, Arkangelo Wanji and I met the ambassador and his staff. The ambassador told us that the delivery of arms to Lagu did not mean that his government was hostile to the NPG or its predecessor. The ambassador also accepted the NPG's proposal to receive a separate arms delivery. We were skeptical of their sincerity but had few other options.

While still in Kampala, a Ugandan newspaper reported that Anyanya officers had overthrown the NPG. Another report said Gen. Taffeng had set up a breakaway administration, the Anyidi Provisional Government (APG).

The following day, runners carrying letters from NPG headquarters arrived in Kampala. We were relieved to learn that the published reports were false but decided to leave for headquarters immediately in any case. When we arrived, Camillo Dhol informed us that Gen. Taffeng had sent 150 armed soldiers from Moroto to the NPG headquarters to put pressure on the ANAF to overthrow the NPG. According to Camillo, negotiations between the force sent by Taffeng and the ANAF had broken down. Taffeng's force launched an attack. The ANAF retaliated and Lt. Col. Michael Lorwe and another of Taffeng's officers were killed. Taffeng's forces then withdrew to Moroto. They were not pursued.

It was all very disappointing. All these years, I had managed to avoid infighting and bloodshed between Southerners. The NPG

War Council was called, and it was decided that a state of emergency be declared. Orders were issued that the ANAF must not carry out any offensive against any Anyanya faction, including that of Gen. Taffeng. The policy of the NPG was not to fight against other Southern groups, no matter the reason. Such infighting would lead to the collapse of the liberation struggle.

Towards the end of 1969, there were constant attacks on ANAF positions by rival Anyanya forces and the APG. The NPG policy of non-aggression remained unchanged despite these attacks. The NPG invited all the leaders of Equatoria, including Taffeng and Elia Lupe Waiwai, to meet in a neutral place to resolve the infighting. There was no response.

The NPG leadership took further steps aimed at reconciliation. An envoy was sent to Lukudu Lokulu, the Kakwa paramount chief in Zaïre, whom we knew had direct relations with some Equatorian leaders and was sympathetic towards the liberation struggle. We appealed to him to mediate between the NPG leadership and opposing groups from Equatoria. We suggested that he should invite both sides to Aba for talks. Chief Lukudu agreed. Unfortunately, the Equatorian groups declined to send a single delegate. That was the end of the initiative. Lukudu apologized for having been unable to help our struggle.

Meanwhile, skirmishes continued between both sides. If the NPG had retaliated, the situation would have become a guerrilla war within a guerrilla war. Still, the skirmishes were minor compared with what followed the attempted coup by Riek Machar and Lam Akol against John Garang in 1991. There was less tribal conflict and rivalry for leadership in the Anyanya than in the SPLA and hence, fewer casualties.

Early in 1970, I went to Aba in response to a foreign invitation. Aba was 15 miles from our former NPG headquarters. The information about this trip seemed to have been leaked. We left Balgo-Bindi at about 7pm on foot, accompanied by a presidential guard, which would turn back as soon as we had crossed into Zaïre. At 12.45am, we crossed a chest deep stream right on the border. A huge tree had fallen across the stream along which we had to walk. After a mile, we heard firing, so we stopped while the commander sent a few men to find out what had happened. Soon after that, we received a report stating that a force from Taffeng's group had been sent to ambush us at the stream crossing, but they arrived late, and we had already crossed. However, they ambushed our reconnaissance party. Taffeng's forces opened fire in the darkness, killing our soldiers and fleeing in fear of retaliation.

I ordered that the whole force return to the scene. We arrived at dawn and saw the bodies of our dead soldiers. Their burials were organized. We sent a message to headquarters informing them of the incident and instructing them to take appropriate measures to secure themselves. We would proceed to Aba.

Several days later, reports from Moroto, Taffeng's headquarters, said that the force that carried out the ambush at the stream claimed to have killed me.

After my return from Aba, we received an ultimatum from Bari speaking Anyanya groups in Western Equatoria: unless we left Equatoria for Bahr al-Ghazal and Upper Nile immediately, food sanctions would be applied against us. The NPG reiterated that Equatoria was part of the soil of South Sudan for which we had been fighting and dying for many years. Nobody had the right to tell us to move out.

Within a week, the cassava plant at the old, abandoned village on which the ANAF depended was systematically uprooted. Consequently, a serious food shortage developed at headquarters. We began to buy food directly from villages in Zaïre, but as our funds were limited it was impossible to buy the required quantities. Despite this, firm orders were issued to the ANAF units in Western Equatoria not to take food by force from the locals.

Akuot Atem Returns from Upper Nile

In October 1969, the former Defence Minister of the SSPG, Akuot Atem, returned from Bor, Upper Nile, where he had gone to implement the SSPG policy of ANAF national integration. With him was a small ANAF contingent, including Maj. Peter Cirillo and Capt. Alfred Aguet Awan.

The force for Upper Nile should not have been sent to Bor but instead been deployed in the center of Upper Nile, within a reasonable distance of the other Anyanya forces in the province. All the Anyanya district forces should have converged on this camp.

Instead, Akuot took the force to Bor district, where he established a base from which he launched conventional military attacks against the government garrison in Bor town. Akuot knew better than anybody that his force, ill-trained and lacking enough weapons and ammunition, was no match for the government garrison.

While Akuot continued his operations with a diminishing force, the Upper Nile Brigade command was awaiting a headquarters force to integrate. They were becoming impatient, and Col. Samuel Gai Tut, the deputy commander for Upper Nile, moved his force to Bor and besieged and disarmed Akuot. He took almost all the arms, leaving only a few for Akuot. Gai Tut's disarmament of Akuot's forces did not result in a loss of life on either side. That was a great credit to him.

The forces under Akuot virtually disappeared. Some went with Gai Tut, another group returned to Western Equatoria, and a small group of senior officers accompanied Akuot back to the NPG headquarters.

The arrival of Akuot and his men aggravated tensions at the headquarters between the ANAF officers and mainly Bari speaking men of Western Equatoria, and the NPG political leaders and the ANAF units comprised of men from Bahr al-Ghazal and Upper Nile. The ANAF officers and men from Western Equatoria formerly in Akuot's force alleged that a "Dinka" officer from Upper Nile, Gai Tut, had mistreated them in Bor. They insisted that Gai Tut was Dinka whereas in fact, he was Nuer. They found it difficult to see the difference between Dinka and Nuer.

Akuot, as one of the founders of the SSPG, was invited to attend the April 1969 NPG convention. He did not attend because he was in Bor. However, when I formed my cabinet, I gave him the portfolio of cabinet affairs. During his short stay at the NPG headquarters, I explained how the convention was held and the NPG formed. I also explained how after careful consideration, I had decided to offer him the post of Minister of Cabinet Affairs. I could not reappoint him as Minister of Defence because the criteria for appointment was no longer based on provincial origin but on capability.

Akuot declined cabinet affairs and insisted he return to defence. I told him that I could not do it as I had already offered the defence post to David Koak, who was well qualified. I promised that in a future reshuffle, it would be possible for Akuot to be moved to another portfolio but not to defence. Akuot was upset but there was nothing more that I could do to make him participate in the NPG. It was regrettable that I failed to agree with Akuot whom I had known for a long time, as a friend and classmate at Loka. To satisfy my conscience, I gave him some time to decide whether he was willing to accept another portfolio.

I received an urgent message from the NPG representative in East Africa that I was required by a diplomatic contact. Just before I left, I called Akuot and spoke to him in the presence of Camillo

Dhol, the Minister of Internal Affairs, who was to act as President in my absence. I asked Akuot whether he had made up his mind about a new portfolio. He answered that he had not yet done so. I said that I would deal with his case as soon as I was back.

Rumors circulated that Akuot was planning an escape from headquarters with some of his supporters and men, mostly from his own area, Bor district. The rumor was that they would head for Moroto to join Gen. Taffeng's APG.

In view of this threat, I instructed Camillo and the Acting Commander-in-Chief, Brig. Guatala, as well as other senior ministers and officers, to take precautions. I made it clear that if Akuot and his force resorted to violence, minimum force should be used in response, to avoid unnecessary casualties on both sides. Under no circumstances should Akuot be killed. Even if he resorted to force, he should be arrested and given a fair trial. If he did not resort to violence, he and his associates should go unharmed.

That was my last encounter with Akuot Atem. Less than a week after I left the headquarters, Akuot, accompanied by five of his officers and men, fled during a dark, rainy night. Two weeks later, reports were received that Akuot had joined Taffeng at Moroto. Other reports suggested that Akuot had instructed Lt. Col. Aquilla Manyuon, the commander of the Anyanya Bor battalion, to move with his forces from Bor to Moroto to join Anyidi. Manyuon refused to comply and instead moved his force to the NPG headquarters, where they were welcomed by the NPG acting president and the senior ANAF officers.

Manyuon's force became part of the ANAF receiving training by military experts. Despite the gloomy situation, there were other developments which maintained morale. Among these was the progress in the military training led by the three foreign experts. At least 2,000 ANAF officers and men were undergoing training,

As time passed, everybody expected a plane loaded with arms to appear in the sky. Nothing materialized and the foreign military expert sent by France, locally known by the name of Bulkueth, was showered with questions. He answered that he did not know. As the delay continued and Bulkueth received no message, we assumed that the French government had reversed its policy for some reason.

Three months later, the two ANAF officers sent to France for training returned empty-handed. They relayed that France could not fly the arms direct to South Sudan, because the Sudanese government had become aware of the plan. Instead, France had decided to land the arms in Chad. We would have to arrange to collect the arms from there. Although we were not convinced, we did not want to discard the possibility altogether. We decided to continue to look for a more feasible alternative.

In early 1970, the Mobutu regime in Zaïre contacted me. An envoy told me that Mobutu would like me to come to Kinshasa to meet on an urgent matter. He went on to say that according to Mobutu, the Sudanese government was training two battalions of Simba rebels to launch attacks against targets in Zaïre. For this reason, Mobutu assured me that his government would help our movement with arms and military advisors. Furthermore, the envoy told me that I would be flown from Bunia to Kinshasa to meet Mobutu. I expressed my thanks and replied that I would willingly meet Mobutu. He said that I would be approached soon.

That such activities by the Zaïrean rebels and the Sudanese government were taking place in South Sudan was already known to the NPG representative in Kinshasa, Francis Mayar Akon. He confirmed that Mobutu would soon send for me. In the meantime, I waited for a signal from the Zaïrean government, but heard nothing more. Later, we ascertained that the Sudanese government had withdrawn its support for the Simba groups. Our hopes for obtaining military assistance from Zaïre dimmed. However, the ANAF were still opposed to the NPG's dissolution and merger with Joseph Lagu's group. I was still willing to accept this for patriotic reasons.

Prospect of the NPG Receiving Foreign Military Aid

That Joseph Lagu became the recipient of the arms negotiated by the SSPG in June 1968 placed him in an advantageous position. This collaboration with foreign supporters allowed him to subvert the NPG. Lagu claimed to be a moderate willing to accept a compromise settlement within one Sudan, compared to the SSPG and others committed to the independence of South Sudan.

I had earlier rejected the ANAF general staff proposal to attack Lagu's base at Owinykibul, Eastern Equatoria. But we had intelligence that Lagu would attack the NPG headquarters and stage a coup since he had more firepower than the ANAF. Those who claimed to know Lagu closely said this was unlikely. They thought it more likely he would infiltrate the military wing of the NPG and attempt a coup from within. Although I did not rule out this possibility, I discounted it. Since the ANAF general staff had rejected dissolution of the NPG and merging with Lagu, I could not believe that the same general staff would allow itself to be used to stage a coup against the NPG. Meanwhile, Lagu and his foreign allies were stepping up rhetoric in the international media and among the troops within South Sudan that the Anyanya military leadership was stronger than its political leadership.

In May 1970, the NPG Council of Ministers convened to review the situation created by the delivery of arms to Lagu. The ministers resolved to send an NPG delegation to East Africa to meet a representative of Israel. This would help us to get a picture of their attitude towards the democratically elected NPG. Did they think Lagu represented the only group who should receive arms and fight for the liberation of South Sudan? Within two days, we left for the Israeli embassy in Kampala, where we met the ambassador and put to him the resolution of the NPG Council of Ministers. We were told that Israel had no desire to take sides among the South Sudanese. Although the ambassador acknowledged Israel had supplied arms to the group led by Lagu, it did not mean that he was favored. The ambassador said that his government was willing to supply arms to us and requested that we send a military delegation to discuss our requirements.

We agreed to send such a delegation without delay. We were skeptical but prepared to risk anything to procure arms. On our return to the NPG headquarters, we briefed the NPG on the outcomes of the meeting. It was agreed that the delegation would consist of Arkangelo Barri Wanji, Minister for Foreign Affairs, Lt. Col. Emmanuel Abur Nhial, now ANAF Chief of Staff, and Lt. Col. Paul Awel, a member of the general staff. They left immediately.

After two weeks, Wanji, the leader of the delegation, returned to the headquarters to report that he had been detached from the delegation. Lt. Cols. Abur Nhial and Awel were accompanied to Lagu's headquarters at Owinykibul by an Israeli official. Wanji was asked to wait for the delegation in Kampala, but feeling humiliated, refused and returned. We suspected the motives of the Israelis. However, we trusted Abur, with whom we had worked harmoniously since his arrival at the headquarters in 1968. Abur had been among the ANAF officers most outspoken against the proposal to dissolve the NPG and merge the ANAF with Lagu's forces.

After another fortnight, the military delegation returned. Abur began by saying that overall, their mission was successful. The only disappointment was that the ambassador declined to allow Wanji to go to Owinykibul, saying that the delegation was required to carry out what he called purely military work, to which a political leader like Wanji could contribute little. We were not satisfied with this explanation but did not want to argue too much, although we requested Abur convey this reasoning to Wanji.

Abur said that everything else had gone well. Israel and Lagu had agreed that the NPG would send an ANAF contingent of 200 officers and men to Owinykibul to receive the first consignment of arms for the NPG. Deliveries would continue until the NPG received sufficient arms to work towards the liberation of South Sudan. Abur said they had seen a variety of arms and had been assured that more would be coming. Military training of Anyanya armed forces in Israel had begun.

One minister asked whether Israel or Lagu had asked them to overthrow the NPG. Abur denied such allegations. I said to Abur that there were rumors of such allegations, but that most of the NPG Council of Ministers dismissed them because we trusted Abur as a loyal South Sudanese nationalist.

The following day there was a more detailed briefing. We agreed that the ANAF general staff would send 200 officers and men from the ANAF to Owinykibul to receive the first consignment of arms and other material assistance. There was a feeling of euphoria in the national headquarters. Despite this, my mistrust of Lagu lingered. I was aware of his mistrust of the NPG, which he regarded as a Dinka movement. I also did not trust the foreigners.

The Overthrow of the Nile Provisional Government

The NPG gave the ANAF general staff freedom to run its own affairs without interference, provided that the minister of defence was kept informed. In view of this, the ANAF general staff met separately under Col. Awel, to select the force to go to Owinykibul. As Brig. Guatala, who would otherwise have chaired the meeting, was on leave, the majority at the ANAF meetings happened to be from Bahr al-Ghazal.

The meeting took place in the morning at the ANAF military quarters. It went on for the whole day without reporting to the minister of defence, which was unusual. However, we continued to wait patiently to hear the outcome. At 4pm, I was sitting outside my house chatting with friends and colleagues when I saw Col. Awel and Lt. Col. Kuol Amoum, followed by more than 60 armed men, walking towards me. I thought that the meeting was over and that they were coming to inform me of the general staff's decision.

Some of the soldiers rushed into the presidential quarters and starting to disarm my bodyguards. I told the guards not to resist. When they were a few yards away, Awel came to attention, saluted, and said that the general staff had decided to overthrow the NPG. He said that the representatives of Israel and Col. Lagu had told the military delegation that unless the NPG was overthrown, no arms would be delivered. He added, "Sir, you are one of our leaders and the NPG has been well organized together with the ANAF. But even with good leadership and good organization, without arms, we will be unable to achieve the liberation of South Sudan."

In reply, I said to the two officers, "You have allowed yourselves to be used by the so-called foreign sympathizers and Lagu to subject me and the NPG to maximum humiliation. What did I say to you in October 1969, following the reports that Israel had delivered arms to the group of Joseph Lagu? I said that the only way out I could see was to dissolve the NPG and the ANAF and to join Lagu. You refused then, and now you are overthrowing the NPG."

As I spoke, I saw a force of ANAF loyal to the NPG arriving, led by Capt. Andrew Makur Thou. Earlier, Makur had promised me that if a coup was attempted, he would suppress it. When I looked around, I saw Makur and he signaled, asking me if he should arrest the coup leaders. I responded by shaking my head. He understood.

I said to the coup leaders, "You have destroyed the deepest

confidence I had in you as Southern nationalists, not power-seeking soldiers. However, I did not join the Anyanya in the bush with an ambition to become a leader and to cause bloodshed among the Southerners. I joined to unite and fight against our common enemy." I accepted the coup and with that, ended the tenure of the NPG.

I was not placed under arrest. Later, when I met Makur, he told me that he was upset by my refusal to arrest the coup leaders. I apologized to him and reiterated that I did not want Southerners to kill one another in a leadership struggle.

I was told by Col. Awel, who despite the coup remained a staunch supporter of the NPG, that Lt. Col. Abur was the initiator of the coup. After a whole day of debate, Abur had managed to convince the ANAF general staff that Israel and Lagu would never allow arms to come to the ANAF unless the NPG was removed. He was asked why a coup was necessary when I had already agreed in principle to the voluntary dissolution of the NPG and the merger with Lagu's forces. His answer was that Israel and Lagu insisted on the military removal of the NPG. After a fierce argument, a resolution to remove the NPG by military means was passed by a small majority.

Abur had been promised the overall civil and military leadership of Bahr al-Ghazal following the demise of the NPG, under the overall leadership of Lagu. He suffered enormous guilt after the coup. Everybody knew how much trust I had placed in him.

Soon after the removal of the NPG, it became clear that there was a power vacuum, since none of the senior ANAF officers wanted to take over the leadership. On the following day, I was told by Awel that Abur would leave soon for Owinykibul with a selected force of ANAF officers and men.

The following day, Elia Duang Arop, the former Deputy Minister of Finance, along with Stephen Ciec Lam, the former Minister of

Information, convened a meeting of the former NPG ministers and members of the general staff, including Lt. Col. Abur. Elia Duang suggested that the recent events should not be allowed to go down in history as a military coup, but as a voluntary dissolution of the NPG agreed by both political and military leaders. This was based on the understanding that the NPG leadership had proposed to dissolve the NPG in 1969 and that it was the ANAF general staff which objected. The resolution was seconded by Ciec Lam and was unanimously adopted.

After that, it was put into writing that the NPG had dissolved itself to promote the best interest of the liberation struggle. Most of us were happy with this compromise. Ciec Lam sent a press release to the media in East Africa and beyond.

Abur then left with a force of 200 for Owinykibul. Everybody was hoping for the arms to be delivered, at which time they would be distributed to Bahr al-Ghazal and Upper Nile. As for me, although I had relinquished my role as NPG president, I still enjoyed respect and influence on both the political and military sides of the camp. Many issues continued to be referred to me for advice and consultation.

Joseph Lagu and Israel Refused to Deliver Arms
In August 1970, a month after the ANAF contingent was sent to Owinykibul, rumors circulated that Lagu and Israel had had a change of heart and had declined to deliver the arms. About a fortnight later the rumors were confirmed: the force returned with no arms.

It was not long before the commanding officer came to see me. He told me that Lagu had convinced the Israeli representatives that the declared dissolution of the NPG was a ploy by its leadership to get arms. He alleged that once we got arms, we would reinstate the NPG and that would put Lagu's leadership of the liberation movement in jeopardy.

On hearing this frustrating news, we began to suspect a foreign conspiracy against the liberation struggle. I suggested that I go to East Africa with Camillo Dhol and meet the Israeli ambassador to find out why they had dishonored their promises. There was no objection to my suggestion since we were no longer officially representing any organization.

Within three days, we met the ambassador in Kampala. He was polite and friendly. I opened by asking why they had gone back on their word. I assured him that the NPG had been dissolved and that the ANAF would merge with Lagu. Camillo added that we were serious and wanted unity among South Sudanese because we believed that was the only way to achieve freedom. The ambassador assured us that his government would reverse the decision to withhold the arms. He asked us to send our men to Owinykibul to collect the promised arms. On our return to Balgo-Bindi, we briefed the senior officers and advised them to send the force to Owinykibul. This was carried out with extraordinary speed.

The Formation of the African National Front (ANF)
We were optimistic that the ANAF would come back with arms. A cordial and friendly atmosphere developed between the former political members of the NPG and the ANAF at headquarters. The NPG's former leaders were gradually being recognized not only as elders but also as advisors on more serious matters.

We used to sit informally under shady trees or around fires at night and spend hours discussing the past, present, and future of the liberation struggle without misunderstanding or tension. New ideas began to circulate. One was that the dissolution of the NPG had created a political vacuum. Some began to think that it was not rational to overthrow the NPG simply because of the arms supply. A conference was proposed to allow both the political and the ANAF leaders to discuss the situation. The date of the conference was fixed for 15 October 1970. It took place just outside the main Balgo-Bindi camp.

On 26 October, after long deliberations, we resolved to form a purely political organization called the African National Front (ANF). Its constitution and aims were the same as those of the NPG. I was unanimously elected as president. I was reluctant because I did not want to become victim to more rivalry and tribal antagonism. I had decided that I would not aspire to leadership again until I was satisfied that South Sudanese had developed a spirit of patriotism and nationalism like we experienced in the Southern Front in the late fifties and sixties. Eventually though, I was persuaded and reluctantly accepted the presidency.

It was unanimously agreed the ANF must not under, any circumstances, become the political wing of a military government. It would carry out purely political activities, including warranted criticism of activities of any military and political liberation efforts. The ANF would strive to define the genuine aims of the struggle.

The executive committee of the ANF consisted mostly of former members of the NPG. It was agreed, for the time being, that the formation of the ANF must be kept confidential. This was to avoid giving the impression of being a rival to military groups, as this might jeopardize the fair distribution of arms to all parts of the South. Joseph Lagu, who despite engineering the overthrow of the NPG, had not yet succeeded in setting up or declaring himself the leader of a liberation organization that could be considered a successor to the NPG and ANAF.

The political degeneration was reminiscent of the period leading up to the formation of the SSPG in 1967. Consequently, in

November 1970, the ANF laid out a proposal to be presented to Lagu and other political and military organizations as a way to achieve greater unity of liberation struggle actors.

We proposed that the various South Sudanese organizations, both military and political, should agree to set up an umbrella national organization under a single leader. A conference to discuss this proposal was convened without delay in Kampala, with Joseph Lagu present. The conference proposed forming a national executive committee, chaired by Lagu, with full executive, judiciary, and military power to enable it to spearhead the movement effectively. We proposed that Lagu lead the liberation struggle in which all the South was represented. In addition, it was proposed that there should be an Advisory Council of 12 members selected from the three provinces, the majority of whom should be political leaders in the movement. This body should advise the overall national committee in all matters pertaining to political as well as military matters.

I believed this was the only way to achieve the elusive unity of the Southerners. We had just received military and material assistance. We would only be able to use it to liberate ourselves if we were united. We all knew that in the previous years of the war, getting military aid was the biggest priority. As he had the arms, Lagu had emerged as a leader.

Other participants spoke in support of what I had said. Lagu said he accepted our proposal in principle, but we should give him time to reflect. He would let us know his decision within three days. This was accepted. After three days we met again. Lagu was the first to speak. He said that he was unable to accept the proposal because the foreign supporters were not in favor of Southern political and military leaders coming together. When he was asked to elaborate and give reasons why they said so, Lagu declined to do so.

It was at this juncture that Camillo accused Lagu of dictatorship. Camillo told Lagu that South Sudan was not his property and that he had no right to lead the movement single-handedly, even with the support of foreigners. Lagu rejected the accusation, and the meeting broke up. We felt that apart from the foreign pressure, Lagu was afraid of leadership or tribal rivalries.

The enemies of our struggle were delighted to see us in disarray at a time when we should have come together and made the best use of the military assistance. The foreign friends who were not committed to supporting full independence for South Sudan were happy to work with a liberation movement led by one man. At the end of the day, they would not be held accountable.

A week later, Lagu invited me to discuss working together. He promised that I would be assigned an important position in his administration if I agreed to work with him. I could sense he was worried about me and the potential for the NPG to be revived and receive military aid. By giving me an assignment, he would have eliminated the threat to his leadership. His fears were baseless. I was not aspiring to challenge him or any other South Sudanese leader.

I said that I would only work with him if he accepted our proposal of becoming the overall leader of the liberation struggle, which he had refused. In addition, I did not want to betray my colleagues in the SSPG and the NPG, and I was angry at him for engineering the coup against the NPG in July. Finally, I was not happy with the humiliation he inflicted on Aggrey Jaden. Just before our talks ended, I asked Lagu whether he had declared himself overall leader of the movement. He denied having done so and said that he was only a military commander of the Anyanya. None of us believed this statement; we knew that Lagu had been aspiring to leadership since the death of Father Saturnino in 1966.

When I met my colleagues, Camillo Dhol pointed out that Lagu was trying to drive a wedge between the former members of the NPG and the ANF. In one of the final meetings with Lagu, I had stated that as the ANF leader, I could not unilaterally decide to work with him. Such a decision would be a betrayal of my colleagues and be interpreted as defection from the ANF.

Whilst in Kampala we met several other leaders, including Joseph Oduho, Akuot Atem, and Elia Lupe Waiwai. Some still doubted whether the NPG had been dissolved. We assured them that it had.

The rejection of the proposal for the formation of an umbrella executive committee by Lagu was regretted by the Kampala conference. The concern was that delays in setting up an umbrella committee would allow the international conspiracy against South Sudan's liberation struggle to continue to sabotage the movement. Before it adjourned, the meeting adopted a resolution urging Lagu to consider the formation of the umbrella committee.

There were many senior Anyanya officers in Kampala at the time, most of whom were in transit from the bush to other destinations. These Anyanya officers were profoundly disillusioned with the political vacuum created by the dissolution of the NPG. Many pressed the ANF to make a public declaration. But we remained opposed to the idea because it would create more divisions and perhaps slow the flow of military assistance. Most of us supported holding more meetings and discussions among the political and military leaders of the movement to open the way for convergence on patriotic ideas.

Among our aims as a delegation was to investigate allegations that Equatoria Province had a political organization separate from the Lagu group. If this was the case, the delegation was to find out if the group might enter dialogue with us on the possibility of a merger. Unfortunately, it was not the case.

At the beginning of January 1971, the ANF delegation returned to the former NPG and ANAF headquarters at Angundri. The delegation presented its report to former NPG cabinet ministers and the senior ANAF officers, most of whom were upset by the negative response by Lagu.

At that time, the ANAF were still receiving training from the foreign military experts. Nevertheless, we could observe a slow process of ANAF disintegration into regional camps, as they were prior to their integration under the SSPG and the NPG. None of the ANAF units had yet left the former headquarters, but they had reverted to regional transit camps, where they intended to wait for the return of the force from Owinykibul with arms.

While the majority of Anyanya soldiers were patriots determined to fight to the death to liberate South Sudan, they preferred to remain and fight in their native districts. This was the main reason for desertion from the national Anyanya military headquarters.

I speculated that Lagu's administration would maintain a centralized national force, equipped to fight a semi-conventional warfare against the enemy. The rest would go back to their districts to continue decentralized hit-and-run guerrilla warfare.

Bahr al-Ghazal Force Returns from Owinykibul with Arms

In January 1971, the Bahr al-Ghazal Anyanya force, part of the group sent to Owinykibul, arrived in Angundri with orders to proceed to Bahr al-Ghazal. This force carried no more than 250 guns of various types and ammunition. The Upper Nile element of the force that went to Owinykibul had been sent directly to Upper Nile. The rest of the Upper Nile forces at the headquarters, under Col. Awel, prepared to leave Angundri for Upper Nile. The Bahr al-Ghazal troops would also leave. This confirmed our prediction that Lagu wanted the Anyanya to function as decentralized units.

I asked Col. Awel whether he could take our foreign military experts to Ethiopia so that they could proceed home. They were

Ronald Gregory, alias "Fashoda", Kirby, alias "Kiir", and Armand, alias "Bulkueth". We had agreed that they would be paid half of the value of whatever booty was seized from the enemy in their joint operations with the ANAF or in the enemy controlled territories. This agreement was to be implemented after the NPG had received military aid from friendly foreign sources. As these men served our struggle, we were determined to protect them, unlike Gen. Taffeng who had allowed Steiner, his German mercenary, to fall into the hands of the Khartoum regime. Kirby, however, was killed by a mine at Bor. The others reached their homes abroad safely.

SSPG and NPG Documents Stolen
One problem which continuously confronted the liberation movement was the security of confidential documents. We were concerned documents would be targeted by the enemy. The SSPG built up a considerable documentation within its first year in office. This consisted of both open and secret documents, letters, press statements, memoranda, and agreements. There was also office equipment: a portable typewriter, rubber stamps, cabinets, and stationery. An ANAF unit of 12 men was assigned the task of keeping the documents secure. The documents were guarded in a special location in the bush whenever the national headquarters was under attack by the enemy.

When I was the SSPG foreign minister, I visited Kampala on a mission in March 1968. As usual, I called upon Lawrence Wol Wol, who was still at Makerere University. He told me that there was an American lecturer at the university who wanted to meet me. The lecturer said that he knew about the SSPG documentation and suggested we hand it over to him for safekeeping. He said he was doing a comparative study of the Rwenzori and South Sudan rebellions. I told him that I could not hand documents over to anyone and that the SSPG had adequate security for them in the bush. The discussion then ended.

As the enemy attacks became more frequent, a hide-out was planned for our documents three to four miles away from headquarters. It became a routine practice that whenever reports of attacks came in, the documents were swiftly removed to a secret location. This is what happened when the enemy attacked NPG headquarters in Balgo-Bindi in 1970. This tradition was maintained until the dissolution of the NPG.

Before Camillo and I left for our last mission to Uganda, we were given a large steel box by Bulkueth into which we placed all the SSPG and NPG documents. We then instructed the commander of the ANAF unit in charge of document security, Capt. Mer Gong, to dig a large hole and bury the box with the documents in it. This was done and we were called to see it. We had decided that the documents would remain buried until we arranged with Father Andrew Makur Macol, or someone else, to deposit them in a secure hiding place in a neighboring country. We explained this to Mer Gong and Col. Paul Awel and left for Uganda satisfied with the arrangements. When we returned in November 1970, we were shocked to learn that the documents had been stolen. I tried in vain to trace Mer Gong. Most of the ANAF officers had gone to Owinykibul and systems at the former NPG headquarters had broken down.

In 1973, I asked an American professor at the University of London whether he had heard of or come across reports concerning the whereabouts of the SSPG or NPG documents or archives. He said he had: the SSPG and NPG documents were somewhere in the State Department in the United States. He added that the documents were obtained through the CIA. I asked whether it would be possible for former members of the SSPG and NPG or South Sudanese researchers to be allowed access to such documents. He said it would be possible and that there would soon come a time when such documents would no longer be regarded as secret.

The Death of Camillo Dhol Kuac

Camillo Dhol and I returned from our mission in Uganda having negotiated the terms of an arms delivery to the ANAF in December 1970. Our return coincided with the arrival of the Bahr al-Ghazal force from Owinykibul. While this force prepared to proceed to Bahr al-Ghazal, Camillo decided to return home with them. I would miss him, and I was worried about his security, so I tried to persuade him to postpone his return. But he was resolute in his decision. He was homesick, his family at home was in bad shape, and he wanted to return before the rainy season began. I sympathized as I too wished to visit my home in Rumbek.

Six months after Camillo went home, news of his brutal murder was received. I was stunned and my heart was broken. Camillo Dhol Kuac was one of the most committed nationalists I ever knew. He had sacrificed everything to contribute to the struggle to liberate his motherland. He was courageous, clear-minded, and of sound judgment.

Camillo was the son of a Dinka Malwal chief, Kuac Mayieldit. Before he joined the liberation struggle, he was a qualified agriculturist employed in the Ministry of Agriculture. He spent many years working in Kargulu, Western Equatoria. He was elected an MP in 1957. Although sometimes misrepresented as hot-tempered by his political opponents, most Southerners regarded him highly. He must have been 49 or 50 years old when he was killed.

The reports were that Camillo was killed by government soldiers. He was spending the night in a hut built on a platform in a Jur Col village deep in the forest, but not far from an Anyanya camp. He had five Anyanya bodyguards stationed underneath the platform.

Unfortunately, they all fell asleep. After midnight, the Arab soldiers arrived, guided by a local spy. They disarmed and shot dead the sleeping guards. Camillo was called by the Arab soldiers to come out. As he climbed down, they ordered his hands be tied so that he could be escorted to Aweil. He knew that he would be tortured and humiliated, and preferred to die, so he defied them and spat in their faces. They shot him dead.

7.

The Addis Ababa Agreement

Second Exile in Zaïre

After the ANAF troops departed Angundri for their respective provinces, I decided to leave the bush. Most NPG ministers had returned to their home provinces under Anyanya control. Anyanya forces controlled the villages around every major town, even when the towns themselves were occupied by enemy garrisons.

I left for Isiro, Zaïre, at the end of January 1971. There were already some South Sudanese refugees living there, including chief Thiongkol Anyijong, the younger brother of paramount chief Macar Anyijong of the Apak section of the Atwot Dinka of Yirol. Food was scarce and the accommodation was bad. There was little income. We depended on what some of our young male refugees could buy with their earnings from manual labor. During this time, I came down with jaundice.

Our staple food was cassava root and the broth of boiled cassava leaves. Rice was occasional and expensive. Whenever possible, we would have salted fish broth as meat was too expensive. There was no shelter for refugees. When I arrived, I joined some other refugees who had occupied an old building with broken windows and doors. Its owners had abandoned it during the Congolese civil war. This house was in an awful state, infested with bugs and lice, which filled our clothing and fed on us day and night.

One day, we felt very hungry. Thiongkol and I decided to visit the UNHCR office and appeal for help, at least with food. The official we met said there were no funds in their budget for South Sudanese. After trying to explain our desperate situation, he gave us the equivalent of two US dollars in local currency to share. He told us not to come to his office again. The money provided for some poor meals for five days. When our situation worsened a month later, assistance from UNHCR did not seem a possibility.

We used to resort to help occasionally from Madam Ageer Gum from Rumbek. She was formerly secretary for information in the SSPG and later became a prominent member of the SPLM/A. She was a great South Sudanese woman leader. Ageer ran a small shop which sold food. She was willing to provide us with free food, but Thiongkol and I were reluctant to abuse her kindness. We persuaded her to accept a small payment from us.

The only solution we could see was to become self-sufficient by cultivating our own food. But we did not have wives to rely on for cooking and who could take care of whatever house one might erect, and we were not sure how long we would be there or where we would go next. I planned to join my former colleagues from the SSPG and NPG in Kinshasa.

The only respite I expected from the outside world was an air ticket to Kinshasa, which Francis Mayar Akon had promised me. I had heard nothing but had not given up hope. One day, a post office messenger delivered a message requesting I collect my ticket. I rushed to the post office. Within a week, I flew from Isiro to Kinshasa. I was welcomed at the airport by Francis Mayar and Agolong Chol Agolong.

The Kinshasa Group and the Build-up to the Addis Ababa Agreement

I had been informed in Kampala in early 1971 that the World Council of Churches (WCC) was trying to initiate negotiations between the Sudanese government and the Anyanya leadership. It was not clear then whether the parties to these negotiations intended to involve the different shades of South Sudanese political opinion. I did not hear further news until I met Rev. Elinana Nglamu in June 1971 in Isiro. He said that consultations were well advanced between the WCC and the Sudanese government. He added that when the time came, I would be one of the political leaders invited.

Nglamu asked for my opinion on the proposed talks. I said that my colleagues and I were not opposed to negotiations in principle. However, we believed it was of paramount importance that all the politicians, Anyanya leaders, and political groups, including those inside South Sudan, must first come together and agree on one objective and on what they thought would be the best outcome for the South. I also told Nglamu that I would be in Kinshasa until November 1971.

One of my aims in Kinshasa was to meet the members of the so-called Kinshasa Group to discuss the future of the ANF set up after the dissolution of the NPG in 1970. We agreed that the ANF should be reorganized, and more members recruited. Its constitution and manifesto should be reviewed, and branches set up among the refugees and exiles. It was also agreed that when the ANF developed into a powerful political organization, it would not need a military wing. We hoped the ANF would be capable of initiating dialogue among different South Sudanese political groups including that of Joseph Lagu, with the aim of uniting the liberation struggle under a single leadership.

Early in August 1971, Lawrence Wol Wol and Enoch Mading

de Garang arrived in Kinshasa and contacted us with an urgent message from Lagu and the WCC: that the Kinshasa Group should send a delegation to the proposed Anyanya – Sudan government negotiations.

In a meeting the next evening, Wol Wol and Mading de Garang explained that their mission was to brief us on the proposed peace negotiations and obtain consensus on the issue. They had come to Kinshasa to meet us, had met Southerners in Uganda, and would proceed to Ethiopia with the same purpose. Wol Wol told us that the WCC had conceded in their preliminary talks with the Sudanese government that all parties must agree to the principle of a united Sudan before the Sudanese government came to the negotiating table. The Lagu delegation tried hard to convince the Kinshasa Group to cease our insistence on independence for South Sudan. They told us it was futile.

The Kinshasa Group had concerns regarding the plans for negotiation with the Sudanese government. We had heard that on a visit of the WCC and All Africa Conference of Churches (AACC) to Khartoum, church representatives had assured the regime that they would do their best to persuade South Sudanese leaders to accept the principle of a united Sudan with regional autonomy for the South. Next, the WCC and AACC met South Sudanese representatives of the movement in Europe. A meeting was arranged in Geneva, attended by Wol Wol, Mading de Garang, and Arthur Akuein. The WCC and AACC representatives told this meeting that the Sudanese government was willing to enter negotiations if certain conditions were met. Wol Wol and Mading de Garang agreed to support and work to promote the WCC and AACC recommendations.

Mading de Garang and Wol Wol proceeded to write to various South Sudanese groups in Africa asking for their views on the proposed negotiations. But the Kinshasa Group was never contacted. Some of the other groups responded positively. On receipt of these replies, Mading de Garang wrote to the WCC and AACC to say that all Southerners had accepted the principle of a united Sudan and the offer of regional autonomy for the South. Both sides thus entered preliminary discussions based on misrepresentation. Wol Wol and Mading de Garang had also informed the Sudanese regime that the majority of South Sudanese had accepted the principle of one Sudan with regional autonomy for the South. But we had not.

The Kinshasa Group maintained that the future of millions was being decided by a few individuals like Mading de Garang and Wol Wol. We felt a body representing all the Southerners: those in exile, Anyanya forces, refugees, etc., should have been consulted. A common strategy should have been agreed before entering talks with the government.

This position was rejected by Mading and Wol as being too idealistic. They argued that since the idea of a settlement other than complete independence for the South was accepted by most Southerners, including the Anyanya leadership, it would be a waste of time to hold further meetings. They said that the WCC had given Southerners a golden opportunity, which we could not afford to miss, because the funds allotted might be diverted to other suffering people in the world, such as the Pakistanis, if we did not act quickly. One Kinshasa Group member asked if we Southerners were being persuaded by the WCC's funds. Wol Wol denied this.

When Wol Wol and Mading realized that we did not accept their aims, they resorted to criticism of our stance. This made it impossible to reach an understanding. The Kinshasa Group accused Lagu's envoys of being opportunistic and conspiring to isolate certain South Sudanese political and military leaders, including Joseph Oduho, George Kwanai, Ezboni Mondiri, Philip Pedak, Dominic

Muorwol Malou, Malek Pajook, Emilio Taffeng, Ali Guatala, and myself. We further asserted that Joseph Lagu had no right to hand-pick South Sudan's negotiation team. This was a national issue.

During the discussion, the two envoys explained that they were collaborating with Southerners who were pro-government as well as the Southern cabinet ministers of the current Khartoum government. The envoys said these Southerners accused the Kinshasa Group, particularly myself, of being extremists and separatists.

We retorted that none of us were extremists. This term was malicious and aimed to taint the image of committed South Sudanese nationalists. The truth was that none of the Kinshasa Group wanted to sell-out the Southern cause, or accept a settlement imposed by foreign, pro-government forces. It was the right of every South Sudanese to give an opinion on how the Southern issue should be resolved.

Lagu's envoys asked us if we supported the idea of federal status for South Sudan, which they proposed to put forward at the negotiations. Our view was that any proposal should guarantee or reflect a probability of achieving a just and lasting solution to the South's chronic problems, as well as be one to which the majority of Southerners freely consented.

Wol Wol and Mading de Garang failed to convince us to accept Lagu's ideas as the way to settle the conflict. As the meeting continued, the Kinshasa Group accused them of trying to dictate views. With no progress being made, the meeting was adjourned.

We resumed meeting the following day. The Kinshasa Group made several proposals as a basis for negotiations with the Sudanese government. First, negotiations should have no preconditions. Second, before attending the negotiations there should be a conference of South Sudanese of different political opinion from all three provinces. This conference would provide a forum to agree on strategies and procedures before entering the negotiations and dispel the fear that Lagu's group might impose its own solution. The same meeting would select South Sudan's negotiating team. Finally, we wanted Lagu to understand that we should not appear as a defeated people in the negotiations. The senior Anyanya officers at the conference must reassure the delegates that the South would negotiate from a position of military strength.

Wol Wol asked how equal representation would be achieved. We replied that the three provinces should be asked to nominate and send their representatives. This was important because there were no political parties in the South at that time, as SANU had been dissolved by the military junta. We also worried that divisions based on tribal differences might resurface if a strong campaign for Southern nationalism and national unity did not intensify.

The Lagu envoys argued that the South Sudan Liberation Movement (SSLM), a political party set up by Lagu to succeed the ALF, SSPG, and NPG represented the whole South. Francis Mayar asked them: "do you expect South Sudan to have only one political party?"

Wol Wol said he and Mading had joined the SSLM in 1970. Mayar asked, if this was so, why they had not informed me, as NPG president, of their intention to join such an organization? It was I who had appointed them as NPG representatives in Europe. If they had changed their allegiance to the SSLM, they had violated the oath of loyalty to the NPG and its president. Wol Wol replied that he was tired of living in exile and since the new organization was likely to open up new opportunities of returning home, he had decided to join. Mayar asked Wol Wol if he was tired of exile why he did not just go home? Wol Wol began to feel angry and exchanged insults with Mayar. They had been friends since school but reached the point of exchanging blows. The meeting ended without a compromise.

Before we parted, Mayar asked Wol Wol and Mading to convey to the WCC our request to financially assist South Sudanese to convene a conference in East Africa, to agree on our demands, and select a single delegation to represent the South at the negotiations. The two envoys agreed, and a written request was handed to them. The Kinshasa Group waited in vain for a response from the WCC.

News of the Addis Ababa Negotiations
In October 1971, I was delegated to visit the Sudan-Zaïre border to understand the state of the armed struggle in the South. During this visit, I was able to meet my wife Sarah, whom I had not seen since I left Khartoum to join the liberation struggle on 13 February 1967. She had already spent three months in Kampala. I could not make it there due to financial difficulties.

My plan to move into exile with my family had failed. The alternative was for my relatives and friends to raise funds to fly Sarah to Kampala from where we could arrange to meet. I arrived in Bunia, in the northeast of Zaïre, three days before Sarah arrived from Kampala. Sarah travelled from Kampala to Bunia by land, accompanied by my relative Antipas Deng Makwac. We were happy to meet after such a long time, but our immediate worry was for our children, who were alone in Sudan. We agreed that Sarah should go back. Meanwhile, I would continue to pursue a family reunion through the UN and the governments of the neighboring African countries.

A few days after Sarah left, I left for Aba to fulfil my mission. I went to the place we used to buy arms when our headquarters was near Yei. There, I was met by members and supporters of our new political organization, the ANF, and some South Sudanese refugees. I spoke of the proposed talks between the Anyanya leadership and the Nimeiri regime. I also informed them of the meeting we had with Lagu's envoys in Kinshasa. We explained our resolve that there must be a conference bringing together all shades of political opinion before any negotiations began. The meeting resolved to support the stance taken by the ANF and the Kinshasa Group leaders.

Two days later, Achol Deng Hot, the civilian Anyanya governor of Lakes region, who had just arrived from Angundri, and I heard on BBC Radio that Anyanya representatives and the Sudanese government had met in Addis Ababa to negotiate a solution to the 17-year war. This news disappointed us as it indicated that the WCC had ignored the Kinshasa Group's appeal for an all-South Sudan conference before any negotiations. Achol Deng and I agreed that I should issue a press release denouncing the talks between the Sudanese government and the self-appointed Anyanya leaders. The press statement warned Nimeiri against any attempt to impose a settlement on the people of South Sudan. Doing so would backfire and cause many complications. Copies of this press statement were sent to newspapers in East Africa, the BBC, the OAU, and the UN Secretary-General.

Visit to Anyanya Camps
In early December 1971, I visited the Angundri transit camp and met wounded Anyanya soldiers. They told me how hard their lives were in the camp. Apart from the wounded, there were some who were ill and waiting to recover before going home. Only those with money were able to buy food from the surrounding villages. Meat was scarce. The security of the camp was provided by a small Anyanya force.

Before returning to Aba, I learned that a well-armed Anyanya force was expected to arrive at Angundri and proceed to Bahr al-Ghazal. I left for Aba on about 3 December, intending to meet the expected Anyanya force on my return.

On 6 December, news arrived that the Sudanese government forces had attacked Angundri. A small, poorly armed Anyanya force was dispersed, and Angundri set on fire. According to the same sources, a well-armed Anyanya force was camped five miles away from Angundri and was ready to engage the enemy despite a shortage of food. Other reports said that the enemy was bombing Angundri by air and that some bombs had fallen inside Zaïre, resulting in civilian casualties.

Fortunately, a foreign gentleman I knew, whose name I am reluctant to disclose, arrived in Aba. I asked if he could help our soldiers. He gave us 120 zaïre, equivalent to 60 US dollars. With this, we were able to buy beans and oil. Achol Deng, other colleagues, and I rushed the food to the border, where it was cooked in large barrels. Word was sent to the Anyanya force to be ready to receive the food. Food was then carried to them by refugee volunteers.

Enemy forces were still occupying Angundri. It was not long before the newly arrived Anyanya force counterattacked. After a fierce battle lasting four hours, the enemy began to withdraw under the cover of darkness. A helicopter was called in to carry away the wounded. It was hit by Anyanya ground fire but managed to get away.

The following day, the defending force returned to Angundri. I was taken to inspect the scene of the battle. There we saw shoes of the enemy soldiers abandoned during the evacuation. I saw a giant tree cut in two by a bomb from the enemy air force. We could see many blood stains on the grass and hundreds of empty cartridges. The Anyanya did not sustain any injuries or fatalities. On the enemy side, the Anyanya told us that they saw many dead and wounded being carried into the helicopter. After I had seen our Anyanya force off to Bahr al-Ghazal, I left for Bunia.

A Giant Step Towards Negotiation

While waiting for an air ticket to Kinshasa, I heard on the radio that the WCC was organizing a conference between the Anyanya leaders and the Nimeiri government in Addis Ababa. The broadcaster added that regional autonomy for the South would be the basis of negotiations and that Abel Alier, Minister for Southern Affairs in the Nimeiri government, would lead the government delegation. Ezboni Mondiri would lead the Anyanya delegation. To the surprise of Southerners, both delegations at the talks were being led by South Sudanese.

Ezboni had been the Minister of Transport and Irrigation in the 1964-65 Transitional government of Sirr al-Khatim al-Khalifa. In 1966, Ezboni joined the Anyanya and was appointed Secretary for Defence in the Azania Liberation Front (ALF), which he held until September 1967. In October 1967, Ezboni fled from custody after being charged with killing some Anyanya officers and men during an attempt to overthrow his ALF administration. It was alleged that this uprising was engineered by some South Sudanese Catholic priests, led by Ferdinand Goi. Ezboni surrendered at the SSPG headquarters at Angundri, where he was provided protection by Akuot Atem, his former colleague and classmate, who was then the SSPG defence minister.

Unfortunately, Ezboni's relationship with SSPG President Aggrey Jaden was poor. Ezboni felt insecure. With the help of Akuot, he fled to Uganda and sought asylum. In 1969, Ezboni and Alfonso Malek Pajokdit formed a two-man organization named Sudan Azania. Consequently, Ezboni was invited to lead the Anyanya delegation in Addis Ababa in early 1972.

The news of South-North negotiations caused disarray among the Kinshasa Group and the ANF leaders. The way negotiations were being conducted indicated the South was on the verge of being sold out by some of its leaders and their foreign sponsors. It was obvious that the WCC and other foreigners were not interested in the views of those Southerners opposed to the negotiations. The hasty negotiations were motivated by a desire to impose a settlement on the people of South Sudan who had fought and died in the hundreds of thousands during the 17-year war. These sponsors were not interested in finding a just and lasting settlement to the conflict.

Nevertheless, the Kinshasa Group ANF members continued efforts to persuade those involved in the negotiations, particularly the Anyanya military leaders led by Lagu, of the need to appreciate the dangers South Sudan would face if the talks with the military government proceeded as planned. The basic fears were the lack of representation from across the South Sudanese political spectrum and that the agreement would fail. The consequences would be disastrous to both sides in the conflict.

Throughout January 1972, I sent letters of appeal to the OAU, Emperor Haile Selassie of Ethiopia, who was hosting the talks in Addis Ababa, President Julius Nyerere of Tanzania, and the UN Secretary-General, among others. I appealed for the postponement of the negotiations to allow the full representation of the Southern people and to allow a free and favorable atmosphere in which the oppressed people of the South could express their aspirations.

Lagu asserted that he had invited me to lead his delegation at the talks and that I had refused. This, of course, was false. The truth was that Lagu knew my stance perfectly well and hence did not invite me. Had he invited me, I would have not accepted. I would have presented the invitation to the ANF Executive Committee for a decision, but I am sure that no member of the ANF would have been sent to the Lagu–Nimeiri negotiations. We were determined to oppose a fraudulent solution to the conflict.

In mid-February 1972, I was still in Bunia. I heard on the radio that the WCC and other organizations were holding a conference in Khartoum to agree how to organize support for the South Sudanese refugees who would return home from exile in the surrounding African countries. This substantiated our belief that the foreign humanitarian organizations were not only committed to supporting an imposed settlement on South Sudan, but that the outcome of the talks was a foregone conclusion to them.

Soon after my arrival in Kinshasa, Francis Mayar and Agolong Chol informed me that Gordon Abyei Makuac, the former SF President, had been sent to Kinshasa by the other former SF leaders, including Abel Alier. Abyei Makuac had come to persuade me and other Kinshasa Group members to support and participate in the negotiations. Abyei Makuac was told that I had gone to the Zaïre-Sudan border where I could not be contacted and that others were not willing to discuss the subject of his mission in my absence. While the talks in Addis Ababa continued, Abyei Makuac decided to wait for my return. When the talks gathered momentum he returned to Khartoum, having been given an outline of our stance, a step which I approved of on my return.

Deportation from Zaïre
As the Addis Ababa talks progressed, it was becoming clear that an imposed settlement was likely. Soon, we heard on the radio that the parties had reached an agreement. The main points were that South Sudan would be granted regional autonomy within a united Sudan according to the 1 January 1956 boundaries; the South would have a government to be known as the High Executive Council, appointed by the President of Sudan and a legislature, the People's Regional Assembly. Arabic would become the official language in the South. Neither the Regional Assembly nor the High Executive Council would legislate or exercise any powers on national matters.

The ANF Executive Committee had closely followed the negotiations and we did not see any logic in waiting for the full text of the agreement. We called a meeting at the house of Francis Mayar to decide how to respond. After a debate throughout the night, we agreed to reject the agreement.

We drafted a press statement, which I signed on 26 February. In summary, it stated that those who claimed to represent the South were self-appointed. They had no mandate from the people of South Sudan, who had not been consulted. The Anyanya had not been fully informed about the negotiations; we had confirmed this with Anyanya provincial commanders.

Instead, opportunistic Southerners had accepted negotiations and claimed that they were willing to accept any agreement negotiated by the parties. The negotiations had turned out to be between Southerners, and the government's representative, Abel Alier, had argued strongly against the legitimate demands put forward on behalf of the South by the Anyanya delegation. The negotiations maintained the current oppression and colonization of indigenous Africans in South Sudan by the Northern Arab colonial regime in Khartoum.

We believed that the negotiations ought to have been held between a fully mandated South Sudanese delegation and the Sudanese government, without preconditions, under the auspices of a neutral organization such as the UN, which would have been able to guarantee the respect and implementation of whatever agreement was reached. We wished to make it known to all African states and the world at large that any agreement was null and void unless negotiated by legitimate representatives of the people of South Sudan. Moreover, the claim that the agreement reached has been accepted by most South Sudanese was false.

On 27 February, the statement rejecting the agreement was reported by nearly all the international radio stations.

The next day at about 1.30pm, while I was at Mayar's house, Mayar and I were arrested by the Zaïrean police. We were accused of attempting to create problems between Sudan and Zaïre and were charged with carrying out political activities against a friendly country from Zaïrean soil. We suspected a conspiracy between Zaïre and the Sudanese government against the ANF leadership in Kinshasa.

The police refused to listen when we tried to explain ourselves. They told us that if we felt we had been unjustly treated, we could speak to their senior officers. We demanded to see the senior officers, but instead, we were taken straight to prison.

Soon after we had been taken away, Agolong phoned the High Court judge who worked with Mayar and informed him that Mayar, the advocate, and I had been arrested. The judge immediately ordered the police to release Mayar. At 8.30pm, a policeman came to the prison and released Mayar in accordance with the orders of the judge. Mayar was saddened that he was leaving detention without me. He assured me that he would do everything possible to effect my release the next day. Meanwhile, he left his transistor radio so I could listen to the news.

At midnight, three policemen came to my cell and told me that I was being deported, without saying where. I was put in their car and taken to Mayar's house to collect my belongings. After that, I was taken to Kinshasa airport. An air ticket was delivered to me there. One of the Zaïrean security officers said at the airport that Zaïre had every right to deport me to Sudan but had a moral obligation not to do so.

Again, I asked one of the officers who accompanied me to the airport to where I was being deported. He smiled and said Burundi. I asked for a document from the government of Zaïre to present to the Burundian authorities on arrival. He said that such a document was unnecessary since the government of Burundi had already been informed. He added that I did not need to worry because the plane was flying directly to Burundi, albeit via Brussels, Belgium, as was the custom between the three countries in those days.

At 1am on 1 March 1972, the plane took off from Kinshasa. Although I felt anxious, I was relieved that I was not being flown to Khartoum. An hour and a half into the journey, the crew announced the plane was flying over Khartoum. From the window, I could identify the beautiful garden of Mogran, the confluence of the Blue and White Niles.

In the morning, we landed in Brussels. I was taken to the immigration office where I was found to have no valid travel document since my Zaïrean travel document had expired. The Belgians had heard from the Zaïrean authorities that I was in transit to Burundi but were unable to understand why I was deported with an invalid travel document.

The Belgian immigration officials said that they would pressure the Zaïrean government to renew the document so that I could continue my journey to Burundi. Eventually, my document was renewed by the Zaïrean authorities. The Belgian officials told me that they had questioned the Zaïrean decision to deport me from Zaïre on the basis that I was a refugee under the 1951 UN Refugee Convention and had been issued with documents to that effect. To the surprise of the Belgians, the Zaïrean government denied having deported me and said that they were investigating the circumstances which led to my removal. Despite this, Zaïre rejected an official request from Belgium to return me to Zaïre.

I told the Belgian officials that my colleagues in Kinshasa had informed me there was evidence that the Zaïrean security officers were bribed by the Sudanese embassy in Kinshasa to expel me, without letting it be known to their government. I asked the Belgian officials whether they knew of such reports. They denied knowing, although they said that they knew corruption was endemic in Zaïre. In the meantime, I was detained at Brussels airport as a passenger in transit.

On 3 March, I was put on a Sabena flight to Bujumbura, via Nairobi and Kigali. On arrival in Bujumbura, I went to the immigration office and told them that I wished to apply for asylum, and that the Zaïrean authorities told me in Kinshasa that there was an agreement between the Zaïrean government and Burundi. I mentioned that before I left Kinshasa, the Zaïrean immigration officials said that they had sent a letter to Burundi on the matter.

The immigration officer took me to his office for a brief interrogation. After answering his questions regarding my identity, background, and whether I was a security risk, he told me to wait. After half an hour, a different officer came and said that Zaïre had not approached Burundi about me. What was more, the Burundi government had refused to grant me asylum. He ordered another official to escort me to the plane, to be returned to Brussels. Since the atmosphere was so negative, I did not see any point of appealing.

Whilst walking to the plane, the official said he could secure asylum for me if I paid him 200 US dollars immediately. I was keen to put an end to this nightmarish air shuttling and was willing to pay any amount for asylum in Burundi, but I did not have even a penny in my pocket. So, I said I had no money on me, but I would be grateful if he would let me in. I would immediately contact my colleagues in Kinshasa to send the money. He declined and that was the end of our negotiations. He handed me over to the pilot of the airliner and told him to return me to Brussels.

On 5 March, our plane arrived in Brussels, and I was taken again to the immigration office. They asked why Burundi had refused me asylum. After my explanation, immigration reluctantly decided to allow me to remain temporarily in Belgium, on the condition that I found asylum in Africa. Unfortunately, my vaccination papers were missing. I think I had left them with the Burundian immigration. So, I was sent to Sabena Airlines hospital to be issued with new health papers. I asked the Belgian authorities whether they could use their influence to make Zaïre change its mind and accept me back because, despite all that had happened, I still wanted to return to Zaïre. Alternatively, I said I would be happy to be granted asylum in Belgium, or I would be equally grateful if they would persuade countries like Kenya or Tanzania to grant me asylum, as I had asked previously. They promised to give due consideration to my requests except for Belgium granting me asylum; for them, it was an African affair.

In the afternoon, the police took me into Brussels, where I was accommodated in the Salvation Army hostel at 27-29 Rue Bodeghem. The next day, 6 March, I was taken to the Ministry of Justice, where I met Madame Laloux, in charge of Police Administration. I was then forwarded to meet two young men, who questioned me again. Then I was returned to Laloux, who reiterated that Belgium would not grant me asylum, nor would it negotiate entry visas for any African states. I would have to negotiate my own asylum. In the meantime, I would be taken into the care of Pastor Rev. Harts of the Protestant Church.

Rev. Harts took me to a secondhand clothing store to find some warm clothing. It was wintry, and it was my first time in Europe. I felt exceptionally cold. I returned to the hostel, which mainly accommodated pensioners, homeless, and disabled people. Specific rules to be obeyed and followed by all residents were explained. I had to go to bed at 8pm and wake up at 5am. Meals were at fixed times.

The breakfast was usually a sandwich of egg, cheese, and ham. We queued to receive the sandwich and sit on chairs laid out in a row. The room was well heated but filled with thick cigarette smoke. The only way to get fresh air was to stand in the freezing cold of the street. Harts used to give me the equivalent of £5 a week as pocket money which I accepted with profound thanks. At lunch, we were provided with a large cup of soup with some bread. After lunch, we were free to go. I had nowhere to go but used to walk and look at the motor traffic, the beautiful shops, and buildings. Coming to Europe had taken me by surprise. While in the bush of South Sudan, I had never envisaged that I would soon be in Europe. I dreaded the cold weather.

A few days later, Harts sent his car to take me to his office where we chatted about the historical background of the conflict in Sudan. With pleasure, I explained it to him, and how I got involved and the role I had played. He said he would speak to the Ministry of Foreign Affairs about helping me to get asylum in an African country, but he was not optimistic.

I wrote to Mayar and Agolong in Kinshasa to inform them of my whereabouts and what had happened. They wrote back expressing their relief. Similarly, I wrote to many of my friends and relatives in various parts of the world concerning my situation. On 16 March, Mayar wrote and promised to remit 600 Belgian francs to me. He also informed me that representatives of Israel were looking for me. On 21 March, I received the 600 francs from Mayar, which I acknowledged with profound thanks.

One day, Rev. Harts took me to the police station to be issued with "Attestation d'Immatriculation No. 3867", on which my passport photograph was placed. Harts instructed me to write a short biography covering the time I had spent in exile, including the time spent in Zaïre. I wrote and delivered it to him. I knew he was going to hand it to some government agencies, but I did not know why exactly.

On another day, Harts took me to meet a doctor who could speak English. A week later, the doctor treated me for "stress."

As time went by, I began to make my own comments on the Addis Ababa Agreement, the text of which was posted to me by a friend. It had not yet been ratified by Nimeiri and Lagu. While at the hostel, I typed up my commentary.

Meanwhile, Agolong sent me a telegram saying that Lagu had changed his mind and had refused to ratify the agreement. I could not believe it. Agolong added that when Lagu turned up in Kampala he had asked for me and requested I meet him at the earliest opportunity. In April, the Israeli embassy in Belgium contacted me to say that Lagu had asked them to tell me that I was urgently required at a discussion in Addis Ababa on the agreement prior to its ratification.

I suspected this might be a ploy to lure me to Addis Ababa. If Lagu actually planned to ratify the agreement, this would be followed by publicity in the media, which would falsely report that I had at last accepted the agreement. I presumed I would not be able to inform the Southerners and the world of my true views after ratification. I told the Israeli diplomat that I would only attend if Lagu confirmed in writing that the discussion would be confined to the Anyanya political and military leaders, including Lagu himself, and those leaders who denounced the agreement, such as Philip Pedak, Arkangelo Wanji, Aggrey Jaden, Francis Mayar, Agolong Chol, Elia Duang Arop, and a few others. The diplomat wrote down my reply and promised to bring me any further reply if any materialized. Several weeks later, the diplomat informed me that their office had received no feedback from Lagu.

Shortly before these events, Elia Duang arrived in Brussels from Kampala carrying a letter from the former acting ANAF Chief of Staff under the NPG, Lt. Col. Emmanuel Abur Nhial. Abur had been reappointed by Lagu as commander of the Bahr al-Ghazal province brigade command. Abur confessed that the so-called Addis Ababa Agreement was a betrayal by Lagu and his accomplices. He wrote that he and other Anyanya officers from Bahr al-Ghazal and the other provinces were disillusioned with Lagu. He wrote, "the rejection of the agreement is no longer yours alone with your other colleagues, but we too have become opponents of such an agreement." He asked I come to Kampala for a conference to meet and decide what to do next.

Although I was skeptical, I considered Abur's letter carefully. I told Duang to give me time to think about it. After two days, I told Duang that I had decided to go to the Kampala conference. According to Duang, the conference would decide whether to denounce the agreement, as had already been done by other groups, and opt for a continuation of the armed struggle.

On 30 April, Duang and I met Harts. I told Harts that I had agreed to attend the conference in Kampala. He was quite pleased and wished me good luck. Harts also suggested that there might be a possibility of obtaining asylum in Kenya through Rev. Ankra of the WCC. He gave me the name of a Kenyan priest who could arrange entrance into Kenya without the usual formalities of obtaining an entry visa in advance. Despite this offer, I was still skeptical.

The same day, Duang and I left Brussels for Entebbe, Uganda. We were taken to the Speke Hotel in Kampala, where rooms had been secured for us by the WCC representative in Kampala.

Conference of Political and Military Leaders of Bahr al-Ghazal, Kampala, May 1972

On 2 May, the conference of political and military leaders from Bahr al-Ghazal opened at the Speke Hotel. The main goal was to discuss the province's stance on the agreement and what concrete steps might be taken to realize that stance. No resolution was adopted by the conference either in support or denunciation of the Addis Ababa Agreement, nor was a program of action agreed upon. In this sense, the conference was a failure.

Attending on the political side were Mayar, Agolong, Duang, Arkangelo Wanji, Paul Duang Yak, and myself, among others. For the Anyanya military were Abur, Lt. Col. Akol Akol and several other senior officers from the Bahr al-Ghazal Brigade. Some senior officers, including Lt. Col. Andrew Makur Thou, Lt. Col. Gabriel Makol Magong, and Maj. Alfred Aguet Awan from Lakes were missing. Later, in London, I was told by the Lakes Regional Anyanya office that they had not received notification of the conference. Presiding over the conference was Abur. By this time, Abel Alier had been appointed as President of the High Executive Council by President Nimeiri. Alier sent Lawrence Wol Wol and some of his supporters to Kampala to lobby the conference. Some Equatorian groups informed us on the eve of the conference that they too were not satisfied with the terms of the agreement and were prepared to support resolutions which might reject the agreement. They sent a few observers led by Daniel Jumi Tungun, a former SSPG deputy minister, to the conference.

Most attendees believed that the Addis Ababa Agreement was a sell-out of the South Sudan cause. As such, they called upon the Anyanya to return to the bush and continue the armed struggle to complete the liberation of South Sudan. For the first two days, it was obvious that a majority rejected the agreement and favored resumption of the armed struggle. But on the third day, a sizeable number of delegates changed their views, due to the work of Abel Alier's lobby as well as war fatigue.

When some of the political delegates became outspoken in favor of resuming the armed struggle, many military delegates, though they spoke strongly for the total rejection of the agreement, did not accept the Anyanya should return to the bush. One said that Israel told us we must follow Lagu, and if we did not, they would not supply more arms. Another officer asked the political leaders if we wanted them to return to the bush empty-handed, without effective arms and enough ammunition, as was done in 1962? He said he was willing to go back if arms were provided. Thus, many Anyanya officers gave their support to "Lagu's agreement," as it was popularly called.

Although many denounced the agreement, there was no desire for the resumption of armed struggle. It became obvious that the conference would end in failure. A dispirited resolution was drawn up, not rejecting the agreement in total, but instead, rejecting "the procedure, particularly the method of forming the South Sudan negotiating delegation, the method of ratification, implementation, and the manner of forming the regional government and the appointments."

The reason for rejecting the procedure was the failure by Lagu to inform the Bahr al-Ghazal Anyanya military establishment and the political leadership. No official representatives approved by the province were present at the negotiations or at the ratification. Bahr al-Ghazal was only informed after the agreement had been initiated.

The majority of the ANF and Kinshasa Group members, including myself, refused to sign any resolutions from the conference. Nearly all the political leaders of Bahr al-Ghazal resolved to maintain their rejection of the Addis Ababa Agreement and dispersed. Mayar, Paul Duang and Agolong returned to Kinshasa to continue living in exile. Elia Duang returned to Italy to continue studying for a university degree. Arkangelo Wanji returned to Kampala where he had already taken up asylum prior to the agreement.

Since the liberation war broke out in August 1955, Uganda had allowed South Sudanese to stay without being formally granted political asylum. This situation changed after Gen. Idi Amin Dada seized power in Uganda in 1971. As a result, thousands of South Sudanese, particularly from Equatoria, acquired Ugandan residency or citizenship. As for me, I was in a fix. I remained steadfastly opposed to the agreement and my living situation remained uncertain since my expulsion from Kinshasa. Perhaps those foreigners and the pro-agreement South Sudanese who lured me to Kampala hoped that I might succumb to the pressure and return to Sudan. Abel Alier wrote to me twice and urged me to accept the agreement and come home. I rejected both his requests.

Before my Kinshasa colleagues left Kampala, Paul Duang and I met Rev. Bob Vassa, the WCC and AACC representative and coordinator for South Sudanese refugee affairs in Kampala. Rev. Vassa told me that he was planning to get me a Kenyan visa, in line with what I was told by Rev. Harts and Rev. Ankra in Brussels.

While still waiting in the Speke Hotel, Daniel Jumi and Elisa Kebi Mulla from Equatoria passed by. They assured me of their opposition to the agreement together with many of their supporters. They added that if Bahr al-Ghazal decided to resume the armed struggle, Equatoria would follow suit.

The same day, I also met Lt. Col. Akol Akol, the commander of the Aweil Anyanya Battalion. I asked what his true stance was on resuming the armed struggle. He said that he was "100 percent" opposed to the agreement but disillusioned by the lack of weapons. However, he said that he would not surrender his forces in Aweil to the Sudanese government.

Sometime around 8 May, two senior Northern Sudanese civil servants, Juba High Judge El Tayek Abbas, and the Commissioner of Juba, invited Francis Mayar, Agolong Chol, Wek Athian and me to meet in Kampala. Both appealed to us to stop opposing the agreement and return to Sudan to resume normal life like other

Southern leaders. I explained what we thought was wrong with the agreement and why we denounced it. I added that more than one and a half million Southerners had been killed in the civil war and we did not want an agreement to be imposed on the South, which could easily lead to another war if abrogated by any future Khartoum government. My colleagues spoke in support of what I had said. The meeting ended without any progress.

On 10 May, a British man came to my room. He introduced himself as the representative of Rev. Vassa of the WCC and told me they were in the process of securing an entry visa to Kenya and an air ticket for me. Shortly afterwards, he returned with a cheque for me to purchase an air ticket. I asked him to confirm that I had been granted an entry visa to Kenya. He said that he did not know about the entry visa but would find out from Vassa. The following day, Rev. Ogwal, one of Vassa's associates, came to the hotel to accompany me to buy an air ticket. He was evasive on the question of the visa to Kenya. So, I gave up questioning the issue and became resigned to whatever would happen in Kenya.

On the morning of 11 May, the plane took off from Entebbe. On arrival in Nairobi, I presented to the immigration authorities and explained that the WCC and the AACC had said that they had contacted the Kenyan authorities on my behalf regarding granting me an entry visa to Kenya. After brief consideration, a document declaring me a prohibited immigrant in Kenya was presented to me to sign. I refused to sign and asked to consult a lawyer. They told me that nothing of that sort could be allowed.

Meanwhile, I was surrounded by policemen who said that the only way out was for me to leave the country. I was not manhandled but was made to board a plane leaving for Brussels via London, instead of being returned to Uganda. Probably, they were afraid that Uganda might send me back. Despite the inhumane attitude shown to me by the Kenyan authorities, I was relieved they did not try to repatriate me to Sudan.

On arrival, I spent the night at Brussels airport without being permitted to enter Belgium a second time. On 13 May, the Belgian authorities took away my temporary permit to remain in Belgium, which had expired on 9 May. They told me they would return me to Nairobi. I asked the reason for sending me back to Kenya when that country had already declared me persona non grata. One Belgian said that this was an African problem for which Africa had to find a solution. He said that Belgium would like to have good relations with the Sudanese government and could not grant me asylum. After this exchange, I was escorted onto a plane bound for Nairobi, via London.

8.

Another Exile

Political Asylum in London

When the plane landed at London Heathrow, I applied for asylum. One of the immigration officers advised I address my application to the Chief Immigration Officer. After an hour, another officer said my application would only be considered if I allowed a search of my luggage. I agreed. Documents and some guerrilla textbooks were taken away with the promise of return. Two hours later, I was given a letter from the Chief Immigration Officer saying that my application had been carefully considered, and rejected, as I was not qualified for asylum in Britain. The letter concluded that I must be ready to continue to Nairobi the next morning at 9.30.

I was stunned. The nightmare was not yet over. I was sure that the Kenyan government would not grant me an entry visa on humanitarian or any other grounds. I was dejected and put myself in the hands of God.

While in that state of mind, a Securicor guard handed me a slip of paper with a telephone number. He said to call and tell the person who answered everything about my case, background, and current situation. I phoned straight away. A man answered and I told him everything. He said he would immediately come to the airport. Within 40 minutes, he arrived and introduced himself as John Ennal, Director of the British Immigration Advisory Services (BIAS). He wrote down my statement and said he would approach the Home Office. He hoped I would not be sent to Nairobi.

The following day, the Home Office did not notify me to get ready for a flight to Nairobi as I expected. I thought this might be the effect of Ennal's contact, but I could not be sure.

I phoned Thomas RH Owen, former governor of Bahr al-Ghazal, now retired in England. I explained my situation and asked if he could help. His response was hostile. He retorted that it had been wrong for me to reject the Addis Ababa Agreement as it was the best agreement we could expect. He said he would speak to the office, but not to pin any hopes on him because former colonial officials became nobodies once retired.

At 5pm, Ennal phoned with good news. He had been in touch with Amnesty International and the Home Office. As a result, he said, "you have been permitted to stay in Britain, during which you will make further efforts to obtain an entry visa to East Africa."

I felt tremendously relieved. I was grateful to Ennal and to my Securicor friend. After three days at Heathrow in the custody of the Securicor guards, where I was well looked after, eating good food and enjoying reading the newspapers, I was permitted a period of one month to remain in the UK, pending the finalization of a decision on my asylum case.

I had never been to London or the UK before, so the question of where I could stay was a bit of a problem. But I did not wish to raise this with the immigration authorities. I recalled I had a list of names given to me by Allen Reid, an American friend who visited

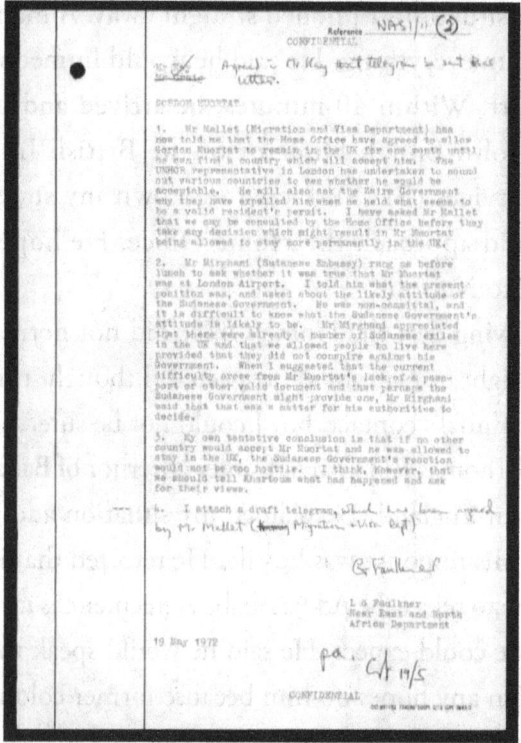

UK Foreign and Commonwealth Office (FCO) letter reporting Home Office decision to allow Muortat to stay in the UK for one month, 19 May 1972

us in the bush during the days of the NPG in 1971. From the list, I picked out the names of Stephen and Sandy Mueweller. Reid had noted that the Muewellers would be happy to let me stay in their house as a friend of his and Elia Duang, although the Muewellers were not politically connected.

On the evening of 15 May 1972, I phoned the Muewellers from the airport. Sandy answered and said she would come to the airport to pick me up. She arrived 25 minutes later. As I walked to the car, my Securicor friend came and bade me goodbye. I have tried my best during my 29 years in Britain to locate him but failed because I did not have his name or address.

On arrival at the Muewellers' house, I was welcomed warmly. They said they would be happy to put me up for a few days, after which they believed I would be able to find other accommodation. One of the problems I had encountered in Europe was the cold weather: to me, it was still wintry. I was taken to a large, warm bedroom and after a heavy dinner, I went to bed and had a good sleep.

The next morning, I left the Muewellers' house for Ennal's office in Stratford. I explained that I needed more long-term accommodation. Ennal phoned UNHCR. Miss Brown, a former CMS missionary, was waiting to discuss the question of accommodation with me at UNHCR. Brown said that I would be taken to Rev. Cannon Arnold's house. Arnold was the missionary who had overseen Akot CMS School in Rumbek from 1930-1945. He was in Rumbek when I enrolled in August 1936 and knew me well.

The following day, Brown arrived at the Muewellers' house in a car. We were going to Arnold's house in Sevenoaks, about 30 miles outside London. I bade goodbye to the Muewellers and thanked them profoundly for their help. Rev. and Mrs Arnold also gave me a warm welcome. Mrs Arnold was also a former CMS missionary, at Yei, before she married Rev. Arnold.

The Arnolds showed kindness beyond my expectations. Rev. Arnold knew the Dinka language well and preferred speaking to me in Dinka. Mrs Arnold took me to London, where she purchased some warm clothing for me. Apparently, the Arnolds had noticed the desperate state of my clothing.

After two days, I visited the BIAS office about my application for asylum. I met Johnny Johnson, one of the deputy directors. He took me to the person handling my case who told me that it was being processed at the Home Office. I would soon be contacted.

Later, Arnold revealed that it was the Archbishop of Sudan, Rev. Oliver Allison, who asked Arnold to put me, his former pupil, up in his house and try to persuade me to accept the Addis Ababa Agreement. I said to Arnold that I was pleased to talk to him about South Sudan and how I became involved in the struggle. I spoke at length on the historical aspects of slavery and oppression, about which Arnold knew a lot.

I told Arnold that the Addis Ababa Agreement was imposed on the South. The South was given very limited powers and was vulnerable to abuse by the Khartoum government at any time. That was why the ANF had rejected the agreement. That was why I had refused to go back to Sudan.

Arnold listened attentively to my explanation. He said that I made sense and that he saw no point in trying to persuade me to accept the agreement and return to Sudan. He did not bring up the agreement again.

One day, Arnold asked whether I would like to visit some other former missionaries. I did. The first visit was to Dr West, who had worked in Leer Hospital for many years. West and his wife welcomed me in their house at Wimborne. In the evening, we had a good chat on the constitutional development of South Sudan, particularly the Addis Ababa Agreement. West was keen to know why the ANF rejected it. I explained the reasons though I suspected that he disagreed with my position.

After two days, West drove me to Rev. Sharland, a former missionary at Akot, Panekar, Gel River, and Malek. I knew him well from his years working with the CMS in the South. Sharland was now working as a parish vicar in Yeovil. Again, Sharland took a lot of interest in talking to me about the agreement and finding out why my group opposed it. Once more, I enthusiastically explained what justified our denunciation of the agreement. One morning,

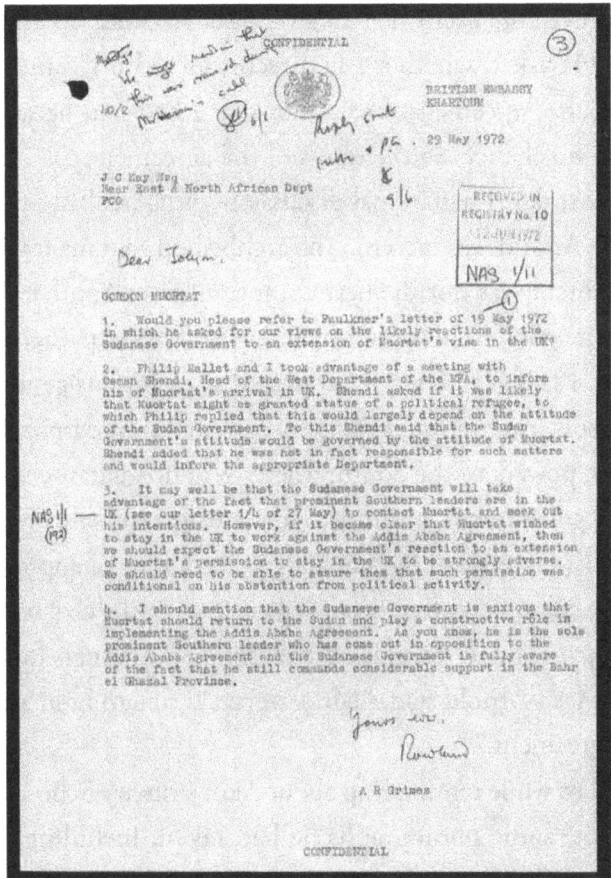

British Embassy Khartoum letter to FCO regarding Muortat and his views on the Addis Ababa Agreement, 29 May 1972

Sharland took me to see the cattle of a local farmer. I was fascinated by what I saw, especially the milking of a cow by machine.

Attempts to Persuade me to Leave the UK

On 1 June, I went to see Ennal about my asylum application. The BIAS arranged a meeting with Brown of UNHCR, who told me that my application was still being considered. To support me while I was awaiting the outcome, UNHCR granted me an allowance of £10 per week.

In the evening, I returned to Sevenoaks. Archbishop Allison had arrived. He asked whether I had reconsidered my stance on the Addis Ababa Agreement. I told him that I had not, because there had been no changes to the terms of the agreement.

The next day, I had a final discussion with Archbishop Allison. This time Arnold was present. The archbishop told me frankly that the agreement was not the best compromise for Southerners, but it was quite good in his opinion, and as such he requested I return to Sudan. I said I regretted if I appeared to be intransigent without good reason. But the agreement had granted limited political and economic powers to the South. There were no guarantees that the Sudanese government, or future Sudanese governments, would not abuse it. The agreement did not address the killing of approximately one and a half million Southern civilians during the civil war, which would nurture lingering animosity among Southerners for years to come. At last, Arnold said, "Mr Muortat is free to hold any views on the agreement."

One day, while reminiscing about Akot Primary School, Arnold showed me some photographs he had taken, including those of young schoolboys in 1938 and 1939, of which I was one. I found it difficult to identify myself as it had been so long. The length of my stay in Arnold's house was approaching a month.

At this time, several friends tried to persuade me to leave Britain. One was Isaiah Majok Akoc, my former SF colleague. He and Henry Bago, both prominent former members of the SF Executive Committee, met me in Hyde Park. They spoke to me throughout the night in a bid to convince me to accept the terms of the agreement, which they said was the best the South could get in the circumstances.

Majok became annoyed because of what he called my persistent intransigence. He later confided that he had a certain degree of mistrust in the policies of Abel Alier. He believed my return to the country to serve in the High Executive would act as a counterbalance. I said that, in my view, holding a position only concerned the short-term interests of individuals. The agreement would be abrogated by the Khartoum government before long.

Akuot Atem had reluctantly accepted the agreement and been appointed as a senior civil servant in the regional government. He also wrote to ask me to return to Sudan. My reply was that of rejection. The list could go on.

The Struggle for Asylum Continues

On 14 June, the Arnolds were preparing to go on holiday. I had to make other living arrangements. The next morning, I spoke to Johnny Johnson at BIAS. He advised me to see UNHCR, who informed me that my period of stay in Britain had been extended by 15 days. As for accommodation, UNHCR said that a room would be provided for me at Friends House in Wimbledon. I moved in with Arnold's help.

I went to the office of Amnesty International to explore the progress of my application for asylum. There I met John Humphreys, who was sympathetic to my plight. After expressing optimism about my application, he raised the issue of a reunion with my family. We agreed to put this aside until the question of asylum was resolved.

On 25 June, Johnson said he had a friend who might help in extending my period of stay in the UK. The following day, we went to the offices of the *Daily Telegraph*, where we met a journalist called David Floyd. He wanted to interview me on the causes of the South Sudan conflict and my deportation from Zaïre. At the end of the interview, he promised that he would look into the question of my asylum in the UK with the Home Office. He said that it was better to keep the issue of my application out of the press, at least for the time being.

Two days later, I met Floyd again. He gave me a lift to go and meet a lawyer called Lionel Block. Block said that Floyd had asked him to become the lawyer on my case and he had accepted. He interviewed me at length. He told me that he was impressed by the genuineness of my case and felt there was a good chance of getting asylum. Block arranged to meet the Home Office on 3 July.

On 1 July, the article by Floyd on my application for asylum in Britain appeared in the *Daily Telegraph*, together with my picture (see p.191). It greatly boosted my morale. I thereafter received many letters from former British administrators, retired missionaries, journalists, and writers who had visited the bush before the Addis Ababa Agreement. They all expressed surprise at my having come to Britain. One of them was GRI Dees, former Lakes ADC and the last DC of Bor District before Sudanization in 1954. I met him and his wife for lunch at Commonwealth House. Dees said he had phoned Lionel Block who had spoken well of me. I was grateful to Block.

On 4 July, Eric Clark, the warden at Friends House, delivered a newspaper cutting which stated that the Sudanese minister of information had called on me to return to Sudan under an amnesty. I posted a reply to the press denouncing the minister's approach as "out of ideas." Clark collaborated with many people who were pressuring me to return to Sudan. It was a really hard time, but I managed to resist the pressure.

Clark warned that as UNHCR and the London Council of Churches had failed to pay the rent, I would have to pay from my own pocket. Clark knew better than anyone that I had no money. I spoke to Brown of UNHCR about the problem and she promised to speak to the Council of Churches. The Council then paid £18.60 to the hostel.

On 16 July, I was visited by Ronald Gregory, alias "Fashoda", one

Sudanese rebel asks Britain for asylum

By DAVID FLOYD

MR GORDON MUORTAT-MAYEN, 45, exiled leader of the African National Front, which fights for Southern Sudanese independence, asked yesterday for political asylum in Britain. He was deported from Zaire in March because he rejected an agreement reached in Addis Ababa purporting to give Southern Sudan autonomy.

Mr Muortat first arrived in Britain in May, and his permission to remain expired yesterday. He has no wish to return to Zaire (formerly Congo Kinshasa) and does not believe he would be safe in any African country.

"I was forced to leave the Sudan in 1967 because I fought against Arab domination of the South and because of the brutality with which they suppressed our movement," he said yesterday.

Helped by friends

Since being asked to leave Zaire he has been shuttled from Burundi to Belgium, then to Kenya, whence he was sent back to Brussels, and finally to London, where, without funds, he depends on the hospitality of a few friends.

Mr Muortat, a former Assistant District Commissioner in the Sudan, served in the Sudanese Government in 1964. Since he came to London President Numeiry of the Sudan has sent messages offering him a Government post.

But Mr Muortat says he cannot accept because he utterly opposes the agreement Numeiry has "imposed on the South." He believes it does not effectively guarantee autonomy, and points out that the Southern Sudanese struggle for independence has cost "at least 500,000 lives."

About a third of the Sudan's population of 15 million lives in the South. It consists of African tribes, many of whom are Christian. The North is mainly Arab and Moslem.

Mr Muortat's lawyer, Mr Lionel Bloch, said yesterday: "If ever there was a clear case for political asylum this is it. Anybody familiar with modern Africa must realise the dangers my client would face if he allowed himself to be tricked into returning."

Mr Gordon Muortat-Mayen.

David Floyd's article about Gordon Muortat in the Daily Telegraph, 1 July 1972. © Telegraph Media Group Limited

of the former British mercenaries recruited by the NPG in 1969 to train the ANAF. He explained his experience after leaving the NPG headquarters together with Kirby, alias "Kiir", following the dissolution of the NPG in July 1970.

He and Kirby travelled on foot with ANAF soldiers returning to Upper Nile. They stopped in Bor at the Anyanya regional headquarters. Col. Paul Awel, in command of the Anyanya force with which they were travelling, requested their help. They agreed and

Kirby went out with a patrol. Kirby was assigned to plant mines. Unfortunately, a mine exploded and killed him.

On another occasion, Fashoda volunteered to lead an Anyanya patrol which attacked and captured a government outpost. During the initial exchange of fire, he sustained a bullet wound to his forehead. It was successfully treated, and he later recovered. After that he proceeded to Ethiopia and from there, back to England.

On 25 July, I was interviewed by Robin White on BBC *Focus on Africa*, about my refusal of the Sudanese government's invitation to return to Sudan. I reiterated my views on the Addis Ababa Agreement. I had several other interviews with White about my views on the future of the agreement during my early years in London.

Throughout July, I waited patiently for the Home Office's reply to my application for asylum. The waiting adversely affected my health. Being cut off from my family was still painful despite having been away for nearly six years. Whenever I needed relief, I visited Gideon Tokmac, an accountant attending a course in London, and Dr Justin Yaac Arop, who was on a postgraduate course, also in London. I also visited Dr Richard Hassan Kalamsakit who was on a postgraduate course in surgery at the University of Reading.

To keep my spirits up, I kept in touch with many of my friends abroad, especially from Zaïre. I could not afford to go to the theatre, cinemas, and other places of amusement in London. My typewriter proved a great help as I spent most of my day typing letters and other political documents on the question of South Sudan. I also spent my time reading newspapers and political books and listening to the radio.

The main content of my letters to ANF colleagues such as Francis Mayar and Agolong Chol in Kinshasa, and Elia Duang in Italy, was how to keep the ANF alive in the face of our difficulties, particularly a

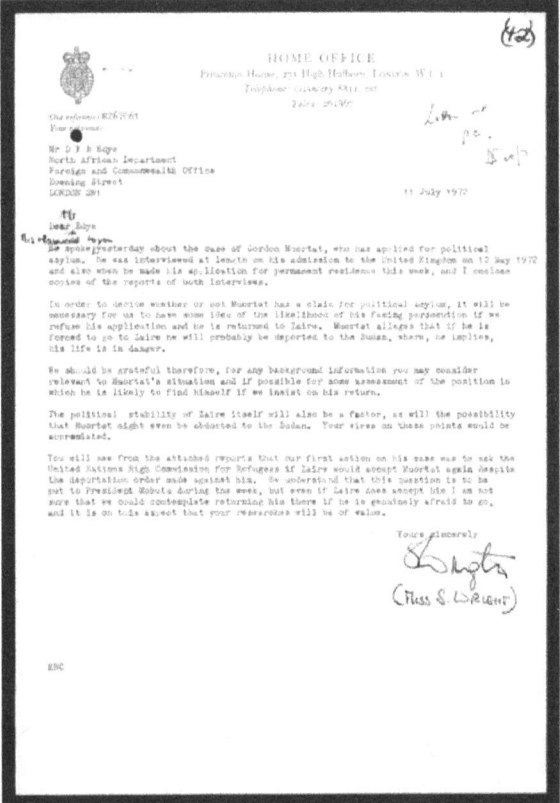

Home Office correspondence about Gordon Muortat, 11 July 1972

lack of funding. At times, we were convinced that it would not be long before the Addis Ababa Agreement collapsed. It was our view that in the event of such a development, there should be a strong Southern political organization ready to re-launch the liberation struggle.

I tried to keep in contact with family in Khartoum and especially my wife, Sarah, who found it difficult to understand why I continued to remain in exile after the Addis Ababa Agreement. The only means of contact was through letters, which had to be sent through reliable persons, as the postal service continued to be censored. However, eventually, Sarah and other members of the family became convinced of the reasonableness of my continuation in exile.

On 7 September, I met my old colleague, Bona Malwal, now a minister in Nimeiri's government. We had a frank discussion during which Bona told me that the chances of serving the people of the South effectively would improve by returning to Sudan. As usual with Bona, he soon came to be understanding and appreciative of my position. We parted amicably with the hope of meeting again.

On 9 September, UNHCR moved me to a bedsit at 20 Gwendolyn Avenue in Putney. The rent was £10.50 per week. The first visitor at my new place was Fashoda. He brought me a warm woolen pullover, to boost my resistance to the cold English weather.

Other government representatives, Isaiah Majok and Philip Ubang, a Southern Sudanese diplomat at the Sudanese embassy, phoned and told me that the Sudanese ambassador wanted to meet for a friendly chat. I told them that I had no time for such a chat.

Permission to Remain in the UK

On 28 October, Christian Aid, through whom the UNHCR was paying my rent, together with my £7 per week allowance, notified me that I should be prepared to leave the Putney bedsit on 31 October. I should not expect further assistance from them: they had been informed that I had been granted permission to remain in Britain. I informed my lawyer, Block, of the news and complained to UNHCR of the short notice received from Christian Aid.

Block said to speak to the officials at the Home Office handling asylum cases as soon as possible and to see him after that. I called at the Home Office and met with a Mr Newton. Newton explained that the British government had declined to grant me asylum, but instead had granted me a permit to reside in Britain for a year and possibly longer. Britain did not believe I would be in danger if I returned to Sudan and did not want to have bad relations with the government of Sudan or the government of Zaïre which had deported me. He endorsed the permit to stay in my *titre de voyage* issued by Zaïre. Newton then sent me to the police officer for alien registration and concluded by urging me to find a job, as there would be no means to support me financially.

Two days later, I met Block to explain the terms of the asylum granted and how most of it was unsatisfactory. Block congratulated me and noted my case was difficult, since it conflicted with the interests of Britain and the other countries involved. He encouraged me to try to make the best of it and keep him informed of developments. I thanked Block for his help, without which I would have not had any asylum at all.

I had no alternative but to go on. I phoned many friends for help to get a job. In Britain, a job was based on skills and experience, for which I was at a disadvantage since the jobs I had held in Sudan were bureaucratic. Here, such positions were confined to British citizens.

In desperation, I called at the Putney police station and explained my situation. The police directed me to the Department of Health and Social Security (DHSS) on Wyford Road in Wandsworth, where I could apply to receive social security benefits. On arrival, I was instead subjected to interview and told to go back to Christian Aid which seemed to have been in contact with the DHSS about me. On 2 November, I met Christian Aid's representative at her office. She had found a room in South London at £5 or £6 per week, where colored people were living. I should keep her informed on how convenient it was within two weeks. Meanwhile, she said, UNHCR and she had agreed to continue paying for my bedsit until 13 November, after which she presumed, I would have found employment.

At Gideon Tokmac's house, I met Tokmac himself, Isaiah Majok, and Philip Ubang, all of whom had been trying to persuade me to return to Sudan. They had heard that President Nyerere of Tanzania had granted me asylum at the request of President Nimeiri. Immediately, I suspected a conspiracy to lure me to Africa from whence I would be forced to Sudan. However, I told them that I would not comment on the information before it was fully substantiated. I refused to discuss the issue with them any further.

On 9 November, I phoned the High Commission of Tanzania in London and asked for an appointment. On 16 November, I met the High Commissioner, who had recently been in Tanzania. He confirmed the offer of political asylum, and that the Tanzanian government would help rectify any points of discontent with the agreement. I would be permitted to visit Tanzania for 2 weeks and then return to the UK. I thanked the High Commissioner. Now that the offer of asylum had proved to be genuine, I would be grateful to know how it came about. Could it be a result of my application first made to the Tanzanian government in 1967 and then from Belgium in 1972? If the answer was yes, definitely, I would not hesitate to accept the offer. The High Commissioner said he could not tell me the source of the initiative. He advised me to go to Tanzania to seek answers there. I thanked him again and said I would consider the offer.

Several weeks later, I phoned the office of the High Commissioner to say that I had decided not to visit Tanzania until I had clear answers about the source of the offer of asylum. The High Commissioner promised to contact his government and get back to me. He never contacted me again, nor did I approach him again on the issue. The agents of the Sudanese government did not raise the matter with me again either.

Surviving in Exile

The 13 November deadline was fast approaching but I did not have a job or alternative accommodation. Fashoda visited and sympathetically said that he would try to find me a room in Earl's Court.

On 17 November, I phoned UNHCR and informed them of my accommodation and employment situation, particularly in view of the notice to quit the bedsit in Putney on 13 November. UNHCR decided to pay until the end of November, sending the payments through Christian Aid. They continued to press me to find a job and accommodation on my own. Meanwhile, my daily efforts to find a job or a room had come to nothing.

On 23 November, I went to Christian Aid at Sloane Square where I was paid £22.50. They said this was the last payment they would make to me. I had never felt so desperate. I could not help but feel that these humanitarian organizations were part of the conspiracy to get me to return to Sudan.

I went to Dalston to see Hoperising Housing Agency which had advertised vacant rooms. The agency sent me to view a bedsit on 59 Colgrave Road, in Leyton, where the landlord, Osuji, an Igbo from Biafra, became sympathetic to my plight. He allowed me to rent the bedsit, paying £6 as an instalment. I moved in the same day.

In desperation, I again reported to the DHSS. I was eventually able to sign up for social security and received a benefit cheque for £12.55.

In late December, I was visited by my son-in-law Joseph Mathubier Guelly, a Sudanese diplomat from Rumbek who had just married my elder daughter Rebecca Acol. I discussed many things with him but mostly, family matters. Like other South Sudanese government officials, Mathubier agreed with the reasons I gave for opposing the agreement but was against my continuing in exile.

ANF Proposed Dialogue with the Nimeiri Regime in 1973

On 16 January, I wrote to ANF members in Kinshasa expressing concern about the future of the ANF. I urged them to come to London so that we could pool our ideas on how to revive the ANF. I was eager to travel myself but was pinned down by a lack of funds and the conditions of my asylum. My colleagues shared my concerns and wanted to travel, but neither would the Zaïre government grant them exit visas, nor would the British embassy in Kinshasa issue them with entry visas. The ANF was becoming a lifeless organization, although none of us would admit it.

On 27 January, Philip Ubang from the Sudanese embassy in London phoned. He had been mandated by the Sudanese government to meet me. They proposed a dialogue to find a solution to my grievances. I agreed to meet Ubang as I thought I had nothing to lose by talking to the government. It would be a good opportunity for us to air our views to the world. But I insisted that enough time be allowed to enable both sides to compose and prepare their respective delegations, agree on a venue and an agenda. Furthermore, the thinking of the Sudanese government that I was the only Southern leader opposed to the agreement was wrong. Apart from the ANF, those who publicly denounced the agreement included Joseph Oduho and Philip Pedak, among others.

Ubang accepted my proposals and promised to convey them to the government. Two weeks later, he informed me that the Sudanese government had accepted the proposals. I wrote to Francis Mayar and Agolong Chol in Kinshasa and Arkangelo Wanji in Kampala to convey the news of the proposed dialogue. I asked whether they approved. If so, would they let me know whether I could suggest a venue and whether they would be able to afford their transport to the venue and back? I also proposed some of the points we might raise, asked them to add their own, and told them that the list of items for discussion would be finalized when we met.

Some of the points were: increasing the economic powers of the South to speed development, including the right to negotiate financial and development aid directly with foreign donors; increasing legislative powers of the Regional Assembly; withdrawing the 6,000 Northern troops from the South; expanding education and healthcare to the same level as the north; fixing a date to review the Addis Ababa Agreement; ensuring that the reviewed agreement was guaranteed by the UN Security Council, as a safeguard to prevent the agreement from being abrogated; and giving the South an equal stake and say in how natural resources were explored and managed.

Not long after I sent my letter, I received a letter from Agolong confirming that the ANF members of the executive committee in Kinshasa accepted the proposal for dialogue with the Nimeiri government. They feared that the agenda which the ANF delegation might put forward would not be accepted by the regime.

As time went on, I received acceptance of a dialogue process from most of the South Sudanese groups in exile. But obstacles began to emerge. A lack of funding made it impossible for ANF members to obtain air tickets and hotel accommodation. Nor could they easily obtain visas for travel. The alternative was for the Sudanese government to pay the costs of the meeting. This was rejected by ANF members as another sell-out, like what had happened during the Addis Ababa negotiations.

The ANF grew to realize that it would enter the proposed dialogue from a position of weakness. It would therefore be futile. The plan for dialogue eventually collapsed.

Finding a Job
Since receiving the right to remain in Britain, finding a job was one of my greatest problems. I applied for the job of a Securicor guard

but was turned down. I completed many other applications without success. David Floyd, the journalist, also tried in vain to find a job for me. I met an official in the Labor Exchange office who asked for a passport. I handed her my British Alien Registration Certificate. She asked why I remained unemployed and reminded me that I would not be allowed to continue depending on the Supplementary Benefit Allowance. I said that I was making all possible efforts to get a job, even as a manual laborer. Getting a job for aliens like me was almost impossible. She dismissed my statement as baseless.

On 16 January, Fashoda informed me that he had spoken to a friend at the Decca Electronics Company who had agreed to try and get me a job. A month later, the efforts of Fashoda paid off. I was offered a factory job at Decca Electronics, on probation, with pay of £23 per week. I would first take a training course for six weeks. If I did well on the course, I would be permanently employed.

On Monday, 27 March, I reported to Decca at 10am. I was issued a uniform and met a man called Bob, whose job was to train the new workers. We were instructed to clock in every morning at 8am. If one came late, it would be recorded. The training went on until 4.30pm when we were allowed to go home. I was given an advance to keep me going until my weekly payment was regularized.

The life of employment was harder than the life I had in the bush of South Sudan; there I still had members of the movement to take care of my affairs. In exile, I had to cook for myself before going to work and whenever I came back in the evening.

Having assessed my performance during the training course, I felt that I would be confirmed as a worker at Decca. I was, indeed, appointed as an employee at the end of the training course. My actual wage would be £23.56 per week. My job was to select the components required for manufacturing various electronic goods and carry these to the respective engineers or technicians.

I was exhausted by the physical work of carrying heavy goods. It was the first time I had worked as a manual laborer. I was not eating well and was struggling to survive in London. The wage was small for someone who was once a civil servant and cabinet minister. But I had no other option.

One day, my senior supervisor called me to her office. She said that something seemed to be wrong with my work, that I was becoming slow, and asked if there was anything I did not understand? In addition, she told me that the assistant supervisor had reported I had kicked a packet of goods instead of putting it in a wheelbarrow. I denied the accusation; it was untrue. I said that my work had not changed, nor had I slowed down.

It was obvious that I was already in trouble, as some of my bosses had developed a dislike for me for one reason or another. I wrote again to David Floyd to ask if he could explore the possibility of getting a new job for me, given my bosses' hostility. He promised to revive his efforts to find me another job. Unfortunately, he did not make headway.

My accommodation was also a problem. At the end of May, my landlord, Osuji, extended my stay in his bedsit by 3 months but said that the rent would go up to £6.50. I had no choice but to accept as I had no alternative. Osuji's place in Leyton was far from my place of work in Raynes Park: a 75-minute commute each way. I had found a bedsit in Wimbledon, nearer my place of work, for £8 per week, but I had to turn it down as my wage was not enough to cover a higher rent and expenses.

Every day, on my return to the house, Osuji informed me that several people had phoned from the Sudanese embassy. I asked him to tell them that I was busy and had no time to speak to them. He promised to do so. I knew that among them were Sudanese government agents trying to watch me and who still hoped that sooner or later, I would be persuaded to return to Sudan.

Gideon Tokmac, who was training as an accountant in London, sent me the news of Nimeiri's visit to London and his desire to communicate with me, which he had conveyed to Tokmac through consul Philip Ubang. Since I had decided to stop contact with anybody from Sudan, South or North, I went underground during Nimeiri's visit. I believed that no purpose could be served by meeting him.

A Visit from Khartoum

On 17 July 1973, Tokmac's wife phoned to say that Sarah had arrived in London accompanied by Gordon Abyei Makuac. It was a great joy to know I would meet Sarah for the first time since Bunia in 1971. This was only the second time we had met since I went into exile in 1967.

Gordon Muortat, February 1973
© *Universal Pictorial Press and Agency / Avalon 2024.*

I was pleased to meet Abyei Makuac, the SF President in 1965, and a native of Rumbek. He had come to Kinshasa in 1971 with the aim of persuading me to attend and support the Addis Ababa negotiations.

The next day I met Abyei Makuac at Tokmac's house in Tooting Broadway. He said that many of our former SF colleagues missed me. In their view, the Addis Ababa Agreement was a great achievement, and would go some way to satisfying the aspirations of the South Sudanese if fully implemented. On their behalf, he appealed for me to return to Sudan to help with its implementation.

Regarding Sarah, he said that, at her own request, she had been provided with an air ticket by the regional government to come and see me after our long separation. He tried to assure me that the central government had played no role in their coming to London.

I thanked Abyei Makuac for meeting me and for helping Sarah to come and see me. It was my ardent desire to reunite with Sarah and my children. I told him, however, that I did not believe in the agreement and that I was convinced beyond doubt that the South had to have complete independence and not feeble regional autonomy.

I said that I had to respect my conscience and remain in exile. At the same time, I did not rule out the possibility of a negotiated settlement. Abyei Makuac, a man of great understanding and honesty, ceased argument. He said that he would convey my position to our former SF colleagues.

The same day, I met Sarah at my bedsit at Leyton. I was overwhelmed with joy and happiness to see Sarah again. The six years of separation from her and the children had tortured me severely. If that pain was due to causes other than that of South Sudan, I would have collapsed and died a long time ago. But I had lived in agony.

I applied for two weeks' holiday to have time with Sarah. She

Gordon and Sarah, London, 1973

was happy to find me in sound health. Our children were well in Khartoum. Daughter Rebecca Acol, aged 22, was now married. Daughter Yolanda Lalwengdi, aged 18, was engaged. Sarah asked whether I was going to return to Sudan in view of the Addis Ababa Agreement.

When I had first left the country, I had planned for the family to join me, but it had not worked out. Then it became imperative to join the movement in September 1967. After I joined the struggle and became the leader of the movement in April 1969, the chances of reunion became even more remote, although I did not give up hope. Joseph Mathubier Guelly, who married my daughter Rebecca, had promised that he would smuggle the family out through Ethiopia.

Unfortunately, I told Sarah I could not return to Sudan to work under the agreement or contribute to its implementation, even if such implementation were possible. I appreciated the suffering that she and the children had undergone because of our separation caused by my participation in the struggle for the liberation of South Sudan. For this aim, both married and unmarried Southerners had patriotic obligations to take part.

I explained that I had applied to the British government for a family reunion, which meant that she and the children might be granted entry visas to join me in Britain. Sarah listened carefully to what I said and agreed to come to Britain for a family reunion if visas were issued.

During the day, I used to go to work at Decca while Sarah remained in the bedsit until I returned. The landlord, Osuji, and his family, went on a one-month holiday to Nigeria, leaving us to look after the house.

During one discussion, I proposed that both of us remain in Britain. Meanwhile, we could pursue a family reunion. Three days later, she told me that it was a good idea, but she would not be able to be separated from the children for so long. We agreed to drop the issue.

On 4 September 1973, I accompanied Sarah to the airport. I pledged that I would do my best to bring about a family reunion.

I suspected that the government had sent Abyei Makuac to make me change my mind and return to Sudan. This was different from the visit of Sarah, who was genuinely adversely affected and depressed by our separation. I detected that the Sudanese authorities hoped that the visit of my wife would complement that of Abyei Makuac and be persuasive. But I was very much encouraged by the conscientious, sympathetic, and understanding stance taken by Sarah. She refused to embarrass me over the pressure by the Nimeiri regime to make me return to Sudan.

More Trouble at Work

There was more trouble on my return to work. I experienced bad treatment from two supervisors. I was accused of delaying the trucks delivering goods to the factory. I tried to explain that the loads were many and I was alone. My supervisor refused to accept this argument and said that as I was tall and strong, I should not have any problems with loads such as these. Although he did not want me to speak, I insisted on explaining that I was not used to manual labor. He was furious and asked why I had come to this country.

The harassment continued. I was accused of sleeping on the job, of taking too many toilet breaks. I was denied overtime. If I came to work in smart clothes, I was told to leave my usual work on electronic components and instead be assigned to unload dusty equipment from the lorries. I was sure this was done purposely whenever I was well dressed.

I was upset and concluded that the supervisors were racists. I was the only black worker. There had been another: a young man from Sierra Leone, who was later deported. I wanted to resign, but finding an alternative job was difficult. Furthermore, I thought it wise to wait for the extension of my asylum, which I was expecting from the Home Office. Being 51 years old was a factor in failing interviews, as was racism, and that I lacked many of the required skills. My health was also giving way. I suffered frequently from rheumatic pains, bronchial coughs, and severe headaches. Most of these symptoms, according to my doctor, were due to stress caused by separation from my family.

The final straw came on 29 April 1974 while carrying out my usual work of bringing electronics from the store to the engineers. I suddenly felt a sharp pain in my right foot. I quickly sat down and took my foot out of my shoe to see the cause of the pain. After pulling off my sock, I found a large stone in my shoe. I removed the stone. The deputy supervisor saw this and became furious. She said, "This is not Africa, you must not show your bare foot for people to see no matter the reasons. In Europe, such sights cause horror to many people who are civilized." I explained what had happened. She reiterated that people in Europe do not show their bare feet. I disagreed and told her that I had seen the bare feet of many people since I had arrived in Europe. She was annoyed and reported me to the supervisor who called me to his office and questioned my behavior. I explained again, but he insisted on issuing a formal warning. He told me to go back to work.

Later, I was summoned to the supervisor's office once more. Without giving details, he told me the deputy supervisor was not happy with my work, and that I would be sacked if I made another mistake. The two supervisors seemed to want to keep me in agony and distress, which they believed would end with me resigning. In June, I formally complained of mistreatment by my supervisors. The case was heard by a panel. For their part, my supervisors accused me of negligence. Fortunately, my trade union representative supported me. He proposed that I be offered a new job in the company. In the end, it was recommended that I take another job of the same nature in the company. I then became a trade union member and in future felt less vulnerable to ill-treatment and racial prejudice.

I was offered the post of an electronic storeman at the main Decca Radar store at Wellington Crescent, about a mile from Kingston-upon-Thames. I accepted without hesitation. On 24 June, I reported to Decca Radar. I met the director, Mr Hind, who offered a warm handshake and assured me that I would not face the same troubles as I had at Decca Navigator. The job had the same responsibilities as those I had had previously. Here, I did not experience any harassment.

Becoming More Settled in London

I had written to UNHCR to ask whether they could find out from the Home Office the reasons for the delay in extending my period of stay. The reply came that the Home Office had agreed to extend my stay. On 6 February 1974, I visited UNHCR to collect Certificate of Registration number 034745, which served as my identity document and showed my status in Britain and the length of the period of stay. This enabled me to move freely throughout Britain without the worry of being harassed. On 28 August, I visited the Home Office in Croydon to meet the officials dealing with my asylum case. They said that my stay had been extended by another year.

On 20 January 1975, I called the Home Office and reminded them of my request for a further extension of the period of my stay. I was told that my period of stay had only been extended for six months. The reason given was that they had been reliably informed that I would soon travel to Africa for a longer period. I denied this was true.

This news coincided with rumors that I was about to visit several African states, where I would be convinced to return from exile. I insisted in my request to the Home Office that they give me a one-year extension and a travel document. They promised to consider my request.

On 2 June, I received a new travel document from the Home Office, the fruit of several years of struggle. I was grateful to the Home Office for their humanitarian gesture. Now I would be able to travel to any country, except Sudan. I had also applied for help with transport for Sarah and my three youngest children, Mary Nyitur, Susan Aciec, and Justin Nyieer, following my application for a family reunion. The UNHCR Office Director promised to consider this request.

I eventually managed to secure more satisfactory accommodation.

Rev. Thwaites helped me secure a bedsit from a Nigerian couple in Tooting Bec for £7 a week. I also enrolled in correspondence courses on journalism and philosophy, although I was not able to complete either; I was again being pulled into political events in Sudan.

Continued Connections with Political Developments in Sudan
I kept abreast of the political, social, and economic developments taking place in Sudan. I continued to receive letters from old colleagues inside Sudan, former Anyanya political and military members, and members of the ANF and Kinshasa Group. I used this information to draft press statements and write letters to heads of state in Africa and the leaders of international organizations.

In my spare time, I wrote and typed a booklet entitled Self-Explanation. The aim was to explain to the South Sudanese people why ANF colleagues and I denounced the Addis Ababa Agreement and resolved to remain in exile. I also produced a press statement which called upon Nimeiri's regime to allow a referendum on the regional autonomy granted to the South under the Addis Ababa Agreement. I took it to the BBC's Robin White, who had interviewed me on the BBC several times. Unfortunately, this statement was not broadcast.

I circulated reports on the situation in the South to the main newspapers in the UK. I informed them of issues like the outbreak of an epidemic in Lakes District, which killed thousands of people, and about which the Nimeiri regime took no countermeasures. I drew attention to violent demonstrations in Juba over the Egyptian activity on the Jonglei canal, which left several dead. I highlighted the clashes between the integrated Anyanya units and the government troops sent to replace them at Akobo in February 1975.

Peter Nyot Kok, who was studying law in London, phoned on 9 July 1974 to say that he had received a letter from my son-in-law,

Joseph Mathubier Guelly, conveying that foreign friends had arranged a trip by air for me from London to Brussels, Kinshasa, Entebbe, and Nairobi, then returning to London, to begin on 17 July. After I met Nyot to discuss it further, I turned down the offer. Its initiators included foreigners such as Jan van Hoogstein, the Church World Service Africa Director, who was heavily involved in structuring the Addis Ababa Agreement. I refused to receive the tickets. My son-in-law and Nyot appreciated the reasons for my refusal to accept the offer.

On 26 July, Agolong Chol, in Kinshasa, reported that a majority of ANF members and other Southern political exiles he met in Uganda, Kenya, and Ethiopia were still adamantly opposed to the Addis Ababa Agreement. In October, Agolong wrote again to inform me that a proposal was recently circulated among ANF members advocating an alliance between the Northern Sudanese opposition and the ANF against the Nimeiri regime. According to him, most members were not opposed to the idea, but felt that the matter needed to be carefully studied before any decision was taken.

All this time, I was still under pressure to accept the agreement and return to Sudan. When former SF colleagues such as Luigi Adwok and Paul Acire came to London, they would ask to see me. On 11 December 1974, I met Ambrose Riiny Thiik, my former SF colleague and member of Abel Alier's regional government. We discussed the agreement at length. He tried to persuade me to accept it and return to Sudan. We parted without making any progress in understanding one another.

9.

The Formation of the Anyanya Patriotic Front (1974-1975)

Southern dissatisfaction with the Addis Ababa Agreement developed for a variety of reasons. Disparity in all areas of development between North and South had worsened since the signing of the agreement in 1972. The regional government had done little to help reconstruct the South. Moreover, a series of incidents had undermined the progress, effectiveness, and implementation of the agreement.

Riots broke out in Juba in September 1974. They lasted for two days, and two Southerners were killed. More than 60 cars were burnt. 200 people were arrested, including members of the Southern Regional Assembly.

There were other incidents. A Northern policeman guarding the Sudan Bank in Wau opened fire on three young Dinka men sitting under a tree nearby, killing one and wounding two. He then went to the market and shot indiscriminately, killing two more. The police succeeded in disarming the shooter and took him into custody.

It was not long before a large crowd of Southerners reacted by beating up Northern Sudanese merchants and looting their shops. The Arab merchants retaliated by opening fire on the crowd. One rioter was wounded in the arm. A police unit composed of the absorbed Anyanya army arrived and dispersed the crowd. It was later reported that three Northern Sudanese civilians had been killed and others injured. After order was restored, the authorities said that the policeman who started the disturbance was mentally ill.

Then, a few days later, a grenade was thrown into a cinema hall in Wau. Seven people were killed and many more injured. Apparently, the grenade was thrown by a Northern Sudanese soldier opposed to the Addis Ababa Agreement and regional government in the South.

Another incident which contributed to the weakening of the agreement was an attempt to assassinate Lt. Joseph Kuol Amoum, a Bahr al-Ghazal Anyanya officer who had integrated into the Sudanese army. After discovering a plot to kill him by a Northern military officer in Wau, Kuol fled to Bussere, south of Wau, and took refuge in an Anyanya garrison yet to be integrated into the Sudanese army.

As news of the assassination attempt circulated, tension grew between the Anyanya forces awaiting integration and the Northern troops. This led to an outbreak of shooting between an Anyanya battalion stationed at Aweil and a Northern unit in the vicinity. Two Dinka caught in the crossfire were killed. The Nimeiri regime swiftly sent Col. Emmanuel Abur Nhial, who had just been integrated, together with some Northern officers from Khartoum, to calm the situation in Wau.

Towards mid-1975, Nimeiri increasingly feared the Southern regional government would gain strength from the deployment of 6,000 Anyanya in the South. Nimeiri and his close colleagues had never been comfortable with this provision of the agreement.

Furthermore, Nimeiri was under pressure from the Umma and the Democratic Unionist Party (DUP), as well as some in the army and the civil service, who opposed making concessions to South Sudan.

Nimeiri responded with a policy calculated to result in abrogation of the agreement. In 1975, directives for the second stage of integration of the forces were issued: deploying 6,000 Anyanya in the South would not occur. Instead, the Anyanya were to be mixed with Northern Sudanese soldiers across Sudan. When this became known, most Anyanya units became suspicious and feared the government was planning to disarm them or transfer them to the North.

Akobo Incident

On 22 March 1975, Peter Nyot Kok informed me that serious clashes had taken place at Akobo, Upper Nile between an Anyanya garrison and a Sudanese army unit dispatched to disarm them. Many government soldiers and some Anyanya had been killed.

According to the Addis Ababa Agreement, 12,000 troops comprising 6,000 absorbed, or integrated, Anyanya forces were to be deployed in the South together with 6,000 troops from the Northern army. The aim of the deployment of the Anyanya in the South was to dispel fears of the Northern army, as many Southerners regarded them as killers. Calming these fears was important for creating stability in the South.

As I have explained, Nimeiri was disturbed by the deployment of the Anyanya forces in the South. Hence, he revived the activities of the so-called Second Military Commission to plot a scheme in which the Anyanya and Northern forces deployed in the South were scattered across Sudan. This plan was endorsed by Joseph Lagu, who had been appointed as military commander of all Anyanya forces in the South.

It was 20 February when action on the new policy was taken. A force of 200 Northern officers and men under the command of Col. Abel Chol Ater arrived in Akobo, where a force of 300 Anyanya was deployed. Just before the Northern force arrived, word had circulated that it had been decided that if the absorbed Anyanya force refused to be disarmed, it would be disarmed by force.

Mixing the two forces was aimed at promoting cohesion and national unity as stated by Abel Alier in his statement on 22 March. Integration was to begin in Akobo and eventually be extended across South Sudan. The Northern force camped on the outskirts of Akobo, not far from the garrison.

Abel Chol tried to explain his mission. The Anyanya refused to accept his explanation. Negotiations between the two forces went on for several days in a tense atmosphere. On 2 March, the Anyanya opened fire on the Northern forces, who returned fire. Abel Chol and some of his soldiers were killed. The rest of his force dispersed.

After some days, government reinforcements arrived from Malakal. Most of the ringleaders of the uprising, such as Cpl. James Bol Kur and Lt. Vincent Kwany Latjor, had already crossed the Ethiopian border and had been granted asylum. The rest of the Anyanya garrison surrendered to the Northern forces. One reason why they agreed to surrender was that those implicated in leading the clashes believed they would not be discovered. However, after being tortured, many were tried and sentenced to death and long-term imprisonment.

Correspondence with John Jack Deang in Gambella
In June, I received a letter dated 24 May from John Jack Deang, a South Sudanese Nuer, writing from Ethiopia. He also informed me of the Akobo incident. According to him, there were 600 Anyanya officers and men at Akobo. The army unit under Col. Abel Chol's

command was not less than 300. When the Anyanya saw the army coming they rushed to the armory, armed themselves, and took up positions.

The next morning, Abel Chol addressed the Anyanya garrison, saying that the president had ordered the mixing of the forces. Anybody who opposed it would be shot. He ordered the store keys to be handed over and told the Anyanya to march out unarmed from the garrison while the army unit remained in the camp. To the Anyanya, this was clearly disarmament. The next day the Anyanya took up positions, indicating that they rejected the order. When Abel Chol arrived in the morning to inspect the troops, Anyanya soldiers shot him dead. The army units tried to withdraw from the garrison, but intense firing began. According to John Jack, 128 soldiers were killed. The Anyanya then took charge of Akobo town after government forces abandoned it. After four days, the Anyanya permitted government officials to enter the town to talk. Divisions were growing between the Anyanya, and some feared betrayal by their comrades.

It was decided that the ringleaders of the uprising should escape to Ethiopia, while as many soldiers loyal to the cause as possible should remain behind to witness any further attempts by the Nimeiri regime to implement its new integration policy. John Jack stated that there were 50 armed ringleaders in Ethiopia.

Although the Akobo uprising ringleaders had been welcomed by the Ethiopian authorities, John Jack asked whether I could find some material assistance for those in Ethiopia. If I wanted to go and meet them, I should let him know and he would arrange it. He also noted that there were more than 500 South Sudanese refugees in Ethiopia already, with more arriving daily.

To respond to John Jack, I sent a verbal message through an Ethiopian called Peter. I promised to reply in writing soon. In the meantime, I welcomed the developments at Akobo and was willing to visit Ethiopia to meet the South Sudanese patriots.

On 17 June, I received another letter from John Jack in Gambella dated 9 June in which he confirmed receipt of my verbal message, together with my London address. He said that the Ethiopian authorities had informed him that my presence in Ethiopia would be much appreciated. Regarding my travel expenses to Ethiopia, the governor of Gambella had assured him that this would not be a problem. The letter stressed the governor's view that my presence as an elder with the young people who had arrived from Akobo was important. John Jack promised to do his best to speed up my arrival and was optimistic about the Ethiopian government's sympathy for our cause.

On 25 June, I replied to John Jack. I wrote that the Akobo uprising had opened the eyes of the Southerners to the weaknesses of the Addis Ababa Agreement. The Anyanya absorbed forces had realized that Nimeiri's new integration policy meant liquidation of the Anyanya. I asked John Jack to advise the absorbed forces to solidly back the Akobo Anyanya forces which revolted against oppression and coordinate a common stance throughout South Sudan.

I stressed that the absorbed Anyanya forces needed good political guidance. This was missing inside the country because Southern political leaders were cooperating with the Nimeiri regime. I expressed satisfaction with the sympathy shown by the Ethiopian government and conveyed my thanks for their offer of transport for me to visit Ethiopia.

I requested John Jack convey a proposal to the Ethiopian authorities: to help transport a South Sudanese delegation to Addis Ababa composed of one representative from East Africa, two from Kinshasa, two from Europe (including myself), two from Ethiopia, and three from among the Anyanya leaders who had mutinied in Akobo. This delegation would hold a secret convention to set up a new national liberation movement for South Sudan. I said I would contact the Ethiopian embassy in London to request an entry visa and asked him to contact me urgently if such contact would undermine his discussions with the Ethiopian government. The government in power was now the military junta which had overthrown Emperor Haile Selassie. The military ruler was Gen. Tafari Benti, who would eventually be succeeded by Mengistu Haile Mariam.

I conveyed my congratulations to the heroes of the Akobo uprising and wrote that their sacrifices would never be forgotten by the South Sudanese. I advised they maintain unity and fundraise to keep going until a new liberation movement was organized.

Political Developments while Awaiting John Jack's reply
While I was waiting for John Jack to reply, some Southern students from Bahr al-Ghazal, including Leo Thuc, wrote to Elia Duang Arop, who remained opposed to the Addis Ababa Agreement and had sought asylum in Italy. The students asked him to come to Addis Ababa to negotiate with the Ethiopian government in light of the Akobo uprising.

Duang and I were in contact regarding the situation post-Akobo. The government of Tafari Benti had invited the leaders of the Akobo uprising and the Southern political leaders in exile to Ethiopia. It seemed that the Ethiopians intended to use us for their own interests. This did not bother us too much as we believed that we could also benefit if we played our cards well.

On 27 August, I received a letter informing me that Elia Duang had arrived in Ethiopia 10 days earlier. He had communicated with the Ethiopian authorities about the issue of South Sudanese refugees and their support for our cause. They seemed to be interested in helping but said that we must first organize ourselves before they considered any detailed request for assistance. They did agree to consider the request for financial help to convene a convention in Nairobi, on 10 September. The funding was limited to cover essential expenses for 10 people.

I received a telegram from John Jack on 29 August. It said, "Come immediately, contact Heathrow Hotel, ask for Bekele on Sunday 31 August before noon." I phoned Ethiopian Airlines at Heathrow and inquired about Bekele. Bekele had gone to look for my house in London. When I returned to the house that evening, I found a note from Bekele saying that he would phone at 9.30pm. He phoned accordingly and we agreed to meet the next day.

I met Bekele near Heathrow. He said I was urgently required to come to Addis Ababa by the Ethiopian authorities and that if I was willing I should prepare to travel. On 17 September, I received a telegram from Elia Duang expecting me in Addis Ababa on 21 September, with the return ticket to be supplied in Addis.

That day, Dr Barnaba Marial Benjamin, who had married my daughter Yolanda Lalwengdi, phoned to inform me that Hilary Paul Logali, a member of the South Sudan regional government, wanted to meet. Logali was a former SF colleague who disagreed with my opposition to the agreement. Barnaba also informed me that Sarah was on her way from Khartoum to see me. At this point, apart from brief visits, we had been separated for nine years, so I was keen to meet her. She was supposed to arrive in London on 18 September.

Logali and I discussed many issues. He appealed to me to return to Sudan, where he said my services were desperately needed. I reiterated the reasons why I was still in exile.

On 18 September, Barnaba informed me that Sarah had not arrived as expected, but he did not know why. I would have postponed my departure had Sarah arrived.

After I agreed to travel to Ethiopia, I applied for four weeks' holiday and two weeks' leave without pay from my job, in case of delay. This was approved.

Return to East Africa

I met Bekele at Heathrow who gave me a one-way ticket. I was worried by the one-way ticket, in case I got stuck in Addis. However, I quickly brushed aside the concern. If the trip was fruitful to the South Sudanese cause, everything else would be secondary.

On 21 September, our plane touched down in Addis Ababa. I was happy to be back in Africa. The brilliant sunshine, which I had missed for three years, greeted us as we were disembarking. As I was in the company of Bekele, I did not face any problems at immigration. I was taken to the hotel where Elia Duang had been staying. Leo Thuc welcomed and informed me that Duang had left for Nairobi the day before. Duang had left some documents to be delivered to me on arrival. One note contained some of the points mentioned in his recent letters and stated that his main objective for visiting Nairobi (and possibly Kampala) was to learn the attitude of the neighboring countries to the situation in Sudan.

Before he left, Duang had sent invitations, dated 25 August, to prominent South Sudanese leaders in exile to attend a meeting on 10 September in Nairobi. Duang explained that the meeting was being convened to determine how the new liberation struggle should proceed following the Akobo uprising. He also explained that the meeting would be held in Nairobi because the Ethiopians thought that meeting in Addis Ababa would be adverse to their interests.

Duang outlined the qualifications of delegates for the proposed meeting. They had to be South Sudanese who opposed the agreement, or have fled recently from Sudanese government oppression, or be volunteer members of the newly formed military of the liberation struggle.

In another document, Duang wrote that John Jack Deang had been stopped from certain activities of which the refugees' organization disapproved. Duang requested I stop dealing with John Jack until I arrived in Kenya. I was upset to read this report because I had formed a good impression of John Jack and of his activities. I was looking forward to meeting and learning more about him.

In the afternoon, I met several Southerners including John Jack, who were pleased I had arrived. They assured me of their confidence in me and the other leaders of the betrayed liberation movement and that they were looking forward to seeing us found a new struggle. The same evening, I met James Bol Kur, one of the leaders of the Akobo uprising, who recounted his experience of the uprising.

The next day, I met John Jack again and thanked him warmly for his letters and telegrams. John Jack explained how he was persuaded by fellow Southerners to serve the cause of the South as a double agent for the Ethiopian and Sudanese governments. This resulted in him losing the confidence of both sides. Some of his political opponents accused him of being a Sudanese government agent. I felt sorry but blamed him for accepting such a role. I urged him to keep in touch and to continue his role as a participant in the struggle and not to worry about criticism from his opponents, because all of us had political enemies.

I also met a group of South Sudanese students in Ethiopia led by Francis Lupai. They were members of the South Sudan Coordinating Committee set up by Duang after his arrival from Italy in early August. Among the issues we discussed was Equatoria's regional representation at the proposed meeting in Nairobi. Lupai alleged that Duang was not enthusiastic about this suggestion. I promised to give the issue special attention.

The next day, Leo Thuc informed me that I was required in the Ministry of Foreign Affairs. Thuc knew some Amharic, the official language of Ethiopia, so he interpreted whenever I met Ethiopians who did not speak English. I was asked to complete an application form for an Ethiopian refugee travel document to enable me to travel to Kenya, rather than travel on my British document. The Ethiopians advised that the British document would not be acceptable in Kenya. The problem of whether my nationality would be recorded as Sudanese or stateless confronted us.

Later, the Ministry of Foreign Affairs contacted Thuc to say my request was being processed and the document would soon be issued. Later, I received a telegram from Duang advising me to stay put until further notice as he was still exploring the political situation in East Africa. On 25 September, Thuc obtained my travel document from the Ministry of Foreign Affairs. He also delivered my new Ethiopian identity card.

On 27 September, Philip Pedak, one of the founders of the Anyanya in the early sixties, who had denounced the Addis Ababa Agreement but had returned to Sudan, visited. We had last met in Khartoum in 1960, when he was one of the radical young South Sudanese leaders. Our views on South Sudan were therefore very similar. He briefed me on the political situation in the South and raised the issue of integration which had resulted in the Akobo uprising. As far as he was aware, the policy was vehemently opposed everywhere. In Upper Nile, the authorities had pushed it through by force.

On 1 October, a telegram from Elia Duang stated that opinion in East Africa favored the meeting in Nairobi taking place only after the Anyanya in Ethiopia attacked Sudanese government forces across the border. I replied that this opinion was unacceptable; the Anyanya should not undertake military action without an organized movement to lead and authorize such operations. The new Anyanya was awaiting a philosophy to be spelt out in order to fight with strong motivation.

The Birth of the Anyanya Patriotic Front (APF)

In early October, I received a letter from Peter Agap de Kuch, a former Anyanya officer from Rumbek. He informed me of a disagreement between Elia Duang and Aggrey Jaden over whether there was a need to launch another organized movement. A few days later, I received a telegram from Duang instructing me to come to Nairobi for the meeting, which was now likely to take place on 10 October.

Contrary to my fears, I got the visa for Kenya without difficulty. Ato Taye Reta, the Ethiopian assistant minister of the interior and the official assigned to our affairs, came to the hotel and said that I had been booked on a flight to Nairobi that evening. I was then taken to the airport.

The next day, Duang arrived and took me to his hotel. I informed him that our delegation for the meeting was being arranged. It would include three leaders of the Akobo uprising. On the same day, other delegates including Joshua Dau Diu, the Southern Regional Assembly member, and Rev. Matthew arrived from Kampala. During the day Duang, Dau, and I discussed holding the meeting even if some delegates might fail to arrive. The agenda was also discussed.

On 11 October, two more delegates, Paul Duang Yak, and John Luate from Equatoria, arrived from Kampala. As we were determined not to lose time and to see the meeting through, discussions began at 11am that day. Rev. Matthew chaired the meeting.

In attendance were Elia Duang, Peter Agap de Kuch, and Paul Duang from Bahr al-Ghazal; John Luate from Equatoria; and James Bol Kur, Joshua Dau, John Omot Omot, Johnny Jock Rasson, and Matthew Cooper from Upper Nile. Aggrey Jaden could not attend because of illness, Arkangelo Wanji had had an accident in Kampala, and Francis Mayar was absent because of his job.

We began by discussing the current situation. We then turned to whether the situation was ripe for an armed struggle for freedom; whether the Ethiopian government would grant material aid as expected; whether there was any feasibility of the new movement receiving aid from any other sources; and, if armed struggle did commence, what administrative methods and policies would be adopted to organize the new Anyanya forces.

Several resolutions were adopted. The first was that it was an opportune time for the Anyanya to be revived and reconstituted into a new movement consisting of a political and military wing. The political wing would be called the Anyanya Patriotic Front (APF), the military to be still known as the Anyanya. The new movement would continue the armed struggle for independence.

Second, the meeting resolved to send a delegation to meet the Ethiopian government to convey gratitude for its support. The delegation would also ask for assistance for the new Anyanya units camped at the border and discuss in greater detail the promised aid, so that the movement could wage a successful armed struggle against the Northern army.

The meeting suggested that the delegation make clear that if the APF started feebly, it would be quickly sabotaged and destroyed like its predecessors. To avoid this, the military assistance would have to be sufficient to make an effective start. We knew that thousands of Southerners would volunteer to take up arms when they heard of new military assistance but would be disappointed when they learned such help was small. The delegation would need to convey that a weak start would expose the civilian population to annihilation by the Khartoum government, given its record of massacres of South Sudanese civilians. Finally, a vigorous start would win us new foreign supporters and support from the masses inside South Sudan.

We agreed the APF would be led by an Executive Committee

with myself as chairman, Elia Duang Arop as secretary-general, Joshua Dau Diu as secretary for information, John Omot Omot as treasurer, John Luate as assistant secretary-general for Uganda, and James Bol as a member of the organizing committee in Ethiopia. Since the APF needed facilities to contact foreign leaders and embassies to win support for our struggle, the vice-chairman and two additional assistant secretaries-general (one for Zaïre and one for Ethiopia), plus two more members in Zaïre and Ethiopia, were to be appointed by the elected members later.

It was also resolved that Anyanya be organized in four zones: Upper Nile, Eastern Equatoria, Western Equatoria, and Bahr al-Ghazal. Each zone was to be run by an organizing committee consisting of two members of the coordinating executive committee and the military commanders of the zone. The assistant secretary-general would be the head of the Zonal Authority. In each zone, publicity and propaganda mechanisms would be set up wherever feasible.

The chairman and the secretary-general were to draft a manifesto for the new movement. We would define the powers of the Executive Committee, the powers of the Zonal Authorities, and complete directives showing how work should be carried out in the bush.

Although I was elected unanimously as chairman and leader of the movement, I expressed reluctance to accept the post. My experience in the liberation struggle, where collective responsibilities and efforts were left to be carried out by a few, gave me reservations. I insisted that unless this attitude changed, I would prefer to contribute in another function. However, after assurances that there would be change, I accepted the role of chairman.

The meeting ended on 14 October. Duang, Luate, and Dau left for Kampala the same day. On the morning of 15 October, I left

Nairobi for Addis Ababa. The next day, we started implementing the resolutions adopted in Nairobi, and delivered the report from the meeting to the Ethiopian Provisional Military Administrative Council (PMAC), better known as the Derg, with a request for urgent action.

On 18 October, Duang arrived in Addis Ababa. We updated each other on our activities since the Nairobi meeting. Then we met the Ethiopian government representative, Taye Reta, who acknowledged receipt of our report on the Nairobi meeting and the formation of the APF. We told him that an official letter to the government would soon follow. We agreed to meet again.

The APF's Requests to the Ethiopian authorities
Duang and I then drafted a letter to the Ethiopian authorities asking for assistance. We had agreed not to request overly extensive help immediately. We wanted to make a start to get them committed and after they were assured that we were serious, we would slowly increase our requests. On 20 October, the memorandum specifying our military, financial, and other short-term requirements was delivered to the Ethiopian authorities. We were told that it would be given serious consideration and that we would soon be informed of the government's decision.

We requested arms and ammunition sufficient to equip three Anyanya companies. The first Anyanya force would consist of 4,000 officers and men, 1,000 to be deployed in each of the four zones. We asked for signal equipment for the deployment: four long-distance radiotelephones to connect the four zones, four medium-distance radiotelephones for each zone to connect the different companies, along with sufficient accessories and parts to last for six months.

We also needed training for military officers and other personnel. Each zone required 20 young intellectuals for first officers' training and 20 senior officers for training in higher command responsibilities. For the younger trainees, we wanted to turn out tough guerrilla leaders who could command operations in difficult terrain. These volunteers would need money for transport to attend training. At the training camps in Ethiopia, the soldiers would also need to be fed.

Regarding technical personnel, we planned to have five radio operators and three radio mechanics. We wanted one medical assistant for each company. Thus, with nine companies in each zone, we had to train 36 medical assistants.

We needed money to run and maintain a variety of services and entities. This included funds to rent an apartment of three to four rooms to serve both as lodging and as an office for the Coordinating Committee. The office needed writing equipment, a typewriter, and a duplicating machine for the publishing of a news bulletin. We would need 300 Ethiopian birr monthly for correspondence and stationery and 150 birr monthly to provide meals.

We requested money for travel, including a ticket for me to London, a ticket for the information secretary to fly from Kampala to Addis Ababa (he had travelled from Nairobi to Kampala on duty after the Nairobi recent meeting), and tickets for the secretary-general to fly to Kampala, Kinshasa, and Geneva. We would also need to be able to buy tickets for flights to Gambella.

We planned to have mobile organizing committees along the borders of Uganda and Zaïre, to receive the soldiers coming from South Sudan to attend training abroad. Each committee would require 250 US dollars per month for food, accommodation, office materials, and transport. A further allowance was required for runners and intelligence personnel to go between Ethiopia and South Sudan.

The APF Becomes a Pawn Between Ethiopia and Sudan

On 28 October, Duang, Moses Malek Chol, and the other new members recently co-opted onto the Coordinating Committee discussed a possible visit to Gambella. The authorities had delayed the trip for several weeks. We agreed not to visit Gambella unless we received a reply to our request for assistance.

That same day, Taye Reta, the Ethiopian official overseeing APF affairs, visited to talk about our request. He spoke positively, though he failed to commit to a date on which action would be taken by his government. He re-emphasized the promises the Ethiopian government had made. Meanwhile, other members of the Committee and its military wing of almost 500 officers and men at the Ethiopia-Sudan border awaited a reply to our request for assistance.

Soon after the Nimeiri government learned of our presence in Ethiopia, it took actions to try and persuade the government of Ethiopia to reverse its pro-South Sudan policies. On 4 November, Radio Addis Ababa announced that the Ethiopian foreign minister had visited Khartoum. This was followed by dialogue between the two governments. After meeting the Sudanese government representatives, the minister declared that the government of Ethiopia was willing to solve the Eritrean problem peacefully. Both governments had agreed to make efforts to end the Ethiopian-Eritrean war. In his statement, Nimeiri added that he would continue to work for a peaceful solution to the conflict in Ethiopia. Two days later, the two governments established a committee to investigate the problems affecting their countries. Although we had no evidence for this, we concluded that Ethiopia might sell out our newly formed movement to the Sudanese government. Alternatively, we might be reduced to a pressure group against the Sudanese government.

There were soon signs that the Ethiopian government would change its mind about aiding the APF, and it was not long before it began dragging its feet. We were told to slow down our political activities. We did not have any military activities at that time, but this was mainly due to the disagreement within the APF on strategy.

We learned that a deal had been struck between the two governments at the expense of the APF and the Ethiopian rebel movements, which were supported by the Sudanese government. The APF, Tigrayan, and Eritrean movements had become pawns in a political game. On the other hand, the Ethiopian government wanted to maintain good relationships with the anti-Khartoum groups from the South, as it did not fully trust Khartoum.

For these reasons, we thought the APF should not always press the Ethiopian authorities for material assistance. Support would depend on whether the Khartoum government would continue to respect the deal between the two countries regarding their respective rebel groups. The APF leadership needed to exercise patience.

Nevertheless, on 8 November, Elia Duang reported that most of our requirements had been approved by the Ethiopian government. Taye Reta would brief us on the latest on 10 November. Leo Thuc also reported that four former Anyanya officers had arrived at the Anyanya camp on the border and been welcomed to the new movement.

The Nimeiri government soon resumed hostile activities against Ethiopia. On 9 November, Sudanese forces committed an incursion into Ethiopia and attacked South Sudanese refugees, killing eight and wounding 30. On 19 November, Sudanese troops killed 13 South Sudan refugees and wounded 40 people in the same area inside Ethiopia.

We stopped pressing the authorities to tell us exactly when the delivery of the assistance we had requested would be made. My leave was running out, and I had not heard about the ticket for my return to London. I had already written to the Ethiopian government about my situation if I delayed my return beyond 15 November, but I had not received a reply. I was anxious about a delay.

Eventually, Leo Thuc and I went to Taye. After a long wait, Taye met us in his office. He started by apologizing for not coming to meet us, as he did at the beginning of our relationship. He said he had a lot of work but assured us of the seriousness of his government. He said it would be a matter of time until the aid we had requested would be delivered. He explained in detail how assistance would be provided. I thanked Taye and his government for the support they had shown to the people of South Sudan. I reiterated the question of the ticket for my return to London, stressing that if I returned to the UK on time it would be easier for me to come back to carry on the tasks. In my absence, the rest of the Coordinating Committee would continue work. Taye said he would refer the matter to his leaders and would convey any decision within the coming week.

The same day, Radio Addis Ababa reported that Gen. Hassan Abbas, security advisor to President Nimeiri, was travelling to Addis Ababa for an official visit. There was little doubt that the Sudanese government was on the offensive, fueled by the presence of the APF leaders in Addis Ababa and the small Anyanya force at Itang, on the border. Apparently, our presence in Ethiopia had caused alarm even in the Southern regional government where the formation of the APF was regarded as a revival of the liberation struggle. I was therefore not surprised that Taye failed to respond as he had promised. Meanwhile, John Jack Deang wrote to say people were waiting for me to arrive in Gambella.

Meeting of APF Coordinating Committee

On 19 November, the Coordinating Committee met to discuss the failure of the Ethiopian government to provide material assistance.

There was disagreement within the APF as to our approach. One group in the APF, led by Elia Duang, the secretary-general, favored launching the armed struggle immediately with the few arms we had. Some felt that if we were offered up to 800 guns, we should accept and start with those arms. Most of the Committee, however, including me, favored starting with a well-armed force. Otherwise, we would simply be dismissed by the Southern population as a nuisance determined to wreck the Addis Ababa Agreement. We needed to avoid the mistakes made in the first Anyanya movement and have a strong launch of the armed struggle.

We agreed to inform the Ethiopian government that if they did not reply to our request for assistance, we would disperse. We also agreed that if too few arms were offered, the offer would be rejected. Given the season, the suitable time to start guerrilla activity in Upper Nile was passing. Morale was deteriorating among the soldiers at Itang and discipline was breaking down. Some of the men believed that the APF's leaders had deceived them. Some groups had carried out premature attacks on the enemy with few arms and ammunition, because they expected assistance was forthcoming. Our forces were vulnerable to attack from the enemy. The Coordinating Committee could not move to the field to implement its activities. So, Elia Duang would proceed to Gambella to inform the military wing that the aid had not materialized. I would return to the UK, and not visit Gambella, to avoid unnecessarily raising expectations.

This letter was delivered to the Ethiopian government by Leo Thuc on 21 November. I had already written to my bank to arrange for my own return ticket to London, to avoid losing my refugee status and job in Britain. Elia Duang, Leo Thuc, and I also tried to follow up our request for tickets. But we did not achieve anything.

On 25 November, the Coordinating Committee met to discuss

the proposed visit of Duang to Gambella. There was again deadlock between those willing to accept small quantities of arms, and those who favoured the delivery of all the arms requested. I still favored the full delivery of arms and declared that if the APF was obliged to resume the armed struggle with few arms, I would resign the APF chairmanship.

Despite the deadlock, the Committee agreed that Duang's visit should take place. On 26 November, Duang, accompanied by John Omot, left for Gambella. On the same day, James Bol Kur, a member of the Coordinating Committee, presented a complaint against Elia Duang, Moses Malek, and John Omot. He accused them of discrimination on tribal grounds and submitted his resignation from the military wing. After speaking with other members of the Committee, I told Bol that his resignation had been rejected. The matter would be dealt with in due course by the APF Gambella Zonal Authority. Bol accepted my decision and promised to reconcile with the others.

Although I was determined not to be frustrated by our Ethiopian friends, I was stressed, and this affected my general state of health. It was a time of great challenge for the APF.

Complaints from the New Anyanya Camp

I received a letter from the Anyanya officers at Itang dated 22 November, reporting the misbehavior of some officers and soldiers in the camp. They also asked whether the South Sudanese students in Addis Ababa could visit the camps to help. Around the same time, I received a handwritten letter dated 19 November signed by Peter Kulang, Samuel Malou, and other Anyanya soldiers at Tiergol, near Gambella. They complained that they were suffering from hunger, disease, and other hardships. They said that they had been waiting for assistance and appealed for rescue.

On 30 November, I wrote to Taye Reta, informing him of the distressing situation of our soldiers at the border, who were expecting an enemy attack at any moment. They would be defenceless unless arms were delivered immediately. I asked if he would let us know whether arrangements to relieve them from distress were underway. The next day, I called Taye's secretary and left a message. I noted that it seemed the government had difficulty in carrying out its promises, and that we would stop pressing for responses. I said I would try to arrange my own ticket back to London.

Shortly afterwards, the Coordinating Committee met to discuss my return to the UK. I urged the Committee that my absence should not adversely affect the APF. The functioning of the Committee and the force at the border would continue until the policy of the Ethiopian government became clear. We also unanimously agreed that if the Ethiopian authorities gave us at least 300 arms, we would accept.

10.

Development of the Anyanya Patriotic Front (1976-1977)

Return to London
On 6 December 1975, I received the money from my bank and bought a ticket to London for 9 December. On 8 December, Taye Reta sent a note to the immigration office to grant an exit visa upon payment of 10 Ethiopian birr.

At noon, we took off for Asmara, Eritrea, before proceeding to Rome. I stopped in Italy for four days to visit Rita Erhart and Dr Mayom Kuel. On 13 December, I left Rome for London.

At Heathrow, I had difficulty entering the UK despite holding a British refugee travel document. Fortunately, the immigration officer who queried my landing was overruled by a more senior officer. I was permitted to enter but was then struck by a series of unfortunate events.

A heavy rain was falling since I arrived at Heathrow. Winter had begun. As I disembarked the escalator at Tooting Bec underground station, I dropped my tape recorder, damaging it. I lost my umbrella, too. Then, when I arrived at the bedsit I had been renting, I found that the landlady had thrown out my belongings and rented the room to someone else, even though I had phoned from Addis Ababa to assure her that I would pay the arrears caused by my delay. I had to spend the night in a bed and breakfast nearby.

On the morning of 14 December, I went to meet the landlady but failed to find her. The new tenant informed me that the landlady had given my things to Rev. Thwaites, who had recommended me for the tenancy in 1973.

I contacted my friend Grish Patel, a colleague from Decca Radar. He said that my job in the company had not been given away. I might be accepted back if I reported immediately. I told him what had happened. He was sympathetic and asked his landlady whether she could find a room for me. She promised to try.

I went to Tooting police station and lodged a complaint against the landlady for giving away my bedsit despite paying the rent in advance, and for only passing on some of my property to Thwaites. My typewriter was missing. Unfortunately, the police declined to open a case and advised me to go to a magistrate at Wandsworth Town Court. Of course, I had no money to launch legal proceedings. I met Thwaites, who unreservedly blamed me for leaving on a long trip abroad without informing him. He said that the landlady was right to throw my things out. I apologized for not having informed him, though as the trip was secret, I could not have informed anybody. Thwaites took me to the attic of his house where my things were covered in dust.

Thwaites put me in touch with Ambrose Riiny Thiik, a lawyer and member of the Southern Front, who had come to study in the UK. Thiik informed me that Sarah had visited London in my absence. Having failed to find me, she had returned to Sudan 24 hours earlier. I was very sorry to hear this.

The next morning, I reported to Decca Radar. To my relief, I was well received. The director told me that I had been away too long – 13 weeks – but that he had decided to keep the job for me. I was told to resume work that day. I explained the loss of my accommodation and was given permission to leave at 2pm to search for a new bedsit.

I complained to the Wandsworth Council officials. They too did not sympathize with my situation and said that I should not have stayed away for three months without paying the whole rent. They recommended I see the Council's Department of the Homeless, near Tooting Broadway. There I was told I would be temporarily accommodated at a hostel on 12 Inner Park Road, near Wimbledon. I had to share a room and bathroom with four other people.

Christmas was approaching and as in previous years, I would be alone in the UK. I wanted to find a church to be with other Christians at this time of year. Since I was back in Wimbledon where I had first landed in 1972, I decided to attend Christmas services at my former church, Emmanuel Church on Wimbledon Hill. On 24 December, I attended midnight mass at St. Paul's Church on Augustus Road in the same area.

My struggle to find a room were as severe as during my first years of life in the UK. Every day, I bought a newspaper and phoned the landlords. Recognizing the voice of an African, they would say, "sorry, the bedsit has gone." The next day in the newspaper, I would find the same room was still available.

In January 1976, I phoned my friend Trevor and asked whether he had found a place for me as life in the hostel was becoming unbearable. He told me to visit on 16 January. I did and he offered me a small room at 6 Bucharest Road in Earlsfield. I hurried back to the hostel and told the lady in charge that I had found a room elsewhere and wished to move out immediately. I would have to pay the whole day's rent, which I did. She helped me find a taxi to Earlsfield. I was offered a legless bed with a mattress, and an electric heater, until I could buy my own. The house was not centrally heated.

Trevor delivered the key and explained the rent arrangements. The landlady had said that I could stay temporarily but did not say how long that could be. I visited Thwaites's house to collect the rest of my luggage. Finally, I had some peace of mind, which enabled me to resume my political activity whenever time was available.

Anyanya Mutiny in Wau and the Deaths of Emmanuel Abur and Alfred Aguet

On 26 March, I received a report from the remaining members of the APF Coordinating Committee in Addis Ababa. One of the most startling events reported was the assassination of the former ANAF Chief of Staff, Emmanuel Abur, who was integrated in the Sudanese army at the rank of brigadier in 1973. According to this report, Capt. Alfred Aguet Awan received information that the Nimeiri regime was planning to disarm the integrated Anyanya forces throughout the South, and that the disarmament had already started in Upper Nile.

On 17 February, Capt. Aguet ordered the Anyanya units under his command in Wau to break into the armory, taking arms and equipment into the bush outside Wau. Government forces assembled to move against Aguet's forces. By the time the government troops mobilized, Aguet's forces were already deep in the bush.

Troops under Brig. Abur's command were ordered to round up Aguet and his deserters. Abur was reluctant to confront Aguet with force; they knew each other well from their Anyanya days. Abur argued to Nimeiri that he could meet Aguet without a show of force and convince Aguet to surrender peacefully and return to Wau.

However, Aguet refused to surrender and ordered his forces to kill Abur, Gabriel Makol Mangok, and the rest of their unarmed comrades. The only survivor was Lt. Col. Lawrence Alew. Aguet then moved with his forces to the Central African Republic (CAR), from where he believed he could revive the struggle.

The Sudanese government dispatched to the CAR a delegation led by Lawrence Wol Wol, which persuaded the Central African government to cooperate with the Sudanese army to crush Aguet. Eventually, Aguet was disarmed by the Central Africans and handed over to Sudan. He and his close associates were court-martialed. His death by firing squad was announced on the BBC World Service on 20 October 1976.

I later learned that it was revealed at the court-martial that Aguet had planned, along with other Anyanya officers integrated into the Sudanese army, to overthrow the civilian regional government and replace it with a military government. The idea was that Nimeiri would have to recognize the military government. If he refused, the military government would declare South Sudan independent. These officers resolved to involve exiled South Sudanese politicians who denounced the Addis Ababa Agreement.

The APF Manifesto

On 8 March, I received a copy of the APF manifesto from Leo Thuc. Elia Duang had edited the text and had it typed.

In sum, the manifesto declared the formation of a new movement to struggle for the total liberation of South Sudan from Northern Sudan Arab domination. We made it clear that liberation included economic, ideological, and cultural freedom, for a new South Sudan based on justice and equality and the belief that people who are politically, culturally, and economically free can develop themselves and their country.

Our aim was also to apply and adopt a socialist ideology suitable to our society. We wanted to eradicate our political and social divisions, recognizing that the enemy had created a privileged class of Southerners which was oppressing and exploiting the masses.

There was a persistent attempt to destroy the integrated Anyanya forces, and thousands were forcefully transferred from the South to North to be used by the Nimeiri regime to crush coups and suppress the Northern opposition.

The APF was therefore not prepared to wait for the fall of Nimeiri's dictatorship. In such an event, the integrated Anyanya forces would be targeted for destruction by the Northern political opposition which would take power in Khartoum. The APF would have to revive its war of liberation before the integrated Anyanya was destroyed.

The APF was committed to armed struggle as the only effective means to achieve a lasting solution to the conflict. At the same time, the APF would not lose sight of any opportunity of achieving its objectives through peaceful negotiations.

Life in London
On 15 March, Trevor's landlady informed me that her children were coming from Canada, so I would have to leave. I called community relations in Tooting Bec to say that I would again be without housing. Their office said it was making efforts to solve my housing problem. On 15 April, I received a reply from Tom Cox, the MP for Tooting, to my recent petition concerning my accommodation, asking me to see him in his office. Cox could do little for me. He advised I continue phoning the landlords whose properties were vacant.

I contacted UNHCR and was given the number of a landlady to call. I phoned her and was offered a small room at £14 per week on Kingston Hill. This was near my place of work in New Malden. I moved my things and was welcomed by the landlady, but learned the room would not be mine alone: I would share it with two others. Although I was upset, I had no choice but to accept. I told the landlady she should have let me know the circumstances at the start.

I would sometimes attend evening political discussions and lectures with my West Indian friends in Peckham. These discussions covered political theory, right and leftwing political analyses, and current affairs. I would inform every member at these meetings about the issues in South Sudan.

I continued to look for a suitable bedsit, as Kingston Hill was not satisfactory. I learned that there was a vacant bedsit at Sarfield Road in Balham. I went and met the landlord, whom I recognized as Odewale, a Nigerian I had met in 1974. This time, his wife was present. They promised to rent a room to me at £11 per week, if I paid four weeks' deposit.

Odewale showed me the room after I had paid. The agreement was then finalized and on 3 October, I moved to Sarfield Road. With great relief, I felt that I had lain to rest one of my main worries, at least for the time being.

That I took political asylum in Britain where there was little sympathy for my cause almost destroyed me politically. The authorities did not hide their feelings from the start. One foreign friend described my situation as being in the political wilderness.

Getting funding for the APF was extremely difficult. Even friendly nations which had granted some limited assistance did not want to know much about South Sudan. Some questioned whether we would be more reliable than the earlier Anyanya leaders. We knew that they understood the just cause of the South, but none wanted to be identified with the new movement since the Addis Ababa Agreement was still in effect. Since it was not put to a referendum, they could not accept our claim that the majority of Southerners were opposed to the agreement.

I continued to read newspapers and magazines and listen to radio and TV. I used to issue press releases and statements on the political situation in Sudan, although there was little interest from media in UK, Europe, and the USA. The only exception was the BBC's *Focus on Africa*, which occasionally broadcast my press statements.

Coup Attempt in Khartoum

On 2 July 1976, an editor of the *Guardian* phoned to say a coup against the Nimeiri government was taking place. He asked what my view would be if the coup succeeded. I replied that the attempt was good news for me, but I could not yet give my stance in the event of its success. The editor said he would come back to me if it was successful. But he did not, so I presumed that the coup had failed.

Later, I heard that the coup was not a typical attempt by army officers to seize power. Rather, it was a massive armed invasion from Libya organized and led by the former Sudanese Prime Minister, Sadiq al-Mahdi. His was a force comprised of mercenaries, most of them black, recruited with the help of the Libyan government from African countries south of the Sahara. Although the force inflicted heavy casualties on Nimeiri's army, the invasion was poorly organized and led. The invading force was not only defeated but annihilated.

Still, had the invasion occurred before the Anyanya forces were integrated, the outcome might have been different. Anyanya forces played a great role in defending Khartoum against the invading force.

The APF would have welcomed the overthrow of Nimeiri, but would not have expected any benefit, because none of the other Northern political forces were sympathetic to South Sudan's liberation struggle. The coup, therefore, was an expression of a power struggle between the Northern political groupings, including the army.

What worried me during the fighting in Khartoum was the safety of my family in the city. I was relieved when I was later informed by my son-in-law Joseph Mathubier Guelly that the family was well.

The Second Invitation to Ethiopia
Major political changes had taken place in Ethiopia since 1975. The government of Gen. Tafari Benti had been overthrown and Col. Mengistu Haile Mariam had become military leader of Ethiopia. Ethiopian-Sudanese relations had seriously deteriorated. As a result, the Ethiopian government wanted to improve its relationship with the APF and invited me to Ethiopia.

Towards the end of 1976, many Southerners, including some opposed to the APF, wrote urging me to return to Ethiopia whenever I could. I told them that I was frustrated by Ethiopia's treatment of the APF and how I had returned to the UK disappointed. However, I promised to carefully consider any invitation from the Ethiopian authorities.

On 9 September 1976, Elia Duang arrived in London. He blamed me for clinging to a job in the UK instead of returning to lead the APF. I reminded him that the Ethiopian government had stranded me in Addis Ababa. I had struggled to get back to the UK. If I had not returned, my asylum status would have expired, and I would have been reduced to begging. I felt that the government of Ethiopia was full of empty promises. I could not be expected to run a movement when the host government was not rendering material aid. We agreed the movement needed a sympathetic foreign source, or that we must be able to raise our own resources from inside the country as we did in the sixties.

On 13 February 1977, a man from the Ethiopian Airlines office in London delivered a letter to me, which read as follows.

Dear Mr Zino Lual (my nickname) alias G.M.

I am writing to invite you for an extended stay here. I have also included a letter from our friend James (Bol Kur), the Defence Secretary.

You shall be very active in the rescue operation that we dreamed about and you shall meet many of your friends. I am inviting them to join you soon. But your coming is vital and indispensable. You do not have to fear for your job security. It shall be provided for.

We have not invited Duang yet. This information is restricted. The only one with some knowledge besides those mentioned in the enclosed letter is Leo Thuc.

I am sure you will have no need for the return trip. Dispose of everything you have on hand at any price...furniture, housing, job, etc. and try to come within 4 weeks.

"The Friend"
PS: You remember that man Taye Reta.

After having read the letter, I told the messenger I would give it serious consideration.

As indicated, a letter from James Bol Kur was also enclosed. Like the other letters I had received from Southerners in Ethiopia, it urged me to return without delay. Bol said that the Ethiopians had learned the Khartoum government could not be trusted and were going to begin serious negotiations with the APF leadership. I also received a letter from Elia Duang stating that Taye Reta expected me to come to Ethiopia imminently. He wrote, "things have boiled down to being implemented only when you come."

I decided to go to Addis Ababa again, despite my experience with the Ethiopian authorities in 1975-76. I was convinced that if I refused their invitation, the Ethiopians would tell the Southerners they were unable to assist our movement. I told the man who delivered the letter that I had agreed to visit Addis Ababa. I also informed Taye Reta I was coming and that it was my hope that we could make progress.

The next day I went to Decca and applied for three weeks' holiday. This was approved on the condition that I came back on time. I was asked to declare in writing that I would return on time without fail. On 25 February, I informed my landlord that I was going to Africa and paid the rent in advance, until 19 March.

I was provided with two tickets, one for Ethiopia and one to return to the UK. However, my departure for Ethiopia was delayed by the expiry of my refugee travel document. It was eventually renewed, and the date of my departure was fixed for 26 February.

Letter from Philip Pedak

Before I left for Ethiopia, I received a letter from Philip Pedak dated 22 February. He would soon be appointed vice-chairman by the APF Coordinating Committee. Pedak reported on his recent visit to Gambella at the Ethiopia-Sudan border. He had met APF members, many refugees, and members of the New Anyanya. His visit coincided with an incident of fighting between the Anuak and the Nuer.

Pedak suggested the efficiency of the APF and its military wing be improved. He felt steps should be taken to promote unity between various tribes in the Anyanya forces to discourage infighting. Pedak criticized Elia Duang and the APF leadership for advocating the

Anyanya establish camps on a tribal basis. This had led to tension and clashes. Pedak also questioned the role of the members of the APF Coordinating Committee who continued their work in the absence of the chairman and the secretary-general. He said there was growing antagonism between the members of the Committee. He criticized some members of the Committee for advocating negotiations with the Khartoum government.

He concluded by saying that many Southerners believed that strong support was needed for the APF leadership. He said that the APF base must be in a neighboring African country and that Elia Duang and I must return to Ethiopia to be among the people. Another meeting must be convened to lay down a new program for the APF.

Arrival in Addis Ababa

On the morning of 27 February, I arrived in Addis Ababa. As I had in 1975, I felt happy to be in Africa again. However, since I planned to stay for less than four weeks, I had to start consultations straight away.

First, Leo Thuc briefed me on the general situation. Moses Malek, the vice-chairman of the Coordinating Committee, was also there. The same day, I met Taye Reta. He explained the policy changes his government had made which were favorable to our movement. He also informed me that his government had decided to invite our people's leaders in exile from various parts of the world.

On 28 February, I met our new contact and liaison with the Ethiopian regime, a colonel in the Ethiopian army. We exchanged views on the improvement of the relationship between his government and the APF. The Anyanya military camp at the border was functioning well and morale was excellent.

The colonel said that although Assistant Minister Taye Reta

would still have a role, the colonel had been assigned to liaise with the APF. He asked that his identity be kept secret and that he should be referred to as "a representative of a friendly government." He thanked me for coming back to Ethiopia and explained that the invitation was a result of several factors, one of which was the deterioration of Ethiopian-Sudanese relations.

We turned to the decision by the Ethiopian government to invite all the South Sudanese political leaders in exile for talks. The colonel told me that I should request they come to Addis Ababa as soon as possible. We could discuss sending one of us to Kinshasa, to urge APF members there to come to Addis Ababa. Air tickets would be made available.

I thanked the colonel for informing me of the new policy of his government. I was discouraged by the bad experience in 1975 with the government of Tafari Benti. The colonel assured me that such troubles would not be repeated.

I promised that we would make every effort to bring the rest of our colleagues to Ethiopia. I proposed to present to his government a new request for material assistance. He agreed and said we would meet again to continue the discussion.

The same day, I met Leo Thuc to discuss his mission to Kinshasa to inform Francis Mayar, Agolong Chol, and Paul Duang Yak to travel to Addis. I wrote letters to colleagues in Kinshasa as well as Joshua Dau, the APF secretary for information, and Arkangelo Wanji in Uganda and Elia Duang in Italy telling them to come to Addis as early as possible.

APF Present a Second Proposal to the Ethiopian Government
On 2 March, I met the colonel for our first formal talks. The colonel reaffirmed that his government was serious about working with the APF. They were willing to consider any request for assistance,

provided it was within their economic means. I assured him that we would take them at their word and not dwell on the bad experiences of 1975 and 1976. As far as the APF was concerned, we wanted to pick up from where our relations had been positive. We planned to request much the same assistance we had proposed in October 1975.

Then the colonel introduced a new subject. He said that there were several Northern Sudanese political groups active in Ethiopia against the Nimeiri government. The largest was the National United Front (NUF) led by Sherif Hussein el-Hindi. He asked if it was possible for the APF to cooperate with the NUF. I told the colonel that it would be impossible; some of the Northerners had been responsible for even worse suppression in the South than Nimeiri's regime. But I said I would take the matter to the APF Coordinating Committee for consideration. The colonel stressed that cooperation would be beneficial because we had a common enemy.

Two days later, on 4 March, the Coordinating Committee met. I was authorized to present the request for support as proposed. As for the issue of cooperating with the Northern parties, the Committee resolved that a delegation be established to negotiate with them through the host government.

I met the colonel and gave him our request for assistance. The colonel promised that his government would honor its commitments. Moreover, the colonel would chair the talks between the APF delegation and the Northern parties in exile. He said that I should get ready to visit the border soon to meet refugees in various camps there.

Visit to Gambella

On 8 March, the representative and I left in a military plane to Gambella. Gambella, in the far southwest of the country, a former British enclave, was returned to Ethiopia by the al-Azhari government in 1956, soon after the end of the Anglo-Egyptian colonial rule. We arrived at noon and were met by the local administrator and a few refugees.

We set off for Itang, the largest South Sudanese refugee camp in Ethiopia. Since the Akobo uprising of 1974, there had been tension between Southern political activist groups, the integrated Anyanya guerrillas, and the Nimeiri government. As a result, many Southerners fearful of another civil war had gone to Ethiopia and joined the refugees who had refused to go home after the Addis Ababa Agreement. The refugees in Itang numbered over 2,000 and more arrived daily. We met many of them, some of whom I recognized.

We were provided with a Land Rover to travel to the new Anyanya military camp of the APF, more than 50 kilometers from the border. There we were welcomed by the New Anyanya force of about 1,500. Capt. Vincent Kwany Latjor thanked us for our visit and explained some of the hardships they were facing. In response, I said that the representative and I were thankful for the welcome. We were grateful to the representative and his government for assisting us with the camp. I expressed hope that such assistance would continue until our struggle succeeded. I encouraged the force to persevere and maintain unity and avoid the past pitfalls of the old Anyanya guerrillas.

When the guard of honor and the military parade was over, we were taken to have lunch and speak with the officers. We discussed the promised material assistance by the Ethiopian government with the representative. He confirmed that his government would deliver the material aid it had promised to the APF leadership in 1975 and that was why they had asked me to return to Ethiopia from London.

A discussion followed between the representative, Kwany, James Bol, and myself, in which we agreed on urgent support for the camp. A limited number of arms would be delivered immediately to the camp. Several instructors would be assigned to train the New Anyanya force. The supply of food to the camp would be improved, from the unground corn presently available. There would also be two medical assistants assigned to, and a dispensary erected in, the camp.

The representative told us that the rest of the aid would be delivered gradually. There would be no deliberate holding back of the promised assistance.

Before we left, I called commanders Kwany and Bol aside and told them I had lost confidence in our hosts because of the bad faith shown in 1975, but that I had come back because so many, including themselves, appealed to me. I explained that I would return to London after two weeks. As soon as I heard that part of the promised help had been delivered, I would resign from my job in the UK and return. We also discussed personal differences between the two commanders. The representative was included in this discussion; he was already aware of these differences. After resolving them, we were ready to leave for Gambella at 11pm.

At 3am, we arrived in Gambella. We called at the house of Joshua de Lual, an Ethiopian Nuer, the Assistant Administrator in Gambella. Joshua was awoken, food was offered to us, and we ate. At 1pm, we left by plane for Addis Ababa.

New APF policies
An APF Coordinating Committee meeting was convened on 10 March. We resolved that a delegation of myself, Moses Malek, and Agolong

Chol, would enter talks with the representative of the host government on all issues concerning material aid. The Committee confirmed that each of the three South Sudan military zones should have a brigade which would gradually be raised to a division as more military aid was received. Recruitment into the New Anyanya should continue until the maximum strength required by the APF was reached. An APF sub-committee would be set up to work with foreign military experts to draw up a training program for the New Anyanya, and to push forward our cooperation with the Ethiopian government.

Whenever true cooperation developed between the APF and the host government, the APF would need political advisors, financial advisors, political education for the grassroots and the army rank and file, and efficient administrative assistance for a period. We estimated our minimum financial requirement at 1,040,000 Ethiopian Birr, about 100,000 US dollars, per year.

The Coordinating Committee meeting ended on 12 March. As my time was running out, it was imperative that the delegated sub-committee established by the Coordinating Committee meet with the representative to agree on next steps and implementation. Other acts would have to be implemented later by the host government, while some matters could await my return.

On 15 March, the sub-committee met the representative. We discussed several issues and agreed to meet again on 17 March. At that meeting, the representatives of the Northern Sudan political parties would also attend.

APF Delegation Meet Members of Northern National Front

On 17 March, the delegation of Agolong, Moses Malek, and I was taken to the house of the colonel, where we found the delegation of the Northern political parties waiting. Introductions were made by the colonel. I could not recognize any of them although I had heard the name of Sherif el-Hindi, the leader of the delegation. Many of them knew of me. The colonel opened the meeting and said that it was his government's wish that the two sides agree to cooperate since we were both opposed to the government in Khartoum. He reassured us that his government was not only friendly to both sides but would make material assistance available to both sides if there was an agreement to cooperate.

On behalf of the APF, I thanked the colonel but clarified that I would not accept cooperation or alliance with any Northern Sudanese party or group because their attitude towards the South was the same. Each of the main political parties represented in the assembled NUF had oppressed the South during the period it had led the government in Sudan. However, I said that we had accepted the advice by the host government to cooperate with the Northern parties in exile opposed to the Nimeiri regime, under certain conditions. First, our relationship would be called an alliance and not cooperation. Second, all contacts between the sides would be channeled through the representative of the host government. Third, any material aid should be equally shared, or the APF should receive a larger share. Fourth, there should be no merger of the political or military wings of the respective parties. Fifth, military operations against the government forces would be carried out separately. Finally, the APF would appreciate if the Northern NUF openly supported our demands for the independence of South Sudan.

El-Hindi spoke after me. He thanked the colonel for bringing both sides together. He expressed his sincere hope that the host government would make all possible efforts to deepen cooperation or an alliance between the APF and his NUF. He expressed sympathy with the Southerners and put the blame on the unwise policies pursued in the South by successive Northern national governments since independence.

The colonel thanked both groups for the frank expression of views and concluded by saying that he and his government would do what was possible to make an alliance a reality. The meeting then ended. Before we dispersed, the colonel told me that he would see me again very soon.

Final Meetings in Ethiopia
We had another meeting of the Coordinating Committee, attended by Joshua Dau Dhieu. He gave a comprehensive report on the political and military situation in South Sudan. He said that the Nimeiri regime was concerned about the activities of the APF in Ethiopia and was doing all it could to persuade the Ethiopian government to stop aiding the APF. He also added that many South Sudanese political activists were under surveillance by the police; some had been arrested, including the former Regional Minister Benjamin Bol Akok.

My stay was coming to a close. Before I left, I had another round of talks with the colonel in his office. I would base my decision on whether to finally move to Ethiopia on the outcome of these talks. I told him that I would be returning to London shortly. I wished to reaffirm that if his government fulfilled its promises, I would resign my job in the UK and move to Ethiopia to lead the struggle. The colonel reiterated that the promises would be fulfilled. We then parted.

I had been booked to fly on Air France from Addis Ababa to London via Paris on 19 March. Unfortunately, on arrival at the airport, we discovered that the plane was flying via Khartoum. After consulting my colleagues, I decided not to board the flight because of the risk of being intercepted by the Sudanese authorities. I made another booking, again through Air France, to leave Addis Ababa at 3.45pm, this time via Cairo and Paris.

On 21 March, I reported to work. My director was pleased to see me; he was afraid that I might turn up late as I had done in 1975.

After my return to London, I received a letter from Francis Mayar dated 28 April, explaining that the colonel and other members of the Ethiopian government met several South Sudanese politicians in exile, including Elia Duang, Agolong Chol, and himself. The colonel briefed them on the program agreed with the Coordinating Committee, which included assistance to be urgently delivered to the APF, and the sharing of the material assistance with the Northern opposition. Francis Mayar informed me that the Southern politicians in that meeting had approved the efforts. Duang had reservations but Mayar and Col were able to convince him to fall in line.

Resignation and Return to Ethiopia
I had promised the colonel and the commanders of the New Anyanya that I would resign from my job in London and return to Ethiopia. I was only waiting for news that the promised assistance had been delivered. Then I would submit my resignation.

In April, another employee of Ethiopian Airlines in London delivered a message and an air ticket. The message reaffirmed that part of the promised material assistance had been delivered to our New Anyanya camp (later to be called Bilpam) at the border. I was pleased and began to prepare to leave for Addis Ababa. It was not long before I received a copy of a letter addressed to Duang from Agolong in which he wrote, "Our friends have at last started to deliver some of our requests."

On 31 May, I informed my supervisor at Decca Radar that I wished to resign from my job and return to Africa. I had to go, even though the reunion with my family was under consideration by the British authorities. Earlier that month, I had received a letter from the Home Office stating that applications for visas to enter the UK had been received by the British Embassy in Khartoum from Sarah for five children and herself. The letter said that the Home Office raised the concern that my income was not sufficient to support a large family. Nevertheless, they instructed me to ask my employer to send them a letter showing my wages. I had given the letter to my manager, and he promised to take the necessary action.

On 20 June, I told my landlord that I was going away for six months and wished to pay for that period in advance. I further added that if I failed to arrive on time, I would remit another payment to cover another period. He was happy and I paid him. To secure my books and belongings, I bought a large trunk to leave in the bedsit.

11.

Last Months in Ethiopia (1977-1978)

I left for Addis Ababa on 25 June 1977. There was confusion about my arrival, so I was not met at the airport. Members of the APF Coordinating Committee visited me later. Leo Thuc informed me that the Ethiopian government was aware of my arrival.

My colleagues briefed me on the relationship between the APF and the Ethiopian government; it had never been so good. More than 300 arms had been delivered to our New Anyanya camp at Bilpam. Food was being supplied to the camp frequently. Morale was high. There would soon be more deliveries because the Anyanya had cleared a good airstrip. I was pleased with these developments.

Francis Mayar Akon and Agolong Chol Agolong from Kinshasa and Elia Duang Arop, the APF secretary-general, had been in Ethiopia. Mayar and Duang had met host government officials and returned to their respective countries of asylum. Agolong was still here. He had gone to visit the border and was expected back soon.

On 28 June, Leo Thuc informed me that my appointment with the representative of the host government was delayed. Our old friend Taye Reta would meet me first. He was away but would soon be back.

Discussions with Rev. Philip Abbas Gaboush

Agolong returned from Gambella. On 30 June, he briefed me in the Pan-Afrique Hotel concerning the situation at the Anyanya camp and the conditions of South Sudanese refugees in Itang and the other camps. He was pleased with the weapon deliveries. Although the number delivered was far from what was required, they were of good quality. Agolong was concerned about the lack of discipline among the officers and men, which he hoped would improve when the training began. The New Anyanya commanders, Capt. Vincent Kwany and Lt. James Bol, were hostile to him. They knew that Agolong was acting secretary-general in place of Elia Duang, who was delayed in Italy. I advised Agolong to not press the issue until we moved to Bilpam and could act. Agolong also told me that Rev. Philip Abbas Gaboush, the former Nuba MP in Sudan, had raised the idea of the Nuba Movement merging with the APF.

My immediate reaction was that we could not accept a merger; it would destroy the South Sudanese nationalist cause for which we had fought for years. I understood that Rev. Abbas had united with the main Northern Sudanese parties such as the Umma, the DUP, and the Communists in opposition to the Nimeiri regime. If the APF collaborated with those parties, the South would lose its cause. Nevertheless, I had sympathy for the idea of cooperation, if the Nuba spelled out their cause for fighting and broke away from the Northern parties. The Nuba would have to organize themselves separately from the Southerners; then we could cooperate as allies against the common enemy. My colleagues agreed. This position became the basis of the APF negotiation with the Nuba elements headed by Abbas.

On 4 July, I visited Rev. Abbas, accompanied by Agolong. Abbas said that we Southerners had been fighting for years and that our grievances were like those of the Nuba people. He said that it would be better for the South, the Nuba, the Fur, and other indigenous African people to join hands and fight for "Black Power" in Sudan. Sudan belongs to black people, he said. "The Arabs are oppressing and exploiting us as if we are a minority. When we join hands we will be able to take over, and the Arabs will lose power," Abbas concluded. He proposed we both join a Sudanese broad front, to include Northern political parties such as the anti-Imperialist Front, the Umma Party, the DUP branch of Sherif el-Hindi, and others, to overthrow the Nimeiri regime.

I rejected his proposals and explained why. I was opposed to the open unity of the black community with the objective of taking power in Sudan because it would leave black people open to accusations of racism. Furthermore, since the black people of Sudan were divided by culture and religion, it would take a long time to bring about political unity. If the Nuba people had awakened politically and were prepared to launch their own liberation movement, the APF would be willing to ally with them. But they would have to state their national objectives to the outside world as we had done.

As for cooperation with the Northern parties opposed to Khartoum, the APF had made it clear to the Ethiopian government that we would fight separately against Khartoum since we had separate causes for fighting.

Finally, I told Rev. Abbas that South Sudanese identity had been fully established and the APF leadership could not allow that to be lost in the high seas of the Northern Sudanese struggle for power. Our talks with Abbas did not make progress.

Other Southern Sudanese groups emerge

Another item discussed when Agolong returned from Gambella was the emergence of several Southern political groups among the refugees in Ethiopia. At that time, these groups had small followings. They were mainly motivated by tribal jealousies and leadership ambitions. Examples were the Southern Sudanese Socialist Movement in Exile led by Akec Mohamed and the Imatong Republic by Gamson Gonda.

These groups emerged because of the material assistance delivered to the APF. This was causing potentially explosive rivalry. Many Southerners in Addis Ababa booked appointments to meet me at that time. Many criticized the APF. Agolong and I answered most of their questions. We said that we were aware of what needed to be done, but full assistance had not yet been received. Even if we received all that we needed, we would have to wait for the Nimeiri regime to abrogate the Addis Ababa Agreement before we embarked on a full-scale armed struggle. We did not want Southerners to blame the APF for having destroyed the agreement.

Meeting the Ethiopian Government Representative

I was still waiting to meet formally with the representative, the Ethiopian colonel. On 18 July, the colonel arrived at my hotel looking unhappy. I introduced Agolong and told the representative I had resigned from my job in London to give my full attention to the liberation movement. The representative accused me of exposing our cooperation because I was meeting many people. I told him that I was sorry to hear such remarks. I assured him I had never exposed any secrets. I reminded the representative that I had been a senior government official, a cabinet minister, and now leader of the APF. I had handled many secrets. I agreed it was vitally important to keep the secrets of our foreign friends. He became apologetic and said the reason they had put me in Pan-Afrique Hotel was to separate me from my younger colleagues, and so that they could meet me without fear of being watched by the agents of the Nimeiri regime.

I was sorry, but I could not isolate myself from my people. No leader should isolate himself from the people whom he is serving.

The representative changed the subject to the issue of the Northern political leaders with whom they were also collaborating. He accused Agolong of disclosing secrets to one of those Northern leaders. We denied this.

The talks then became progressively more friendly. We said that we had rejected the attempts by the Northern opposition parties in exile to merge with the APF. We would have had nothing to do with them had it not been for the advice by the host government. Even so, we had agreed to operate separately from them while sharing the material assistance offered to us.

The representative then briefed me on how the host government had implemented the agreement on assistance to the APF and Anyanya forces. In addition to the material assistance already delivered, six military instructors and some medical supplies would soon be sent to the camp.

Another visit to Gambella

On 19 July, the representative visited again, and informed me that arrangements had been made to fly me, my colleagues, and the six military instructors to Gambella on 21 July. I thanked him and said it was my intention to move to Bilpam to establish my office there.

On 21 July, we left in a military plane for Gambella. On arrival, we learned that Capt. Vincent Kwany was unwell and had left the camp. Soon after, I received a message from the Acting Commander, Lt. James Bol Kur, welcoming us and the military instructors who had travelled with us.

I wrote back to instruct Bol to prepare to accommodate and feed the instructors. Unfortunately, our onward journey to Bilpam was postponed because the boat provided was too small for all of us. On 24 July, a new boat was provided. We left for Bilpam the same day.

To get to Bilpam, we travelled the River Baro, known in South Sudan as the River Sobat, which flows into the White Nile near Malakal. Our boat was piloted by Cham Adhom, a South Sudanese intellectual who had graduated from Khartoum University. He also served in the first Anyanya and like us, did not go home after the Addis Ababa Agreement because he was opposed to it.

After an hour, we went ashore at Akado, a small American missionary station with two white missionaries, a man and a woman. One of the Southerners to meet us there was Opong, a former Anyanya officer who served in the Upper Nile Brigade under the command of Col. Joseph Akuon and his deputy, Lt. Col. Gai Tut. Opong volunteered to resume active service in the Anyanya. I said that he and others would be welcomed. Opong added that thousands of young men in Upper Nile were eager to join. We then returned to the boat and continued our journey.

At noon, we reached the point where we had to disembark and walk. We had to cross a swamp of knee-deep water. It took us three hours to get to Bilpam. We were met by Bol, who invited me to inspect a guard of honor commanded by a new Anyanya officer. After that, we were taken to our quarters. After we had taken refreshments, Bol briefed us on the general camp situation and Kwany's condition.

He said that because of the military assistance received, the morale of the new Anyanya had improved, as had its discipline. Kwany's health had also improved, although he was still mentally unwell. His illness was exacerbated by his consumption of alcohol.

The report about Kwany was a shock. We expected Kwany and

Bol to have made much progress in organizing the Upper Nile front into a national headquarters. In any case, we thanked Bol for his comprehensive briefing and asked him to make the military instructors as comfortable as possible.

I then wrote to Kwany to ask him to return to the camp to meet us if he felt he had improved. Kwany returned the same day. Agolong and I asked how he was feeling. At the start, Kwany thought that he had malaria, but as time went on, he felt mentally unwell. He left the camp and began treatment. Regarding his mental disturbances, he had had similar attacks on previous occasions and been treated. He denied that he had been drinking. He had been examined by a doctor but said that he was feeling quite normal now. This pleased us. We decided he should resume his duties until we could arrange for him to go to Addis Ababa for further examination and treatment.

We then called another meeting, attended by Bol and a few of the junior officers. On the agenda included recruitment of those young Southern Sudanese who were arriving from various parts of the South. It was agreed that every South Sudanese volunteer of the right age should report to the camp's recruitment center. They included former Anyanya servicemen, former students in Addis Ababa University, and other educated people, some of whom could be trained as officers. Bol was opposed to the recruitment of the educated young men from Addis Ababa and certain former Anyanya. He did not give clear reasons why. So, I overruled his opposition with the support of Agolong, Kwany, and others at the meeting. Bol also objected to the recruitment of Opong, whom we had met at Akado. Bol accused Opong of causing a fight between the Nuer and Anuak in 1975 and made several other accusations against him. These were denied by Opong, but as there were witnesses, we decided to suspend his recruitment. Towards the end of the meeting,

I also promoted several soldiers recommended by Kwany and Bol.

Within the week of our arrival, the military instructors started work. The whole force in the camp was scheduled to undergo refresher training. A program for training new recruits was also being drawn up.

The implementation of a training course as part of the promised assistance to the APF raised the morale of both the political and the military wings considerably. On 29 July, we witnessed a sizeable force of the New Anyanya undergoing weapons training in new tactics. It was impressive.

Agolong and I met Kwany and Bol to discuss administrative issues in the movement and their roles as commanders of the New Anyanya force. We were concerned at the serious differences between them. This was worsened by Kwany's parlous mental health, which had undermined the respect for Kwany from Bol and some of the other officers. Most seriously, Bol had criticized Kwany, even to the representative of the host government. We feared the representative might use these differences to keep them divided, particularly as his government was not yet fully committed to supporting the APF.

These talks gave us an opportunity to promote reconciliation between them. We determined to do this, not only as APF leaders but as their elders, since they were young and lacked experience. The discussions appeared successful, and the two commanders promised us that they would, from then on, work harmoniously.

On 3 August, Kwany invited me to speak at a parade organized to celebrate our visit. The newly received arms were displayed and the audience applauded with satisfaction. Before the parade dispersed, I gave the recruits a chance to ask questions and give brief comments. The main question asked was whether the arms were sufficient to start an armed struggle and if they were, why were we not beginning to fight? I gave several reasons why the APF should wait. First, the number of arms was not adequate and some of the most effective weapons had not yet been received. Second, we had to wait for the complete abrogation of the agreement. This was to avoid being used as a scapegoat by those Southern leaders who signed the agreement in Addis Ababa. Third, our benefactors were opposed to the APF embarking on military operations before their approval, because they feared that it might undermine the efforts of both governments to achieve peace on both sides of the border. Lastly, the APF needed time to establish a strong, well-trained guerrilla army which could be operational throughout South Sudan.

The next day, another meeting was convened to discuss recruitment. It was agreed that a massive recruitment drive should be launched despite the uncertainty hanging over material assistance. We resolved to prioritize ex-Anyanya officers and men, who would immediately go through the planned refresher courses. Following them would be volunteers to be enrolled from all over the South.

It was soon realized that the air deliveries of food supplies had suddenly stopped, leading to a food shortage. The only food left was corn flour, unground corn, cooking oil, and onions. We did not know why deliveries had stopped. At night, many soldiers went to the Baro River and caught fish, which often began to rot before they were cooked. We had no option but to eat them. I wrote urgently to the representative of the host government informing him of the food shortage and the adverse effects it was having. I asked for the food deliveries to be resumed. I wrote to John Jack Deang, the senior member of the APF Coordinating Committee in Addis Ababa, and told him to deliver my letter by hand to the representative and urge action.

Having no immediate response, I wrote another letter to Maj. Wandarad, the Chief Administrator in Gambella, appealing to him to remedy the situation in the camp and to coordinate the resumption of food deliveries with the authorities in Addis Ababa. As the situation grew bleaker, Agolong and I decided to visit Gambella to discuss the situation with Wandarad in person. I wrote another letter to him to send us a boat.

The next day, Wandarad sent us a boat. We left for Gambella taking Kwany, who would proceed to Addis Ababa for medical treatment. Bol and a newly commissioned officer, James Tab, accompanied us as bodyguards.

We stopped at Itang refugee camp and spent the night there. We met the committee of South Sudanese refugees and discussed their hunger, ill-health, and lack of land for cultivation. The following day, we continued to Gambella. Our boat developed engine trouble twice, but we eventually arrived. We went straight to Wandarad's office and briefed him on the grave situation. Wandarad promised to take appropriate action but warned us that communications between Gambella and Addis Ababa had been disrupted for the past two weeks.

While in Wandarad's office, I sent a telegram to the representative in Addis Ababa, again highlighting the food crisis. Wandarad informed us that a few lorries would leave for Addis Ababa the next day. We decided that Agolong and Kwany would proceed to Addis Ababa, while I continued to wait for a response in Gambella. Before they left, I wrote another letter for Agolong to take to the representative concerning the situation in the camp. In the evening, we received a telegram from the representative saying, "We regret we are unable to normalize the situation in the immediate future due to unforeseen circumstances."

On 5 August, I felt violent stomach pain. The pain worsened and continued throughout the night. In the morning, I went to Gambella Hospital to see a doctor. A test revealed that I was suffering from amoebic dysentery. I was treated and improved after a few days. Members of the movement paid for my treatment.

Once I recovered, I spoke with Opal, an Ethiopian Anuak junior administrator, about the shortages in the camp. It had been agreed that a small boat would leave for Bilpam the next day with a limited supply of food. The following day, I met Kalashew, the UNHCR representative, to discuss the food shortage and lack of health care for the refugees. He promised that steps would be taken to deal with the situation.

I met Wandarad again along with the boat captain, Cham Adhom, at 5pm. Wandarad informed me he had changed his mind and would not send emergency food to Bilpam. Meanwhile, I heard that the shortages had worsened, and 26 soldiers had run away.

The negative responses to my appeals justified my suspicion that the Ethiopian government was deliberately using food shortages at Bilpam to drive a wedge between the APF's political leadership and the Anyanya guerrilla army. This was reminiscent of what had been done by foreign powers prior to the Addis Ababa Agreement.

On 12 August, Wandarad informed me that he would visit Bilpam to see things for himself. I insisted that we go together but he refused. In the evening, he returned with a letter from Bol. The letter explained the worsening situation. The number of trainees had reduced to 100. He wanted to know why the camp was not being supplied with food.

After seeing the conditions at Bilpam, Wandarad promised to send food, even without approval from Addis Ababa. The boat was sent with 12 sacks of corn. I expressed my gratitude.

On 13 August, Wandarad gave me a note from the representative saying I was urgently required to return to Addis Ababa. I told Wandarad to inform the representative that I could not return before I completed my mission to Bilpam. He promised to convey that message to the representative.

I sent a telegram to the representative repeating my verbal

message and another to Agolong urging him to send a report on his mission to Addis Ababa. I also asked Agolong to find out why I was required to return to Addis Ababa. On the same day, Wandarad informed me that large quantities of food had arrived in Gambella, enroute to Bilpam. This was a great relief.

I received a letter from Agolong explaining he had met the representative, delivered my letter, and done what he could to explain the desperate situation. The representative promised to take steps to resolve the crisis in Bilpam. But the representative expressed doubt over any quick solution, particularly as it was the rainy season and the roads were flooded, causing difficulties in transporting supplies. He also alluded to the APF's internal problems.

Their meeting ended without a serious commitment from the representative. He did, however, pay 5000 Birr, about 500 US dollars, into the APF accounts to meet expenses. As agreed, Agolong would bring the 11 educated Southern recruits to join the training at Bilpam. Kwany had been admitted to hospital, but the doctor was optimistic that he might soon be discharged. The representative was quite upset to learn of Kwany's condition.

The representative also asked Agolong about the Northern political parties, and particularly about Rev. Abbas of the General Union of Nuba (GUN). Apparently, Sadiq al-Mahdi of the Umma Party had returned to Sudan. We did not know about Sherif el-Hindi of the DUP.

There was no further request for me to return to Addis, so I decided to wait in Gambella. After a few days, Wandarad confirmed that the large quantity of food brought in by lorries from Addis Ababa was in Gambella and was being slowly transported by boats to Bilpam.

I again asked Wandarad to arrange a telephone call with the representative. He said he would try again. That afternoon, I spoke to the representative who expressed regret for the shortages and promised that the situation would soon be remedied. He told me I was required in Addis for important consultations, after which I could return to Bilpam. He confirmed that 11 educated cadres would leave with Agolong to join the training. I confirmed I would return to Addis Ababa soon.

Soon after, Cham Adhom, the boat pilot, informed me that Acting Commander Bol was leaving Bilpam for Gambella. Cham asked whether I had been informed. I had not. That afternoon, I asked Wandarad whether Bol was coming to Gambella on his own initiative, or if he was being called, and if so, by whom. Wandarad said Bol was coming to see him. He had called Bol to Gambella to proceed to Addis Ababa, as required by the Ethiopian government representative. I asked Wandarad why he had not told me. Wandarad said he was answerable to his superiors, not the APF.

I told Wandarad I viewed Bol's coming as mutiny, and I held the Ethiopian government responsible. I returned to my hotel. Shortly after, Wandarad came and repeated that my presence was urgently required in Addis Ababa. I agreed to go.

On 19 August, Bol arrived in my hotel to inform me that he was on his way to Addis Ababa because the representative had called for him. I was furious. I ordered him to return to Bilpam. I would find out why Bol was wanted in Addis Ababa and why I had not been informed. Bol promised to return to Bilpam and left the hotel amicably.

At noon, I went to Gambella airport. Agolong and the 11 young, educated Southerners on their way to join the New Anyanya had arrived. I greeted Agolong and thanked him for his report on his mission to Addis Ababa. I briefed him on the slightly improved situation in the camp and informed him that I was going to Addis Ababa as requested by the representative. I also explained that I had ordered Bol to return to Bilpam but did not know whether he had.

Agolong was upset by the development. He felt that there seemed to be a change of policy by the Ethiopian government towards the APF after our move to Bilpam. The mood was more hostile, but he did not know why. However, they had been quite cooperative in organizing the transport of the 11 educated cadres.

As we spoke, Bol turned up. He informed us that he was on his way to Addis Ababa to meet the representative. I was stunned; Bol was clearly insubordinate. Agolong asked Bol, "Didn't the APF Chairman order you this morning? Are you prepared to disobey his orders?" Bol said, "I am complying with the instructions of the representative who asked me to come to Addis Ababa. Moreover, I have the obligation to go and meet Rev. Abbas. We have been working together with the approval of the representative in the absence of the chairman." I could not understand what was going on. To me, it felt like Bol considered himself the alternative leader of the APF. It appeared that I was no longer considered the leader of my own movement.

Bol went on to tell Agolong that he had seen the 11 cadres who had arrived and opposed their journey to the camp to join the training. He said that he had informed the representative of his position and that the representative supported Bol's view.

If Bol had behaved like this when we were at the camp, I would have ordered his arrest. So, I approached Wandarad who had come to the airport to see me off. I explained Bol's insubordination. I asked him to place Bol under arrest in Gambella. Wandarad pleaded that he was not in any way involved in the relations between the movement and his government and that he could not arrest Bol.

I said if Bol could not be arrested he should at least be prevented from flying to Addis Ababa. Again, Wandarad declined and said the representative was expecting Bol. He did not know why I had not been informed. He suggested that the 11 cadres should remain in Gambella until we had resolved the disagreement.

Further talks with Wandarad seemed pointless. I said to Agolong that we should go to Addis Ababa to find out what was going on. Meanwhile, we agreed to leave the 11 cadres in Gambella pending further instructions.

Return to Addis Ababa

Bol, Agolong, and I left for Addis in the same plane. I did not want to be put up in a hotel again, so when we arrived, I went to a room rented by the APF. Senior members of the APF who visited were frustrated by Bol's behavior. Since foreigners might take advantage of the situation, we had to try to avoid being emotional.

Our colleagues briefed us on the war between Ethiopia and Somalia, which was escalating daily. We were aware these developments might adversely affect our relationship with Ethiopia.

On 21 August, I received a letter from Joshua Dau, the APF secretary for information, in Kampala. He wrote that there had been a mass arrest of Southerners accused of political activities against the Nimeiri regime, some of whom were found in possession of what the government called subversive documents from abroad.

On 22 August, I instructed Leo Thuc to inform the Ethiopian colonel that I had returned and wished to meet him. Later, Tusai, one of the host government officials, visited. He mentioned that the colonel was aware of our return and that he would meet us on his return.

Meanwhile, I met an official of UNHCR responsible for the refugees in Gambella. I explained the grave food shortage facing South Sudanese refugees in places like Itang. Healthcare was also poor. The UNHCR man thanked us for our concern and promised that his office would take steps to remedy the situation.

Capt. Kwany arrived, after having been discharged from the hospital. The medical report stated that he had recovered from his mental illness but that future attacks could not be ruled out.

Meeting with the Representative in Addis

On 28 August, we met the representative, the Ethiopian colonel. Present from the APF were Agolong, Leo Thuc, Kwany, Bol, and myself. After the colonel had greeted everyone, he asked everyone other than me to leave.

The most serious issues to discuss were the food shortage and Bol's insubordination. I told the representative that I suspected that there had been a fundamental change of policy by the Ethiopian government. There had never been such shortages before my arrival in the camp on 24 July. I sent many messages requesting the resumption of food deliveries but received no reply.

I went to Addis Ababa in the same plane with Bol after he had refused my order to return to the camp. It was my view that if Bol was required to be in Addis Ababa, I should have been informed.

The colonel said he did not want to argue and would explain to Bol that he had made a mistake. The colonel went on to say that it was my mistake to have gone to the camp without a letter of introduction from him to Kwany and Bol. With an introduction, the commanders would have not disobeyed my orders nor shown disrespect.

I told the colonel that I had been elected leader of the movement and that I did not need an introduction to my own organization. Besides, his accompanying me to the camp in early 1977 implied introduction. All members of the APF, including Kwany and Bol, understood that the APF was operating inside Ethiopia with the latter's permission. But under no circumstances did we imagine that the Ethiopian authorities could control the movement to exclude its own leaders.

I gave the representative copies of letters which Bol had written to foreign embassies and leaders such as Fidel Castro of Cuba, as well as a copy of an APF draft constitution, which Bol and

Rev. Abbas of GUN had jointly drafted. I asked the representative whether he was aware of these activities. He said he was not.

The representative did not say much more. He then recalled the rest of the APF members. To them, he said that Bol had disobeyed my orders at Gambella on 19 August. He reprimanded Bol for contacting Rev. Abbas and other opposition figures, as well as embassies, without my knowledge or that of the Ethiopian authorities.

When the representative finished, I thanked him for acknowledging the insubordination and misconduct of Bol. In my capacity as APF Chairman and commander-in-chief of the New Anyanya, I reiterated my orders that Bol be suspended until tried by court-martial at Bilpam. He was to be placed under arrest and be held in custody of the Ethiopian authorities and transferred to Bilpam.

The representative replied saying the host country did not want our movement to face problems before having matured. He repeated that I was mistaken for having moved to Bilpam before word was sent to the camp leaders through Administrator Wandarad. Agolong intervened, saying that we had sent a message about our visit on 21 July. This should have been sufficient unless the representative insisted that the APF chairman and secretary-general must be permitted to enter their own camp by their own officers.

Bol was given the floor. He said that since I had been in the UK and struggled to come back, the host government was in sole charge of the movement.

To our surprise, the representative did not dissociate himself from this claim. His only reaction was to say that Kwany and Bol are soldiers and should not speak in a political meeting. I responded that officers like Kwany and Bol are political leaders too and may speak at a political meeting if they maintained strict discipline.

The attitude of the representative emboldened Bol, who burst out saying that the 11 cadres are likely to pose a danger to the movement, should they be permitted to enter training. Agolong challenged Bol to produce evidence against these young Southerners keen to contribute to the struggle. Bol failed to give a satisfactory explanation. He and the representative seemed to have a common concern: a fear of educated Southerners finding their way into the movement and consolidating its strength. It was not in Ethiopia's interests to have a well-organized, strong Southern movement, as this would compel the Sudanese government to retaliate by strengthening its support for Ethiopian rebel movements operating inside Sudan. Bol saw the incorporation of young Southerners better educated than him as a threat to his position.

Eventually, the representative asked Bol to apologize for his insubordination at the camp and at Gambella. I was prepared to forgive Bol on all counts except for his refusal to allow the 11 to join the training. This was unacceptable and contrary to the resolution of the 26 July meeting at Bilpam. I said that to prove his patriotism, Bol must obey my orders. The representative urged Bol to accept the 11 cadres to join the training. However, Bol remained adamant against their participation. Nothing could convince him otherwise.

The representative then proposed to send the 11 cadres elsewhere in Ethiopia to receive a comparable military training course. Bol immediately rejected this proposal. Agolong and I did not favor it either. We suspected the host government would take advantage of our divisions and assume control over our military wing.

Bol then threatened to resign from the movement because Agolong and I were against him. As the row reached its peak, the representative appealed to Bol, Agolong, and I to calm down. He appealed to us to unite for the common cause. I said that unity was essential, but we faced a clear challenge to the APF's unity from Bol's lack of discipline. The situation was being made worse because the representative was undermining my authority by supporting Bol.

The representative reiterated that we should unite. If we could not, he said that we should hand over control of Bilpam and the Anyanya to the host authorities. Of course, we rejected this. The representative then apologized for making this suggestion. He asked all present at the meeting to forgive one another.

I spoke again, stressing that for relationships to be rebuilt, Bol must carry out my orders. There were other important issues: I must be allowed to return to Bilpam, our food supply must be resumed, and the Ethiopian government should formally recognize the APF. Yet again, the representative evaded these issues. Instead, he said we should shake hands and accept reconciliation. I accepted this with difficulty. I suspected the representative of being behind most of our setbacks. I knew the future of the relations between the APF and the host government was uncertain. Even so, we all shook hands.

Pessimistically, Agolong and I thanked the representative for attending. We also drew his attention to the unresolved items on the agenda, such as the shortage of food in Bilpam. He promised another meeting.

More meetings in Addis
On 30 August, the APF Coordinating Committee was briefed on the meeting between the host government representative and APF leaders. In view of the reconciliation at the meeting of 28 August, Kwany and Bol attended as ex-officio Committee members. It was agreed that despite the apparent change of policy of the host government towards the APF, we should continue to exercise patience. In the same meeting, APF financial affairs were discussed, and a budget was passed.

Our main concerns remained the shortage of food and deteriorating health conditions in the camp. This was interrupting training. We needed negotiations between the host government and the APF to resume. There had been slow progress in the implementation of the promises made by the host government in 1975. The APF had submitted its annual budget requirement, but no reply had been received. We were also increasingly weary of the Ethiopian authorities dealing with the APF political leaders and commanders separately.

The Coordinating Committee resolved that these issues be discussed by an APF delegation of the chairman, the secretary-general, and the two commanders.

On 4 September, the Ethiopian representative met the APF delegation in his office. He requested the APF write to the Ethiopian government about the objectives of the movement. Since Ethiopia was poor and had numerous problems of its own, the Ethiopian government had no objection to us seeking material assistance from any African country. They would allow assistance to pass through Ethiopian territory on the way to South Sudan. He also offered the APF a broadcast on the former Voice of Gospel Radio station.

We explained that our objectives had been put in writing when we first appealed to their government in October 1975. I reiterated that the APF was a successor to the former Anyanya and its various political wings. The aim of the APF was to struggle uncompromisingly until South Sudan attained independence from Northern Sudanese oppression.

Turning to the second point, we thanked him for keeping our options open, but were still in need of Ethiopia's help in facilitating our contact with other African states.

We were also thankful for the offer of radio broadcasting. This would enable us to educate the outside world on the gross human abuses Khartoum was perpetrating against South Sudanese civilians.

The representative said that his government was puzzled when it saw South Sudanese leaders, especially those participating in the Nimeiri government, betraying the APF. For example, during the recent OAU conference in Freetown, Sierra Leone, certain Southern ministers attacked the government of Ethiopia, accusing it of subverting the government of Sudan by supporting the APF and remnants of the Anyanya.

There was a great deal more that we wanted to discuss, but the representative was evasive. Agolong did ask about the Northern opposition parties active in exile. The representative said these opposition parties had requested the Ethiopian government support them in their struggle against the Nimeiri regime in 1976. This request was not rejected or accepted. It was not true that the host government supported a merger of these parties and the APF. They accepted my view, which accepted cooperation, but not a merger.

The representative made it clear that he had no wish to discuss the other items on the agenda of 28 August, such as solving the food shortage at Bilpam, why I had been recalled to Addis Ababa, finding a solution to the training of the 11 cadres, or implementation of the agreement on assisting the APF. Asked whether he could agree when these issues could be definitely discussed, he remained evasive.

On 24 September, the Coordinating Committee met Johnny Rasson, who had just returned from Gambella. He said that there was no improvement in the food situation at Bilpam. Healthcare was still bad. The training had stopped.

Contact with the Derg

There was a stalemate between the movement and the representative, which we suspected was the policy of the host government. After consulting with senior members of the Committee, Agolong contacted the PMAC (Derg) Secretary-General through a junior official. Agolong met the junior official briefly and explained the relationship between the APF and the Ethiopian government. On

27 September, word came from the PMAC Secretary-General's office asking we meet him tomorrow.

An emergency meeting of the Coordinating Committee was convened to discuss our options. Some members thought a meeting with a top PMAC member would imply accusing the representative of failing in his duty and would turn him against the APF. Others felt that we had had enough delays and that it was time for us to look beyond the representative and find out the true policy of the host government. Most members favored meeting the PMAC Secretary-General, so we proceeded with the appointment. On 28 September, Agolong and I met the PMAC Secretary-General at 11.45am in his office.

We were cordially received. We explained the background of relations between the host government and the APF since 1975. We expressed thanks for the progress made between 1976 and August 1977 and disappointment about the recent problems, including a lack of communication between the APF leadership and the representative of the host government.

The PMAC Secretary-General listened carefully to what we had to say. He said that there had not been any change of policy from his government, and that their resolve to help our oppressed people was intact. He promised to find out what had caused the stagnation in our relationship and do his best to return the relationship to normal. We went away hopeful that significant changes, even if they might not fully favor the APF, would soon emerge.

In the same meeting, we asked the position of his government on the APF's objective of South Sudan's independence. Without hesitation, we were told that the government disagreed with the objective of fighting for the independence of South Sudan. Since Ethiopia was fighting the Eritrean rebels whose aim was to achieve independence from Ethiopia, it would be contradictory for them to support the APF in fighting for independence from Khartoum. The policy of the host government in supporting the APF was to assist it to achieve a solution of the South Sudan problem within the framework of a united Sudan.

I said that the causes of Eritrea and of South Sudan were different. Ours was a colonial case. The Northern Sudanese took over South Sudan in 1956 and ruled it as a colony with an iron fist. That was why the APF did not believe in any other settlement than independence. We had little doubt that this was now the main point of disagreement between the APF and the Ethiopian government.

The APF Keeps a Low Profile

In early October, the representative came to Agolong. He had been instructed to tell us that we should scale down our operations within Ethiopia. This included APF Committee meetings, press statements, and military activities. We were not surprised, because of our recent difficulties. We asked if he could give us the reason. He said that there had been a remarkable improvement of relations between the Sudanese and Ethiopian governments, following mediation between them by some African states at the OAU meeting in Freetown.

We convened the Coordinating Committee. After a lengthy discussion, we agreed to wait it out. Many felt that Khartoum would not be able to resist pressure from those Arab states committed to supporting Eritrea against Ethiopia. When that time came, Ethiopia would resume its sympathy for the APF.

Some blamed the weakening of our relations with the host government on the infiltration of the Ethiopian government by Northern opposition parties, who posed as rivals to our liberation movement. Ethiopia was simply interested in the overthrow of Nimeiri's regime and hoped for a new, socialist government in Sudan. In such an event, Ethiopia would discard the Southern liberation movement, particularly because of the issue of independence for the South. Independence was unpopular among the OAU member states, which did not want to change the colonial boundaries on which their independence was based.

I had written to Mengistu on 16 July 1977 in response to the letter sent to him by Rev. Abbas. Abbas had claimed the existence of a "Sudanese Provisional Government in exile," with troops along the borders of Sudan in Zaïre, Uganda, and Ethiopia. This suggested that the Northern political parties in exile had merged with the APF. I told Mengistu this was false, and that I had only accepted a loose alliance between political organizations against the current regime in Sudan, based on equality and common friendship with the Ethiopian authorities. Each organization must operate from its own territory.

When the oppressive regime was removed, a fair share of power would have to be negotiated. The alliance members must agree on a solution acceptable to the majority of South Sudanese. This view was accepted by the host government. It was ludicrous for Abbas to think that the South Sudanese were so docile as to be pushed about like in the old days of North-South politics. Another major difference with Abbas was that he favored launching a war against the Nimeiri regime without proper preparations. The APF wanted to begin with a guerrilla war and slowly develop a conventional one. I concluded by reassuring Mengistu that the APF was willing to negotiate the terms of an alliance with the Northern opposition parties in exile under Ethiopian mediation.

Negotiations with Libya
The situation in Bilpam was not improving. The attitude of the host government remained unpredictable. The APF's political and military activities had been scaled down. In these circumstances,

we initiated contact with the Libyan government with a view to ask for their material assistance.

On 25 September 1977, Agolong wrote to Muammar Gaddafi of Libya. Enclosed with the letter was a detailed memorandum, which explained the historical background and the continued failure by successive Northern Sudanese governments to address the problem of the South. We denounced and rejected the Addis Ababa Agreement. We explained our requirements from his government. We wrote that we knew Nimeiri's government was hostile to Libya and assured him the APF leadership was resolved and determined to support Libya. We appealed to Gaddafi to give our memorandum his full consideration. To put our grievances and requirements across in greater detail, we asked for permission to visit Libya and speak with Gaddafi personally. Agolong visited the Libyan Embassy in Addis Ababa to deliver the letter. The embassy promised to send it to Tripoli.

On 4 October, Agolong conveyed a message from the Libyan Embassy confirming an invitation to send a delegation of two to Libya, which turned out to be Agolong and me.

On 9 October, Agolong and I met the Libyan ambassador. He told us that tickets would soon be made available. Then we casually met the representative of the host government who asked our reasons for visiting Libya. I reminded him of what he had told us more than three months ago, advising us to seek material assistance from an African country and that his government would have no objection. He laughed and apologized for having forgotten.

The next day, Agolong and I had blood tests and vaccinations in preparation for our trip. We took our travel documents to the Embassy and were told to collect them once entry visas had been stamped. We had been booked to fly from Addis Ababa to Tripoli via Rome on 14 October.

On arrival in Tripoli, we were met by two Libyan officials. Journalists covered our arrival. We told them that giving publicity to our visit to Libya might adversely affect their relations with Khartoum, but they said that they did not care.

On 16 October, two officials met us. They introduced themselves and told us that for security reasons we should not reveal their identities to anyone else. We assured them that we would not do so. Then, the talks began. We communicated in English, although we switched to Arabic occasionally. Agolong's Arabic was better than mine. The leader of the Libyan delegation said that our visit was appreciated by Gaddafi, who passed his greetings and good wishes to us. I expressed our gratitude at being received. I explained that we had outlined our requests in the Memorandum sent in September, which the Libyans confirmed had been received. We went on to present our requests in more detail. Our short-term needs were material assistance for our struggle. Long-term requirements included the training of our people in both military and civil skills.

We continued the talks over several days, with a day's break for sightseeing on the Mediterranean shore where we saw fascinating Roman ruins. As the discussion progressed, Agolong and I gave more details on the origins of the conflict. We also explained how the hostility of the Nimeiri regime to Libya gave the Libyan government and the APF a common interest. Both needed to cooperate to bring about the demise of the Nimeiri regime.

The head of the Libyan delegation said that his government was willing to grant assistance to the APF if the Ethiopian government permitted the APF to assemble 200 men inside Ethiopia. He asked that the APF obtain travel documents for these men so that Libya could issue them entry visas and fly them to Libya for military training. As soon as they completed that training, the

Libyans would help airlift the men to their bases in South Sudan in accordance with the arrangements made by the APF. I accepted this offer with thanks but said that we were currently uncertain whether the Ethiopian government would agree to issue our men travel documents. Instead, I asked the Libyan authorities to provide travel documents. The Libyan delegation insisted that the APF should first try to obtain documents from Ethiopia. If these attempts were unsuccessful, they would consider what steps to take. Matters were left there.

The head of the Libyan delegation said there was no fraternity left in their relations with Nimeiri and his regime. Gaddafi knew perfectly well that most of the people of South Sudan wanted independence from Sudan. He reiterated that Libya was willing to support the independence of the South.

During our negotiations, the BBC reported that a joint Egyptian-Sudanese meeting of 600 parliamentarians was taking place in Cairo. It seemed that the meeting was a step toward a merger of the two countries. This was followed by an announcement of a military pact between the two states. These developments were undeniably relevant to the discussions. Agolong asked the Libyans if this news made them feel isolated. They replied that their government was determined to do everything possible to overthrow the Nimeiri regime. One Libyan commented that they were waiting to see what Sadiq al-Mahdi, the Umma Party leader who was clearly opposed to the unity of Egypt and Sudan, would say.

I added that if unity between the North and South of Sudan continued to be imposed, Southerners were bound to suffer more oppression as a minority in a merged Sudan and Egypt. Just as in 1953 when Egypt and Britain agreed on the unity and independence of Sudan, Southerners would not be consulted. We feared that Egypt would then send troops to the South to assist the Nimeiri regime to violently suppress the legitimate struggle of the Southerners.

On 27 October, one of the officials assigned to us took Agolong and I out for more sightseeing. This time we were driven in the direction of Tunisia to see a large agricultural scheme. There were many orchards of oranges, lemons, and olives. We visited a luxurious restaurant to enjoy coffee and delicious food. We were then taken to Zawiya town, where we had a look at the shops. Most of the shopkeepers were Arabs. We did not see any indigenous black Africans, and we refrained from asking questions about the racial composition of the population. We were also taken to another town, Sabratha, and saw more Roman ruins. We then returned to our residence.

The TV in our residence showed nothing other than Islamic cultural films and the call to prayer. We were told that cowboy Western films were shown on rare occasions.

My bronchial cough worsened so I was taken to a local clinic which gave me medication. I had to pay for my treatment.

What struck us as quite wonderful was the absence of alcohol in the shops. However, if one approached foreign business individuals discretely, alcohol could be obtained, but we were not very keen to drink.

On 6 November, the delegations met again. The head of the Libyan delegation told us that Gaddafi was pleased with our visit. He assured me that the agreements we had made would be implemented in the near future. They would be in touch with Mengistu and would coordinate the assistance for the APF. He emphasized that the most important point was the willingness of Ethiopia to cooperate with Libya. They would do everything in their power to convince the government of Ethiopia to cooperate. We raised another important issue: we would like to open an office and appoint a representative to work in Libya. The head of the Libyans said that he would talk to Gaddafi, but in his view, a South Sudanese presence would be too distinctive, and would be vulnerable to attack by Nimeiri's agents. When we tried to argue, he told us to leave it for consideration by Gaddafi.

On behalf of the movement, I thanked the Libyans for the positive response to our request for assistance and for their hospitality during our visit. We did not raise our desire to meet Gaddafi himself.

Our talks were over. Air tickets were given to us. They bade us farewell and left.

Visit to Rome

On 7 November, we were taken to the airport. At 11.30am, we left on a Libyan Airlines plane to Rome, intending to stop for a few days to meet Elia Duang Arop. Unfortunately, Agolong was refused a transit visa by the Italian authorities because his refugee travel document was Zaïrean. I was allowed to land because my refugee travel document was from the UK, which allowed me to land in any country within the European Community. Efforts were made to obtain permission for Agolong. With further contacts by Rita Erhart, a European sympathizer of South Sudan, Agolong was permitted to remain in Italy for 48 hours. We contacted Father Bechana, a former Catholic missionary in South Sudan, and asked if he could persuade the authorities to extend Agolong's stay in Italy. Father Bechana promised to try. The following day, Agolong was given an extension for seven days.

This gave us an opportunity to exchange views with Duang. However, Duang surprised us by announcing his resignation from the movement. He intended to return to Sudan. Duang argued that since Sadiq al-Mahdi was returning to Sudan, the APF should cease its activities and return to Sudan; to remain as the only opposition force in exile would be ineffective. Agolong and I disagreed. We reminded him that the movement had operated militarily and politically in the country and in exile independent of any Northern Sudanese parties since 1962.

After our talks with Duang, Agolong said that he would like to visit Kinshasa briefly and from there would return to Addis Ababa. He suggested that I proceed to Addis Ababa where he and Francis Mayar would join me. I proposed to visit London for a week or so before I returned to Addis Ababa. This was agreed.

On 8 November, Father Bechana informed us of an invitation for dinner from Baron, a German resident of Italy. Baron had visited Anyanya controlled areas in South Sudan, particularly in Equatoria, in the late sixties and early seventies. He knew the three of us. Father Bechana took us to the Baron's house, 35 kilometres outside Rome. We passed through Italian farmlands and enjoyed the beautiful, green countryside. Baron welcomed us warmly. To our surprise, he greeted each of us by name, despite being over 80. He had many female servants. After we were served refreshments, we were taken to a restaurant nearby, where we had an excellent dinner. We discussed South Sudanese politics at length. At night, we returned to Rome. The next day, I booked a flight to London.

A Surprise Family Reunion

I arrived in London with nowhere to spend the night. I phoned my former landlord, Adewole, with whom I left my luggage in May 1977. I asked whether he could find me a room for a week. I revealed that I had just returned from the trip I began in June. Adewole had unexpected, good news: my wife Sarah and two children had arrived on 17 September from Sudan and were being taken care of by UNCHR. They had asked where I had gone. Of course, Adewole did not know. Adewole said that Jacob Marial Makur, a relative of mine and a student in the UK, knew where my family was in London.

An hour after Adewole phoned, Marial arrived and confirmed that Sarah, my youngest daughter Susan Aciec Muortat, and my youngest son Justin Nyieer Muortat, had come from Sudan due to my application to the Home Office for a family reunion. As it was already late, we agreed that Marial would take me to my family the next morning. Meanwhile, Adewole accommodated me in the same room where he had stored my luggage.

At midday on 11 November, Marial accompanied me to 51 Rye Hill Park, Peckham, where I met Sarah, Susan, and Justin, in temporary accommodation provided by UNHCR. The last time I saw Sarah was in June 1973; Susan, on 13 February 1967, the day I left the country. Justin was born on 28 February 1967, 15 days after I had left Khartoum to join the movement. There was a lot of emotion. My children wept because they had thought that they might never see me again.

Two days later, I met the UNHCR representative, whom I thanked for all they did to bring my family out of Sudan. He said that it was good that they had been able to locate me, because otherwise they would have had no alternative but to return my family to Sudan. I appreciated the support UNHCR had given my family. If there was a problem extending my refugee status, I would apply to any African government to grant them refugee status. In the meantime, I would have to leave them in the UK and return to Africa. I had only come to Britain on a brief visit, but I would try to find a solution to the status of my family.

On 17 November, I phoned Agolong and informed him of the arrival of my family in the UK. I explained that I would rejoin him after the family was settled. While I remained in London, Radio Moscow announced on 22 November that the OAU Committee in Sierra Leone was still working to reconcile Sudan and Ethiopia. This justified our suspicion that Ethiopia had been persuaded by the OAU to cease efforts to show sympathy with Sudan's dissidents.

Before I left the UK, I wanted to make sure that Sarah and my two children were treated as refugees in their own right. So, on 28 November, I met Miss Brown from UNHCR. I explained that I had to return to Africa and that Sarah and the children should be treated as status refugees. I undertook to visit them frequently until I could reunite with them permanently, after a lasting settlement for the South Sudan cause was achieved or if I found alternative refugee status in Africa. Brown did not reject or consent to my return to Africa but said that Sarah and the children could remain as refugees. There would be no reason for them to be returned to Sudan.

Return to Ethiopia

On 7 December, I bade farewell to my family. I reassured them that I would visit as often as possible and that under no circumstances would I again be separated from them indefinitely. A taxi took me to Heathrow from where I flew back to Addis Ababa via Rome.

At Rome Airport, I was met by Elia Duang, who took me to the house of Rita Erhart, the APF sympathizer. Duang informed me that Agolong was still in Kinshasa. I then decided to fly to Kinshasa, so that we could review the situation together. However, I was refused an entry visa by the Zaïrean embassy in Rome.

While I waited to proceed to Addis Ababa, Duang again raised his returning to Sudan. I was still opposed. He handed me a resignation letter, which I refused to accept. I proposed that since the APF was a democratic organization, he should submit his decision to return to Sudan to the Coordinating Committee for consideration. Duang rejected this and said that the decision was his to make. We ended without compromise. I told him that I would bring the issue to the attention of the Coordinating Committee.

On 15 December, we heard on Radio West Germany that the Vice-Chairman of the PMAC, Col. Atnafu Abate, had been executed in November in Addis Ababa. This was shocking news. We began to analyze whether such a terrible event would affect the relationship between the APF and the government of Ethiopia. The next day I received a telegram from Agolong advising me to proceed to Addis Ababa. He would soon return to Addis himself.

On 18 December, I flew to Addis Ababa. Leo Thuc informed me that the representative occasionally asked when the APF mission to Libya would return. Thuc had told him that it would be soon. Since Thuc remained the APF contact point, I told him that Agolong and I planned to meet the representative together as soon as we could, but as Agolong had been delayed, I would brief the representative on our visit to Libya alone. In the meantime, I would brief the APF Coordinating Committee. A few days later, I presented a verbal report on our visit to Libya to the Coordinating Committee. I told the members that we would present a detailed written report after Agolong returned from Kinshasa.

On 20 December, Thuc arranged a meeting with the representative. The atmosphere was, unsurprisingly, not quite cordial. I said that our talks with the Libyan government had ended in some success, since Libya had agreed to provide the APF military assistance, food, clothing and money, contingent on the willingness of the Ethiopian government to issue travel documents to 200 military recruits to be assembled inside Ethiopia and then airlifted to Libya This would be followed by another similar recruitment; the process would continue until the APF was satisfied with the size of its forces.

I explained that we would provide a written report of our talks with the Libyans soon. The representative said that he was impressed with the outcome and thanked us for the confidence in him and his government. When we had submitted our written report, he would pass it to his government. We would be informed of their decision.

I also explained that before I returned to Addis Ababa, my family had arrived in the UK. Since I had refugee status in Ethiopia, I would be grateful if they could be granted the same status so that they could join me here. The representative advised I put this request in writing so that he could forward it for consideration. Three days later, I gave him the necessary letter.

On 23 December, I delivered the written report on the mission to Libya to the representative. He read it and promised to convey the decision concerning our request for help in implementing the agreement with Libya soon. While we awaited a reply, the press published the agreement between the governments of Ethiopia and Sudan to cooperate and normalize their relations.

On 26 December, the representative visited us unofficially. He was passing by and had stopped to say hello. As we chatted, I asked him whether a decision had been made. He said that his government had not yet considered the report. On the issue of asylum for my family in Ethiopia, no decision had been made, though he believed that accepting my family in Ethiopia would not be a problem.

However, he said that all South Sudanese refugees would have to move to Gambella and not live in Addis Ababa or elsewhere in Ethiopia. I explained this would be hard for the refugees as food supplies were always scarce in Gambella, but that we would let him know the APF stance on the issue soon.

Ethiopia and Sudan Normalize Relations

More news was appearing on the normalization of relations between Sudan and Ethiopia. Before our visit to Libya, we had been instructed by the host authorities to scale down our activities until further notice. We did keep a low profile. Nevertheless, we convened a meeting of the APF Coordinating Committee on 24 December.

Those present were Moses Malek, Johnny Rasson, John Hoth Guor, James Bol, and me. The items on the agenda were the agreement between Sudan and Ethiopia to normalise relations and the resignation of Secretary-General Elia Duang and his decision to return to Sudan.

Regarding the normalization of relations between the two countries, the Committee resolved that the APF must remain patient and friendly to the government of Ethiopia. This was based on the belief that things would one day change in our favor, particularly when Khartoum turned hostile again.

Regarding Duang, the majority proposed to defer a decision pending Agolong's return. He knew Duang best.

On 29 December, Agolong returned from Kinshasa. In the evening, I met him at Leo Thuc's house and briefed him on the developments since we had left Libya.

On 31 December, the Coordinating Committee met again at Agolong's place. Agolong and I informed the Committee of the reasons for Duang's resignation. The letter of resignation was read out. Many expressed dismay and several others said that they appealed to Duang to change his mind, but he declined to do so. I said I had done my best to persuade Duang and argued that the return of Sadiq al-Mahdi from exile had nothing to do with the APF. I told the meeting that I had said to Duang that I would not accept his resignation before presenting it to the Coordinating Committee.

Many members paid tribute to Duang for his contribution to the struggle. The majority reluctantly recommended acceptance of Duang's resignation. I had no option but to accept. I later wrote to Duang informing him accordingly.

I recommended to the Committee that Agolong be appointed secretary-general. It was unanimously passed. I also recommended that Moses Malek be appointed APF vice-chairman. This was also unanimously adopted.

We also discussed the representative's position that all South Sudanese refugees be moved to Gambella. Our stance was that this would cause much suffering to the refugees because of the food scarcity in the region. The only way forward would be to encourage international relief organizations to supply food to the area.

We hoped that the host government would respond positively to the agreement reached between the APF and the Libyan government. We hoped that the APF would soon embark on the training and deployment of the New Anyanya throughout South Sudan in 1978.

A Coordinating Committee meeting was called to discuss APF security. John Hoth Guor, the security officer, conveyed that spies had been sent to Gambella to report to Khartoum on the activities of the APF. The Sudanese government spy network, well established throughout Ethiopia, had been put into operation after the Akobo uprising of 1974. Spying intensified following the establishment of the APF and the Anyanya camp in October 1975.

The APF leadership continued to receive reliable information on the developing political crisis between the South and the Nimeiri regime over the constant violation of the terms of the Addis Ababa Agreement. The Nimeiri government devised many divide and rule policies among the Southern people, such as breaking up the integrated Anyanya. Many Southerners were also aware of skirmishes between the leaders of the Akobo uprising and government forces in 1975 and 1976. The Southern Regional government had no choice but to support the central government, although some regional ministers supported the APF. Sadly enough, some integrated Anyanya units and the regional police clashed with the New Anyanya, who had not yet been ordered by the APF to begin operations against Khartoum's forces.

The End of the APF

It upset us to realize there was a degree of hostility on the part of the host government. Nevertheless, there was very little we could do about it. All we could do was keep calm and remind the representative whenever opportunities presented themselves.

Soon, the representative got back in touch. The report of the APF's objectives had been carefully considered by the Ethiopian government. His government would not support our fighting for independence of South Sudan, because it would contradict their own opposition to the Eritrean fight for independence from Ethiopia. They would support the APF if it changed its objective to that of fighting for a solution of the conflict within one Sudan.

Supported by Agolong, I swiftly replied that this suggestion was unacceptable. The aim of fighting for independence was conceived and declared in 1962. We had given the reasons why the Southerners took up arms. Furthermore, attempting a solution within one Sudan had proved disastrous. The representative then asked for the meeting to be adjourned until another day.

On 3 January 1978, we received a message requesting Agolong and I come to the representative's office urgently. He opened by saying, "Our meeting is not going to last too long. My government has instructed that you two, Gordon Muortat Mayen, Chairman of the APF, and Agolong Chol Agolong, the APF Secretary-General, must leave Ethiopia." He said this would be until the Ethiopian government asked for us to return; air tickets had been arranged.

We were initially speechless; it was the last thing we expected. I broke the silence and asked if we could meet Mengistu before leaving Ethiopia. The representative was quiet for a few seconds. Eventually, he said he would convey our request to Mengistu and let us know the response. We asked whether he could reveal the reasons for our expulsion. This action by his government amounted to shutting down our movement. We wanted assurances that this move would not end the friendship between Ethiopia and the oppressed people of South Sudan. We also wanted to know what the Ethiopian government had decided about the cooperation with Libya.

He said the decision to ask us to leave was a diplomatic and political necessity. As far as the relations between Ethiopia and South Sudan's oppressed people were concerned, there would be no change. With regards to the elements of the movement who would remain in Ethiopia, everything would be fine until we were called back again. The decision was only temporary.

I knew the APF Coordinating Committee would not be active in our absence. So, I asked for approval for Agolong to remain in Ethiopia as a student since he had been granted a scholarship by an international humanitarian organization. The representative said that he would have to raise this with his government. He went on to apologize for the failure to decide on our requests, including the application for asylum for my family. The meeting ended gloomily. Agolong and I knew that there would be no other meetings with the representative before I left. There was a faint hope that the representative would arrange a meeting for us with the Derg Chairman, Mengistu.

On 5 January, a full Coordinating Committee meeting was convened to discuss the grim situation. I said that something fundamental must have persuaded the Ethiopian government to act against the APF leadership. Even though this government had shown us much sympathy, we would have to accept that they were closing us down. However, I was pleased that the APF had not been uprooted totally. The Ethiopian government knew that whatever agreement was concluded between Ethiopia and Sudan, they could never trust an Arab government in Khartoum.

I urged the members to remain courageous and determined. This was not the first time our movement had been shut down by foreign powers. The Congolese government closed the offices of SACDNU after the assassination of Lumumba, expelling its leaders in 1962. In 1966, Joseph Oduho, Aggrey Jaden, and others had to flee Nairobi and Kampala after the ALF and the SALF were shut down. Those remaining in Ethiopia had to remain united and keep in touch with those abroad. There was no problem of communication in these modern times. Those remaining in the country in the leadership should keep a low profile so that rank-and-file members also be allowed to remain.

Many members expressed frustration and disappointment at our deportation. Some were not surprised because the government's attitude towards the APF had been hostile since July 1977 when they stopped supplying food to Bilpam, ordered me to leave Bilpam, stopped the military training of the New Anyanya, and supported Bol's insubordination.

One member felt that we had to ascertain why the Ethiopian government changed its policy towards us. He added that the Ethiopian government had ignored the Libyan offer to coordinate its material assistance to APF with Ethiopia. Another said that it was a terrible upset that APF leaders were being deported when they had almost made a breakthrough in obtaining assistance for the movement. A third member said that the APF was a victim of the Freetown Conference of 1977, in which some African states undertook to reconcile Sudan and Ethiopia at the expense of the APF.

In rounding up the discussions, it was my hope that with the ongoing political situation in Sudan, we would soon be reinvited as had happened in the past. I advised the members to pull together and keep active quietly and effectively until the mood of the host authorities changed. We had been informed that the Ethiopian authorities would allow Agolong to remain in the country as a student. We were grateful as this would allow him to keep working with them in various ways.

Elia Duang's resignation from the APF and return to Sudan may have contributed to the weakening of our relations with the host government. Any defection by leaders of the movement could be taken as lack of seriousness by outsiders.

I thought back on the last few years of activity in Ethiopia. After my election as APF Chairman, I led the delegation which negotiated with the Ethiopian government for political and material assistance. In late 1975, when these negotiations failed to achieve concrete results, I returned to the UK. In early 1977, I returned to Ethiopia at their government's request and resumed negotiations. At that time, I was convinced that the Ethiopians were taking our relationship seriously. So, I resigned from my job in London and returned to Ethiopia. Now, the same authorities were sending me away. Still, I would never get discouraged no matter the humiliation to which I was subjected.

I began to prepare to leave for the UK. On 11 January, I flew to London to reunite with my family.

12.

Second Waiting to be Recalled

I did not believe that my return to London was temporary, despite the apparent promise to recall us from the Ethiopian government. We were resolved to move to any country willing to accept us.

In 1977, after sensing the Ethiopian uneasiness to continue hosting the APF, we approached some African states with our desire to be hosted by one of them. Responses were courteous, but no offer was made. This left us with no alternative but to return to the countries which had granted us political asylum: the UK, Zaïre, and a few others. I was ready to stay with my family in the UK until a suitable host for the APF was found. The UK was not a suitable place from where to run the APF. It was too far from Sudan, and there were no funds to support the work.

After a week in London, UNHCR told me to register for unemployment benefit. The head of UNHCR knew that I had been politically active as a South Sudanese leader in exile. He also knew that my family members with refugee status had the right to receive social security independent of me. But despite telling him that I would return to Africa, he remained adamant that I must work to support my family. I registered at the unemployment office the following week. I signed up weekly for unemployment benefit, which was insufficient to support my family of three. But there was nothing we could do until I found employment. On 20 January 1978, I went to find schools for my still young children, Susan and Justin. They were accepted at different schools. Mary, a few years older, was to arrive shortly from Sudan.

One of my adult children, Paul Madong, aged 26, had managed to enter Britain on his own with the promise of a scholarship, which did not materialize. Paul was later granted residential status and I managed to get him a scholarship from the African Educational Trust. The rest of my adult children were still in Sudan in precarious circumstances.

I decided to try and find an African country which would accept me as a resident, even on a temporary basis. On 13 February, I visited the Embassy of Liberia. I chose Liberia as an African country which understood the cause of South Sudan. I was met by an embassy official to whom I explained my objective. I was asked to put my request in writing, which I did the following day. I was told the request would be forwarded to the Liberian government for consideration.

Ethiopian Government Threatens to Ban the APF

On 17 February, I received a letter from Agolong Chol, who was still in Ethiopia, informing me that the Ethiopian government was threatening to ban the APF. The Ethiopians alleged that some APF leaders, including Agolong, were agents of the US Central Intelligence Agency (CIA). Agolong wrote to the Secretary-General of the Derg declaring these accusations false. At the time of the Addis Ababa Agreement sell-out, the CIA had supported the deal.

Another letter received from Agolong on 4 March explained

that the accusation originated from the representative assigned to APF affairs. His relations with the APF leaders had been difficult for years, because of the food shortages at Bilpam and his encouragement of insubordination against me by James Bol.

Some sympathizers of the APF within the Ethiopian regime advised Agolong and I not to leave Ethiopia. They would try to change the decision to send us away. We refused because we thought that it would damage the movement if the gap between the pro-APF group and others within the regime widened. One of the friendly group, after having read Agolong's letter, exclaimed, "He, the representative, is the real CIA agent."

I was upset by the allegations made. I wrote a letter of protest on 26 February to the Secretary-General of the Derg to express my dismay at the false accusations. I reminded him that the APF was among the poorest liberation movements in the world, which would hardly be the case if we had been supported by the CIA. I appealed to the Secretary-General to ask the accusers to produce evidence for their allegations.

I believed the root of the allegation was that in 1977, we had petitioned the representative regarding the failure to implement the 1975 agreement between the APF and the Ethiopian government. Then, the Secretary-General queried the representative, and had told us that he and his colleagues in the government were not aware of the delay in implementing the agreement. The Secretary-General assured us that there would be an investigation into the delay and that appropriate action would be taken to remedy the situation. It was soon after that episode that the representative grew hostile and told Agolong and I to leave the country.

After Agolong and I left Ethiopia, we expected a military takeover of the APF by Bol. But, according to a letter dated 19 April, this did not occur. Moses Malek, the APF Vice-Chairman wrote,

"The representative who accused APF leaders of being CIA agents is angry with us because he insisted that the accusation was not official." Recounting the representative's words, Malek reported that the representative was queried by his bosses and asked to explain why he had caused the APF leaders to be deported from Ethiopia. The representative had no more convincing option than to invent the story that the leaders were CIA agents. Malek also wrote that the Derg Secretary-General asked the Ethiopian colonel to prove his allegation. The colonel responded that he had no evidence to produce: "I just wanted these people to leave the country."

Another letter dated 22 April came from Bol saying, "The shortage of food at the camp remains desperate. Our friends have done nothing about it." He asked me to find supplies and send it to the camp. I wrote back to Bol that the only way out of the impasse was for the members of the APF Coordinating Committee still in Addis Ababa to persuade the Ethiopian government to allow the Libya/APF agreement to be implemented.

On 5 May, Sarah received the news that her father Col Ahoc had died on 10 April in his house in a village outside Rumbek. We then entered a process of mourning according to tradition.

Death of Joseph M. Guelly, my Son-in-Law

On 19 June at 1pm, when we were still living in Rye Hill, Peckham, Dr Barnaba Marial Benjamin, Judge Bol Alueng, and Kon Bior, a Sudanese embassy official, arrived. Bol Alueng broke the news that my son-in-law Joseph Mathubier Guelly had been killed in a car crash on the road between Juba and Yei in Equatoria. The news was crushing. The previous week, Guelly had written to say that he, my daughter Rebecca Acol, and their four children, would soon pass by London on their way to the Sudanese Embassy in Czechoslovakia, where Guelly had been due to take up an assignment.

Move to 40 Huntly Road

On 3 July, we moved from Peckham to a 3-bedroom house in South Norwood, London, offered by the British Council for Aid to Refugees (BCAR). The house was unfurnished and without central healing. When winter came, it became too cold for us. We complained to BCAR but received no positive response.

Sarah's visit to Sudan

Our daughter, Rebecca, was not recovering from her grief following the sudden death of her husband in June. The family agreed that Sarah should return to Sudan to be with Rebecca. On 16 August, Sarah left for Khartoum. I accompanied her to Heathrow. From Khartoum, she would proceed to Rumbek to meet Rebecca. Sarah's status in the UK allowed her to visit Sudan and return to the UK at any time.

Proposed Dialogue with the Northern Opposition

After the Nimeiri coup against the al-Azhari government on 25 May 1969, some of the Northern opposition leaders fled into exile. With the aim of opposing the military regime, they created a new organization, the Sudanese National Front (SNF). SNF's policy regarding armed struggle was not clear, if not non-existent.

SNF initiated contact with us in 1970. They sent a letter to me as President of the NPG, appealing for cooperation against the Nimeiri regime. They pledged to collaborate with the NPG in overthrowing the regime and in finding a lasting solution to discontent in South Sudan. The matter was presented before the NPG Council of Ministers, but before a decision was made, the NPG was dissolved.

Two years later, the Nimeiri regime signed the Addis Ababa Agreement. Some Northern leaders in exile, such as Sadiq al-Mahdi, reconciled with the Nimeiri regime and returned to Sudan the year following. The DUP faction led by Sherif Hussein el-Hindi continued the opposition to the Nimeiri regime in exile, in loose association with some members of GUN led by Rev. Abbas.

In 1976, almost a year after the APF was set up, the Mengistu government arranged for me to meet el-Hindi, the leader of the Northern Sudan opposition, in Addis Ababa. The objective of this meeting was to create a basis for the two groups to work together. As I mentioned earlier, the meeting to bring about cooperation failed because the APF refused to accept the proposed strategies.

On 26 June 1978, el-Hindi phoned and suggested we meet at a venue on Cromwell Road, London to again discuss cooperation between our two movements. I accepted and met him there. El-Hindi asked whether we could agree that our two movements work together given our clear common interests. After a lengthy discussion, we agreed to cooperate. El-Hindi was well spoken of as one of the few Northern Sudanese leaders who sympathized with the South Sudanese, although he did not support the right of the South to become independent. I said that I would not negotiate without consulting the Coordinating Committee, most of whom were in Addis Ababa and Kinshasa. We agreed that I should arrange for an APF delegation to come to London as soon as possible to join me at the talks. I told el-Hindi that I would keep him informed regarding the arrival of the APF delegation in London.

On 27 June, I telegrammed Francis Mayar, the roving APF foreign secretary, Agolong Chol, and Paul Duang Yak in Kinshasa, asking them to attend the proposed negotiations in London in about two months' time. I also sent telegrams to Addis Ababa to Moses Malek, the APF vice-chairman and acting chairman, Johnny Rasson, the deputy foreign secretary, Leo Thuc, secretary for special functions, and the two Anyanya commanders, Vincent Kwany and

James Bol. On 20 July, Agolong replied that he and Duang were preparing to attend the conference. Mayar was facing some problems which he hoped to overcome shortly. All that we could do was wait.

The Proposed Dialogue Between the Northern Parties in Exile and the APF Continues

On 20 July, I received replies from the APF members in Kinshasa confirming their willingness to attend the meeting in London if air tickets and visas were arranged. El-Hindi and I resolved to send them air tickets as soon as they were ready to fly to London. This message was conveyed to them. Meanwhile, Johnny Rasson and Paul Wal wrote from Addis Ababa and requested air tickets as well. They also said that the Government of Ethiopia was opposed to the conference for reasons unknown.

On 27 July, I received another letter from Moses Malek, also signed by Vincent Kwany, James Bol, and John Hoth Guor, the secretary for security functions. The letter reported that the proposal to hold the conference was unanimously approved by the Coordinating Committee. The letter also confirmed the Ethiopian government's opposition to the conference. Committee members would try to persuade the government to change its attitude in favor of the conference.

On 8 August, I received a report from Addis Ababa that the Ethiopian authorities had arrested Johnny Rasson, along with other APF members. No charges disclosed against them were disclosed. On 11 August, I posted a petition to Mengistu protesting the arrest of Rasson and his colleagues without charge. I appealed for their immediate release. In London, I delivered a copy of my protest to the Ethiopian ambassador who assured me that he would do his best to ask Mengistu to consider releasing those under arrest.

Through the months, I received messages from various APF members invited to attend the proposed London conference. It was clear that delegates were facing difficulties in obtaining travel documents and exit visas from their concerned host countries. I therefore contacted el-Hindi and we agreed to postpone the conference.

On 22 September 1978, I received a letter from Rev. John Malou informing me that Sarah, Rebecca, and her four children, had left Rumbek and were on their way to London. We had requested the Home Office grant visas to Rebecca and her children to join the rest of the family in the UK, as visitors on a humanitarian basis. On 12 November 1978, Sarah, Rebecca Acol, and the children Ater Guelly, Sammy Guelly, and baby twins Awet Guelly, a boy, and Angair Guelly, a girl, arrived at Heathrow.

Vigorous Attempts by Nimeiri to Convince me to Return to Sudan

Since early July 1978, rumors had circulated that the Nimeiri government would send a delegation to the UK to try to convince me to return to Sudan. On 25 September, I received a letter from Omer el Sheikh, chargé d'affaires at the Sudanese embassy in London, advising that Clement Mboro, Amir Gamal Eldin, and Ezekiel Macuei Kodi, had arrived in London to see me. El Sheikh wrote that their mission was part of Nimeiri's initiative for consolidation of national unity, and that the delegation was ready to meet with me at any time The same day, I received a letter from Mboro, my former colleague in the Southern Front, and now speaker of the Southern Sudan Regional Assembly, confirming that he had arrived in London with Gamal Eldin and Kodi on behalf of President Nimeiri to talk to me.

I responded to Mboro that I was not opposed to talking, but that a delegation comprising mostly Southerners would not help, because the conflict was not between Southerners. I also pointed out that I should have been informed well in advance of the arrival of the delegation to have time to assemble my delegation. On the telephone the following day, Mboro said: "When we meet the Sudanese ambassador tomorrow, I will find out why you were not informed in time."

On 26 September, I met Mboro at the Savoy Hotel in London. He explained why Nimeiri had sent the delegation. Nimeiri feared that I might launch a new South Sudan liberation struggle, Mboro said. As for the composition of the delegation, Mboro said he was made to lead the delegation because he and I were leaders of the Southern Front and old friends. "But Nimeiri is not aware that I am one of the Southern leaders inside the country who support your activities in exile," he confided. I insisted that my colleagues and I were willing to talk to anybody anywhere. Mboro disclosed that the other Southern delegate, Ezekiel Kodi, Regional Minister of Commerce and Trade, was included because he was my relative. Gamal Eldin, a member of the Sudan Socialist Union (SSU) Political Bureau, was included to testify on the talks.

I asked Mboro why the Sudanese government gave us insufficient time to prepare. He said that he did not know that I was given such short notice. His understanding was that the delegation was sent to speak to me alone because the government believed that I was alone. I said that that was disappointing to me because everybody knew that I led a group of Southern political leaders who rejected the Addis Ababa Agreement. I cited some names: Francis Mayar Akon, Agolong Chol, and Paul Duang Yak in Zaïre, Arkangelo Wanji in Uganda, Moses Malek, Johnny Rasson, Vincent Kwany, and James Bol in Ethiopia.

On 28 September at 12.30pm, I met the whole Sudanese delegation at the Hilton Hotel. Mboro said that the delegation's terms of reference were to extend to me and my colleagues (if any) the need for reconciliation in the same way as it was conveyed to other Southern groups previously. Gamal Eldin and Kodi spoke in support of Mboro.

I replied that I could not accept to negotiate alone and needed time to form a delegation from among the APF members in Africa. I was critical of the way the government delegation was composed, giving the impression that the proposed talks would be between the South Sudanese, and noted that this evoked the composition of the Sudanese government delegation at the Addis Ababa talks in 1972. I proposed that the London talks be postponed pending the arrival of the APF delegates, which may take three to four months, bearing in mind the problems of obtaining travel documents, visas, and tickets.

Mboro, after consulting his colleagues, said that they would like a few days to inform the government and that they would meet me again. I agreed and the meeting adjourned. On 6 October, the delegation met me again. Mboro stated that my proposal for more time was accepted by Khartoum. We agreed to appoint William Bior of the Sudanese embassy in London as a liaison between the two sides. The same day, I telegrammed APF members urging them to attend the talks. On 7 October, I briefed the delegation that the APF participants had positively replied. Arkangelo Wanji pledged to come to London at any moment. On 9 October, I met the government delegation at the Bedford Hotel, where the reading and correction of the minutes of the meetings that had been held so far took place. Some of the government delegates skeptical that the APF members would arrive on time pressurized me to negotiate alone, but I refused. After a brief exchange of views, it was agreed by both sides that the meeting would be adjourned until 16 November.

On 11 October, Mboro informed me that the delegation had

decided to return to Sudan. William Bior would keep the delegation informed on the arrival of APF delegates in London. Mboro stated that the government delegation would then return to London without delay. On 12 October, I wrote to Nimeiri to thank him for his desire to bring about a just solution to the problem of the South, which he had shown by sending the delegation to London. I reiterated in my letter that most of the government delegation were Southerners and I disagreed with the rationale for such a composition, since the conflict we were trying to resolve was between North and South and not between the Southerners. I articulated my continued advocacy for the independence of the South because of the injustice, oppression, domination, and mass killings of Southerners by successive Khartoum governments since 1954. I ended by writing that I hoped that "when it became possible for the two delegations to meet in November 1978, they will be able to create an atmosphere conducive to the type of understanding desirable by both sides."

Visit to the Cuban Embassy

On 27 October, I visited the Cuban embassy to confirm the report that my sons Thomas Mawan and Isaiah Mayen had received scholarships to study in Cuba. An embassy official denied the news. I persisted that my intention was to be told about the terms of the scholarships so that I could give my opinion and blessing if necessary. Later, I was informed that the scholarships never existed. Mawan and Mayen later told me that one of their friends, Thomas Korou Tong Aleu, had applied to the Cubans on their behalf. The Cubans had promised grants, but these did not materialize.

My Throat Operation

I had been suffering from a painful swelling on the right side of my throat for some time. Doctor Gifford sent me for tests. Gifford informed me that there was a likelihood that I would have to undergo an operation to remove a gland. On 19 November 1978, I was admitted to Princess Alexandra Ward, Croydon Hospital. The same evening, I was allowed visits from Sarah and my son, Justin. The service by the doctors and nurses was the highest I had so far come across.

On 20 November, I had more medical tests throughout the day. The consultants assigned to operate on me were Doctors Sutcliffe and Panama, who told me that I would be operated on the next day. On the morning of 21 November, I had a bath, then my beard was partially shaved. At 12.45pm, my clothes were removed and replaced with an operation garment. I was taken to the operation theatre upstairs and injected with anesthetic. My consciousness slowly faded away. Later in the evening, about 7.30pm, I came round and realized that I was back in the ward. Sarah was sitting by my bed. I felt great pain and had difficulty speaking. The pain continued for most of the night.

On 22 November, the pain had almost gone. I was able to speak to Sarah and others. On 26 November, I was discharged and returned home in the company of Sarah. I eventually regained my health and resumed normal life.

William Bior Report

In the meantime, continued obstacles for APF delegates had meant the proposed conference in November had been postponed. On 29 January 1979, William Bior informed me that Clement Mboro had phoned from Khartoum to say that his delegation would only be ready to attend talks in April 1979. Bior also confided that certain South Sudanese individuals in the government were pressing Nimeiri to give up the idea of negotiating with the APF and me. For now, Nimeiri remained determined to resist them. I thanked Bior for letting me know. I added that the talks faced numerous obstacles and that we were not optimistic that the event would take place.

On 31 January, I received a letter from Paul Duang Yak from Kinshasa. He, Agolong, and Mayar were still making efforts to get air tickets but had not yet succeeded.

Appeal Against the Arrest of APF Members in Addis Ababa

On 19 February, I received a letter from Simon Jock in Addis Ababa informing me that Moses Malek, John Hoth, Bol Kiir Diew, Leo Thuc, Paul Wal, and others had been arrested by the Ethiopian government for having agreed to attend the proposed talks between the Sudanese government and the APF.

On 20 February, I posted my appeal to Mengistu to release the members of the APF Coordinating Committee. I also wrote to the UN Secretary-General appealing for his intervention to help release those in detention in Addis Ababa. When I received no response after two weeks, I further appealed to the Secretaries-General of the OAU and the UN, as well as UNHCR. None replied, although I was sure that they had received my messages.

On 26 February, I appealed again to Mengistu to release the members of the Coordinating Committee, noting that these young men had been law abiding in the years that they had been living in Ethiopia. So far as there were no charges against them, they should be released. Although my letter remained unanswered, I was pleased to learn after several months that my colleagues were released from detention. On 4 May 1979, I received a letter from Paul Wal that all the members of the APF Coordinating Committee except for Moses Malek had been released from detention by the Ethiopian authorities. Johnny Jock Rasson had been deported to an unknown foreign country.

On 23 March, I received a letter from Francis Mayar and Agolong Chol in Kinshasa. They had changed their minds and were now against the proposed dialogue in London, as they believed it would be futile. I was disappointed by this reversal. They knew that I held the same view as them; nevertheless, we had agreed that we would lose nothing by entering into dialogue. Rather, it would promote the cause of our struggle and give publicity to the APF.

On 27 March, Bior informed me that Mboro had phoned to say that Nimeiri had decided to reconsider the dialogue with the APF. I suggested Bior send me a copy of the letter he received from Mboro, so that I could inform Arkangelo Wanji to postpone his coming to London if need be. I then wrote to Mayar and Agolong, rejecting their change of mind against the talks and re-emphasizing that the APF had nothing to lose by entering those talks.

Arrival of Arkangelo Wanji at Gatwick Airport

On 6 April, I received a telegram from Arkangelo Wanji, the former SSPG deputy minister of defence in 1968, and former NPG minister of foreign affairs, that he would arrive at Gatwick Airport on 9 April. I contacted Bior who confirmed that he would meet Wanji at the airport and put him in a hotel, in accordance with the instructions from Mboro. Mboro said that he had a budget from the office of the President to cover the expenses of the talks.

On 9 April, Wanji arrived as anticipated. I met him at the airport and brought him to my house. Bior did not come to the airport, so I phoned to say that Wanji had arrived and was at my house. When Bior arrived at my house, he apologized to Wanji for not having met him at the airport. Bior said he did not come to the airport because he was busy arranging Nimeiri's visit to the UK.

I spoke to Mboro who told me that the funding for the dialogue had not materialized as promised to him by Nimeiri. He had learned that a Southern minister working in foreign affairs, whose name he was unwilling to disclose, blocked the funding.

I apologized to Wanji for the misunderstanding, and on 14 April, Wanji returned to Lusaka, Zambia, where he was a university lecturer.

After the Wanji visit, it was obvious that the plan for dialogue was failing. We still lacked funds for air tickets, accommodation, and to sustain our delegates, and we were unwilling to accept funding from the Sudanese government. Some of the host countries refused to grant exit visas and did not agree to facilitate air tickets for delegates.

I was still optimistic that it would not be long before we made a breakthrough with another country to render the APF with material assistance and political support. I visited the Libyan embassy and requested a visit to follow-up to that of 1977. I was well received and given promises, but none of them were fulfilled. Nevertheless, I did not give up hope in Libya because Gaddafi was in serious conflict with Nimeiri.

I Take a Job
In early October 1979, I met the factory manager of TI Plasero, a plastics company in West Croydon, who offered me the job of a cleaner, working at night. I asked whether I could be offered a storekeeper's job. There was no vacancy for a storekeeper, but when the role became available I would be offered it. I accepted this for now. My wage was a little more than £60 a week.

By the beginning of 1980, the cleaning job was affecting my health. I suffered from bronchitis, cough and cold, infections, ulcers, and conjunctivitis. According to my medical friends, most of these ailments were caused by dust containing plastic and other chemical elements.

In February 1980, Dr Gifford wrote to my employer to point out that my job was the cause of my ill-health and asked for me to be employed in another position. On 3 March, I delivered Gifford's letter to Don Bowman, the factory foreman. Bowman said: "Let the doctor find another job for you." I told Bowman that I had no alternative but to consider leaving the company. He did not respond. On 11 March, Bowman called me to his office and said that he had discussed my case with his boss and that they could not meet my request.

I tried to find another job. I was keen on being a guard, as it related to my police experience and was better paid. Unfortunately, despite attending many interviews, I had no luck. Consequently, it was impractical to drop the TI Plasaro cleaner's job. Becoming dependent on unemployment benefit was the worst choice I could make. The wages were higher than benefits and getting another job would not be easy. TI Plasaro were reluctant to sack me because my cleaning was superb. My weekly pay was the minimum wage in England at that time. It was not enough to cover the cost of food, rent, gas, electricity, water, and telephone bills.

Contrary to the traditions in South Sudan where the husband was supposed to be the breadwinner, Sarah took up a job washing linens with the New Eva Company on 8 May in a factory less than half a mile from our house. Her weekly wage was only £25.

As the cleaning job continued to affect my health, I stepped up seeking another job. On 4 September 1980, I met the owner of *The Variety of Fashion*, a textile company which I had read about in the newspapers. After I answered a few questions, the owner asked me to meet his brother, the co-owner of the company, in Croydon on 8 September. On that date, I met BH Singh. He agreed to employ me on a salary of £4,000 per year. This worked out to being paid £333 per month. There would be no breaks, no sick pay, nor pension, nor insurance. Pay would be reviewed in December. There was no overtime except on Saturdays and Sundays, which would be paid in cash. I accepted this offer. On 10 September, I gave notice to TI Plasaro that I had found another job and would leave next week. I was asked to write a short letter of resignation.

At 7.30am on 15 September, I reported to Joseph, a supervisor at *the Variety of Fashion*, who showed me around the factory and explained the textile printing machine. I started work at 8. Rolls of cloth and rolls of paper were provided on which different patterns were drawn. When a roll of cloth and a roll of paper were inserted together into the machine, beautifully patterned cloth was produced.

On 26 September, I learned that I would be doing different jobs, including cleaning the factory, carrying the rolls of paper to the printing machine, and printing the textiles. I knew it was going to be hard, but I had no choice, so I agreed. Some rolls were extremely heavy, and I found it difficult to lift these. I managed to do so with the help of a wheelbarrow.

I did this job throughout 1980 and the winter and summer of 1981. I worked from 8 to 8 every day. It was tiresome. Those in such jobs were known as slave laborers: the work was hard, working hours were long, and wages were low. Trade unions had no access. Since it was forbidden to break for meals, workers pooled money so that someone could go out to buy food for everyone.

On 30 September, I asked for the day off to attend the case of my son, Paul Madong, who was facing the charge of being an illegal immigrant following an argument with a British worker at his place of work. The charge was false because Paul entered Britain legally as a student of one of the colleges of Oxford University in 1977.

His lawyer, Errol Reid appeared on his behalf. Paul was eventually discharged by Bromley Magistrate Court on 13 April 1981.

Moses Malek Released from Detention in Ethiopia

On 25 June 1980, I received a letter from Moses Malek stating that he had been released from detention on 7 June. Many APF members, including the detainees themselves, believed that the APF members had been released because of the pressure mounted through the external media, the Ethiopian authorities' fear that further detention could damage the hope from the Southerners that Ethiopia was sympathetic, and the pressure on the government by Ethiopians who believed that South Sudan would, in due course, be useful to the cause of Ethiopia.

Dialogue with the DUP Continues

Despite the virtual collapse of dialogue efforts with the Sudanese government, attempts to bring about a dialogue with the DUP faction of Sherif el-Hindi continued. The hostile attitude of the Ethiopian government towards the APF, the reluctance by the Libyan government to fulfil its promise of assistance to the APF, and indifference by other African states forced us to review our liberation stance, at least temporarily. We therefore decided to seek assistance from any nation, or organization, with genuine sympathy for the people of South Sudan, even if such a nation or organization was Arab. To be precise, this meant collaborating with some Northern Sudanese opposition parties. This policy might be interpreted as the end justifying the means.

Hence, contrary to the earlier refusal to ally with el-Hindi and his faction of the DUP in exile, as urged by the Ethiopian government, the APF became willing to enter negotiations with el-Hindi. On 14 September 1980, after been fully delegated by the APF

Coordinating Committee in Addis Ababa, I entered talks with el-Hindi. El-Hindi tried to persuade us that he was different from other Northern Sudanese Arabs who had ruled Sudan. He argued that to achieve genuine national unity, we had to strive to eradicate inequality, ethnic and racial discrimination at all levels in Sudan. Our talks resulted in drawing up a Charter, eventually published in April 1981, as the basis of an alliance between the APF and the DUP Abroad.

The Charter established the Sudanese United National Front (SUNF) with the aim of liberating Sudan from Nimeiri's dictatorial rule. It would comprise the DUP and other Northern political parties other than the Umma Party, which had returned to the country, the APF and other political organizations, groups and individuals opposed to Nimeiri. The Charter noted that the Nimeiri regime was illegitimate, and consequently all means necessary to eliminate the regime should be used. The SUNF resolved to grant full autonomy or a federal structure to South Sudan. In autonomy, the center would relinquish most powers to the region except for foreign affairs, defence, and finance.

The Charter set out that during the armed struggle, APF forces would operate separately against the regime. However, a joint SUNF delegation would visit friendly Arab and African countries and any other countries to seek assistance for the struggle against the Nimeiri regime. Any assistance obtained would be equally shared between the APF and DUP. Moreover, as soon as funding of the SUNF materialized, separate offices for APF and DUP with their own budgets would be opened.

On 14 April 1981, the APF issued a press release to announce the SUNF. Despite our reservations about promises made by the Northern Sudanese, we congratulated el-Hindi for his boldness. Our press statement noted that while many Southerners appreciated the stance taken by El-Hindi in signing a charter with the APF, in view of the bitter experience of many broken promises, whether anything good for the South could come out of the old Northern political parties remained a question. Belatedly, the press release was signed by me as APF Chairman on 16 June 1982. The reason for this delay was that it took time for ratification of the Charter by the APF Coordinating Committee.

The Sudden Death of Sherif el-Hindi

At 8.30am on 15 January 1982, Ahmed Zein Abdin of the DUP phoned to say that Sherif el-Hindi had died in Athens, Greece, of a heart attack. This confirmed reports circulating since early September 1981. I asked Zein Abdin for the date on which el-Hindi died. He said that it was in September 1981, but he was not sure of the exact date.

The news of el-Hindi's death saddened me. He impressed me as one of the very few Northern Sudanese leaders desirous of finding a lasting solution to the South Sudan problem. Before el-Hindi died, we had agreed to send six men for training in how to drop arms from a plane, but the Ethiopian government refused to issue visas to the men chosen for the course.

I asked Zein Abdin who would succeed el-Hindi. I suspected he aspired to the post. Whomever it was, I doubted whether el-Hindi's successor would continue to implement our agreement and pursue the alliance. Zein Abdin told me that no meeting had been held by the DUP members, but many senior members felt that he should act temporarily until proper elections were held.

I protested the apparent marginalization of the APF. I reminded Zein Abdin that el-Hindi had promised to pay for air tickets for APF delegates from Ethiopia and Zaïre to attend the anticipated SUNF Conference in London. I expected Zein Abdin to make the money for the tickets available. At the same time, I pointed out that the APF had no intention of depending on the DUP financially. These arrangements were temporary pending common funds being made available to the APF.

Zein Abdin said that el-Hindi did not tell him where he kept the funds for the opposition movement. Zein Abdin said this was the main problem facing the SUNF. "Despite this, I will try to keep the SUNF active," he said. By February 1982, it had become clear that Zein Abdin rather than Abdel Magid Abu Asabu had succeeded el-Hindi; the latter was reluctant to live in exile.

Progress in the Efforts to Bring APF Delegates from Ethiopia
According to Moses Malek's letter of 3 March 1982, the Ethiopian policy of restricting the movements of the APF had changed. Malek reported that APF members were now allowed to travel abroad. Consequently, we only needed air tickets and British visas to enable the APF delegates from Ethiopia to attend a DUP/APF conference in London.

In the same letter, Malek conveyed that the APF forces in Bilpam were still demanding from Mengistu the return of the APF leadership to Ethiopia. Malek added that the Anyanya continued to carry out guerrilla attacks against Nimeiri's forces inside South Sudan, regardless of advice from the Ethiopian regime and the APF leaders still in Ethiopia not to do so. As the Ethiopian authorities did not supply them with food and other necessities, the forces acted this way. I asked Malek to convey to the APF forces operating inside South Sudan that I understood their problem of the lack of food and other supplies but that under no circumstances should they attack, rob, or ill-treat South Sudanese civilians.

On 12 March, I raised the urgent need for air tickets to be made available for the APF delegation then waiting in Ethiopia to attend the DUP/APF conference in London. Zein Abdin instructed a young DUP activist, Ahmed Saad, to arrange for air tickets to be issued to the APF delegates. Saad promised to do so immediately.

On 21 April, at 11am, Moses Malek, Leo Thuc, and Bol Kiir arrived at Heathrow, where I met them. We had some problems at immigration. After my status in the country was checked and assurances given as to when the trio would leave, they were released. We went to their hotel where I chatted with them briefly and left them to rest. When I returned to my house, I phoned Zein Abdin and informed him of the APF delegation's arrival.

On 24 April, I returned to the hotel and met the delegation for several hours, during which I explained the basis of the SUNF alliance and charter. I told the delegation that the greatest setback to the alliance had been the death of el-Hindi.

El-Hindi had worked single-handedly. His successor, Zein Abdin, was not confident whether implementation would be carried out as previously agreed. I said that this would be a key matter on the agenda of the London conference. Moses Malek thanked me for the briefing and agreed that the question of implementation must be on the conference agenda.

On 1 May, I invited the delegation to visit my house on 3 May. They accepted.

London Conference Commences

On 4 May, at 4.30pm, the conference commenced at Farlie Hall near Zein Abdin's house in London. Attending for the DUP were Zein Abdin, Omer Abdalla, and 13 DUP youth members, who were not introduced to us. Besides the former two, most of the older figures of the DUP were absent because they were still in Sudan. Attending for the APF were Moses Malek, Bol Kiir, Leo Thuc, and myself. Among the items on the agenda was ratification of the alliance, financial cooperation, and coordination of military operations.

The meeting was opened by Zein Abdin. He praised the formation of the Alliance and the possibility that other opposition parties from both North and South might join in due course. He said that although Sherif el-Hindi used to keep him informed about the talks to establish the alliance, he was not actively involved. He cherished the determination of both sides to bring about the overthrow of the Nimeiri regime. Zein Abdin concluded that he would do his best to make the alliance a success despite the problem of funding.

I spoke next. I covered the main points on which the alliance was based, including the sharing of ideas to find a lasting solution to the South/North conflict, the sharing of military and material means needed to defeat Nimeiri, and how to implement the SUNF Charter.

Then, Zein Abdin proposed the APF dissolve and that its leaders and members join the DUP. We furiously rejected this. We demanded Zein withdraw the proposal in which we saw an intention to wreck the conference. On behalf of the delegation, I told Zein Abdin that the alliance was not in itself a solution to the South/North conflict. He should know that the only solution would be the complete end of Northern Sudanese rule in South Sudan. What el-Hindi and I intended in the Alliance was to help the APF and DUP work together on issues of common interest as well as learning to understand one another. Summing up, I said that neither merger nor dissolution of the sister organizations was the way forward. My rejection was supported by delegates from both sides except Zein Abdin, who remained unconvinced.

On 9 May, the meeting resumed at the same venue. Although Zein Abdin did not apologize for his hostile proposition, other DUP delegates, such as Omer Abdalla, spoke conciliatorily and expressed strong support for the alliance, equality between its members, and the need for confidence building. A vote was taken on the need for, and desirability of, the alliance. The majority voted in favor.

Other proposals included establishing a joint delegation to raise funds, opening an APF office in London, organizing a propaganda campaign, setting a budget for the APF headquarters, and maintaining the APF's military wing in Ethiopia. These were all approved. Before the meeting adjourned, Zein Abdin warned the delegates that obtaining funds for these agreed projects remained a serious problem.

On 12 May, I phoned Zein Abdin about the desperate financial situation of the APF delegates, including the hotel's threats to evict them because the bills had not been paid. He promised to act immediately.

On 20 May, another meeting took place at Zein Abdin's house. The following items were discussed and passed unanimously: a mini-budget for the APF for the current year, renting an office for the APF in London, the membership of the SUNF Executive Committee, the composition of a fundraising delegation to tour some of the Arab countries and a proposal to hold another meeting in Athens, Greece, within the next three months. Finally, we declared our determination to implement the conference resolutions of May 1982. The meeting marked the end of the conference. The delegates were ready to disperse.

APF Delegates Review the London Conference

On 22 May, the APF delegation met at Leo Thuc's hotel, under my chairmanship, to review the work of the conference. We agreed that the way Zein Abdin had conducted himself meant that the prospects for SUNF were bleak, even though the attendees had declared their determination to honor the alliance and its charter.

The APF delegation was not fully satisfied with the response to the proposal that a SUNF joint delegation tour some Arab countries to fundraise. Zein Abdin had repeatedly said that he did not know the whereabouts of the funds set aside as the DUP contribution to SUNF. Another point of the APF delegation was the promise el-Hindi had made to make funds available to run the APF office in London. At the conference, Zein Abdin refused to answer this question adequately. The review ended with a resolution that the APF must intensify efforts to raise its own funds.

Attempts to Subvert the APF
Bol Kiir, the third delegate from Ethiopia, raised the issue of a meeting in Tripoli hosted by the Libyan and Ethiopian governments in August 1981. Members of the APF Coordinating Committee in Addis Ababa were invited, as were leaders from several Western Sudanese political organizations opposed to Nimeiri's regime, including the Sudanese Popular Revolutionary Front (SPRF) led by Yacoub Ismail. The APF members who attended this meeting were Moses Malek, Johnny Rasson, Bol Kiir, and Paul Wal. Southerners who were not members of the APF, such as David Dak Gash, also attended. The purpose of the meeting was to create a new movement under the SPRF, to include the APF and other Sudanese organizations, which the two governments would equip to overthrow the Nimeiri government.

Leo Thuc added that the intention was to set up a new movement to exclude separatist leaders such as myself, Agolong Chol, and Francis Mayar Akon, who were committed to the cause of an independent South Sudan. The two governments persuaded the Sudanese groups represented in the Tripoli meeting to unite under the SPRF and abandon the APF. Efforts were being made to convince the APF military at Bilpam camp to form the spearhead of the new movement. An Executive Committee was formed, and David Gash was appointed secretary-general of the new movement.

The governments undertook to provide necessary funding and equipment. According to the letter of Johnny Jock of 18 January 1982, the Government of Libya had granted one million US dollars to the SPRF to be paid through its embassy in Ethiopia. Payment would depend on the progress made, the letter went on. it was clear to me that the intention of the sponsors was to set up a new movement aimed wholly at removing Nimeiri from power. If that was the case, why should the APF join as a member organization and its members as individuals? The truth was that even if the Nimeiri regime was removed, the APF would continue its struggle against the new government in Khartoum until the South achieved full independence.

I objected to the participation of the APF in the Tripoli meeting. I therefore accused the APF members who attended the Tripoli meeting of ulterior motives and betrayal of the Southern cause. Moses Malek agreed and said, "As APF members, we should have declined to accept the invitation to the Tripoli meeting. Furthermore, Gordon Muortat Mayen, as the Chairman of the APF, should have been consulted before we attended." Moses Malek declared that they had made a mistake. After that, the APF delegation agreed to put aside the differences of its members. We reaffirmed our stance of struggling for complete independence.

On 24 May, Leo Thuc left for Addis Ababa. The next day, Moses Malek and Bol Kiir followed him to Ethiopia.

Efforts to Accelerate SUNF Activities after the London Conference

On 2 June 1982, I met Zein Abdin and discussed how the resolutions of the London conference would be implemented. Among these were the sending of the fundraising delegation and the opening of the APF London office. Unfortunately, we failed to agree on the steps to be taken. Zein Abdin kept repeating that we had to trace the whereabouts of the funds held by el-Hindi first. "Meanwhile, we have to wait," he said.

That was the position in which we remained indefinitely. It looked as if the conference had been futile. The same fate befell the promised APF branch office, which was supposed to follow the opening of the London office. In the meantime, our strenuous efforts elsewhere did not yield the funds needed to execute the APF's plans.

Zein Abdin and I were supposed to maintain contact, despite the failure of our organizations to make progress. Instead, he avoided me. Telephone calls went unanswered. Contact with Zein Abdin became rare. The small expenses which el-Hindi used to pay for APF work stopped.

The End of the Alliance

On 3 July 1982, I began circulating a report on the deteriorating relations between the DUP and the APF. The objective was to expose the differences and the breakdown of communication between us and the DUP following the London conference of March 1982.

Zein Abdin had little respect for the APF. He was unwilling to cooperate and work together with the APF on an equal basis. The APF was a South Sudan liberation movement. Its leaders were still angered by the DUP proposal at the conference that the APF should be absorbed into the DUP. Zein Abdin also refused to implement every agreement signed between el-Hindi and the APF.

The effective end of the Alliance gave me more time to follow up on the affairs of the APF. In the last five years, I had tried to get an entry visa to visit Ethiopia to improve the work of the APF. The

Mengistu government had been reluctant to allow me to come. They would not tell me directly that I had been banned from entering Ethiopia, and kept saying, "Your application is being processed; we will let you know soon."

Thus, I had confined myself to correspondence with the APF Coordinating Committee in Addis Ababa and elsewhere, and with other members of the APF. I had to content myself with leading the movement from exile. I wrote a lot of articles, booklets, and pamphlets, gave speeches, radio broadcasts, and press conferences, and attended local and international conferences. All these were related to the cause of South Sudan.

Postscript and Thanks

While Gordon Muortat's written account of events concludes in 1982, marking the end of his direct engagement in the armed liberation struggle, he remained politically active for the rest of his life.

As Muortat's text foreshadows, he lived to witness the dismantling and collapse of the Addis Ababa Agreement. Muortat welcomed the resulting resistance which emerged from a new generation of South Sudanese and Sudanese. Some of these younger cadres and soldiers would go on to form the Sudan People's Liberation Movement / Army (SPLM/A). When divisions arose within the SPLM/A, Muortat engaged its leaders, urging unity.

In addition to supporting the SPLM/A, Muortat continued to campaign for the cause of South Sudan in the UK and continental Europe. He helped found the South Sudan Human Rights Organization. He continued to write, participate in demonstrations, and lobby the British government and the African diaspora about South Sudan. Beyond South Sudan, Muortat also supported other liberation struggles.

In 1994, the SPLM/A chairman, John Garang, appointed Muortat as his advisor. As a guest of Garang, Muortat witnessed the signing of the Machakos Protocol in 2004.

Following the Comprehensive Peace Agreement of 2005, Muortat returned to Sudan. In 2006, on the recommendation of the elders of Lakes State, President Salva Kiir appointed Muortat to the Southern Sudan Legislative Assembly, the regional parliament. In that role, he championed unity among South Sudanese, sustainable development, and the protection of marginalized communities. His commitment to these aims helped lay the foundation for South Sudan's independence, which he sadly did not live to see.

The Muortat Family would like to thank all who provided encouragement and advice in bringing Muortat's memoir to publication. Particular thanks to: Helen Dollo, who advised Muortat; Helen Mursal, who helped type the manuscript; Kwesi Kwah Prah, who advised Muortat and read an early version of the manuscript; John Ryle, Cherry Leonardi, Charlotte Martin, and Zoe Cormack, who read the manuscript and advised the family; Peter Lual Deng for his support and encouragement; and Aly Verjee, for his exceptional editorial work.

For more historic photographs from the Muortat Family collection, please scan this QR code with your mobile device.

www.ingramcontent.com/pod-product-compliance
Lightning Source LLC
Chambersburg PA
CBHW010824070526
44583CB00022B/2923